MONTESSORI

WHY IT MATTERS FOR YOUR CHILD'S SUCCESS AND HAPPINESS

Montessori Children's House of Durham
Montessori Education Since 1977
2800 Pickett Road
Durham, NC 27705

Montessori

Why It Matters for Your Child's Success and Happiness

*Why the principles of the
Montessori Method are optimum for a
child's proper development*

Charlotte Cushman

Published by:
The Paper Tiger, Inc.
722 Upper Cherrytown Road
Kerhonkson, NY 12446-1331

www.papertig.com

Cover and text design by Mark Van Horne

ISBN: 978-1-889439-39-6

To Ayn Rand, who gave me the proper philosophy to understand;
to Maria Montessori, who gave me the tools to understand;
to my father, who taught me how to understand;
and to the children who gave me the understanding.

When we talk of "the opening of the mind," we mean a creative phenomenon, which is not the weak result of an impression violently made from without. The opening of the mind is the active comprehension which accompanies great emotions and is therefore felt as a spiritual event.

I once knew a motherless girl, who was so much depressed by the arid teaching of her school, that she had become almost incapable of study and even of understanding the things which were taught her. Her life of solitude lacking in natural affection, was a further aggravation of her mental fatigue. Her father decided that she should live for a year or two in the open country like a little savage; he then brought her back to town, and placed her under the private direction of a number of "professors." The girl studied and learned, but remained passive and weary. Every now and then her father would say, "Is your mind opening again?" and the girl always replied, "I do not know. What do you mean?" Owing to a curious coincidence in my life, this girl was confided to my sole care; and it was thus that I, when I was still a medical student, made my first pedagogic experiment…One day we were together, and when she was at work on organic chemistry, she broke off and looking at me with beaming eyes, said, "Here it is now! I do understand." She then got up and went away, calling out loud, "Father, father! My mind has opened!" The joy of father and daughter and their union at that moment made me think of the joys and the well springs of life which we destroy by enslaving intelligence.

MARIA MONTESSORI

Table of Contents

Foreword

In November 2012, I was approached by Fred Weiss of Paper Tiger Books about writing an introduction to a book he planned to publish. Knowing of my background as a professor of philosophy of education, with a specialty in Montessori education, he thought (correctly) that a book on "why Montessori matters" would be of special interest to me. I've written and lectured about Montessori's philosophy and was Board chairman of the Montessori school my daughter attended in the 1970s, so Montessori has been an important part of both my academic and personal lives.

With limited time available, I was reluctant to give the manuscript a close read, but I agreed, and the more I read, the more enthusiastic I became, eventually getting involved editorially. True, from the title I could tell that the book was on an important topic, one that responded to the crucial need for parents and teachers to understand the value and uniqueness of a Montessori education. However, it's one thing to write on a worthy topic but quite another to produce a book worthy of that topic. And Charlotte Cushman has done just that.

To summarize the virtues of this book: It is aimed at teachers and parents (and grew out of independent pamphlets for her school near Minneapolis), and it is written for those audiences, not for academics or those already expert in the Montessori method. Charlotte Cushman's explanations are clear, essentialized and replete with examples that make her points easily understood. At the same time, she possesses an ability to identify in clear terms the "why's," i.e., the important ideas on which classroom practice is based. Not only is she philosophically astute, but her long experience as a Montessori teacher and her sensitivity enable her to provide a multitude of anecdotes, including conversations with children, that keep the discussion in "the real world." She also answers questions and doubts that parents have raised over the years and applies her knowledge of Montessori to matters (e.g., computer use) that post-date Maria Montessori. The result is that a Montessori parent—including me with four decades of hindsight—can say, "Oh, that's what's going on with my child" and "that's why he's doing that in class." But just as important, a parent who is considering sending a child to a Montessori school will learn the most important lesson from Charlotte Cushman's book: why Montessori matters for a child's success and happiness.

Michael Berliner
Founding executive director, The Ayn Rand Institute

Preface

Shortly after I received my AMI Montessori diploma,[1] I began to teach at a small, private Montessori school owned and operated by a group of parents. Even though the parents liked the positive results they saw in their children because of the Montessori experience, they did not understand why it worked. They requested that I write short essays explaining the method that could be distributed to the rest of the parents in the school. I have continued that practice at every school I have worked at since then.

Parents and teachers alike have found the articles of value and have urged me to get them published in book form. *Montessori--Why It Matters for Your Child's Success and Happiness* is the result. This book explains various aspects of the Montessori Method and normal child development for children ages two and a half to six years of age and some characteristics concerning the elementary and middle school child. It is significant to note that this is not just a book that mouths the teachings of Maria Montessori, the person responsible for the development of the Montessori Method. The mouth is my own. My conclusions are based on what I have observed about how children learn and how they think. I did not attempt to make Montessori work because it sounded like it should work. I instituted the method and then observed over and over with my own eyes that it, in fact, does work. Montessori is a philosophy of education that encompasses more than just classroom learning. It is an integrated, consistent approach to the child which promotes his independence. I have, therefore, also explained from my perspective, how Montessori applies to issues such as electronics (computers, television, video games), uniforms, summer vacation and other issues that Maria Montessori herself never wrote about.

Dr. Montessori indicated that parents and children are at odds with each other. I never fully understood what she meant by that until I tried to answer the myriad questions and misconceptions about children that

---

1 AMI stands for Association Montessori International, an organization founded in 1929 by Maria Montessori in order to protect the integrity of her work and to ensure it would continue after her death.

parents had expressed throughout my career as a Montessori educator.

When children are disrespected, it is usually because they are misunderstood, not because they are unloved. Adults need to get inside the mind of the child to appreciate how enormous a task it is to grow up. Children have to learn everything from scratch because they start out knowing nothing. Imagine what it must be like. You come into the world with a blank mind. You see light, hear sounds and move your limbs in reaction. As you grow you begin to recognize your parent's face and voice as more sensations come in: different sounds, colors, textures, temperatures, weights, odors, lights. At this point, objects in the environment seem like globs. You are bombarded with information and you are eager to put it all together, to make sense of it all. You are excited, like an explorer on virgin land or an astronaut on a new planet. What is it? What is out there? You can hardly wait to crawl so you can discover and explore your world with your hands. But most adults don't remember this part of their childhood.

During the first three years, the child's mind is in chaos; during the next three he[2] will learn how to put the whirlwind of information into order, organizing his mind as a kind of mental filing cabinet. The method by which he does this will determine the cognitive functioning of his subconscious. The question is, what method will he use? Will he be active or passive? Will he continue to explore or will he stop? Will he become independent or dependent? Will he continue to want to learn or will he become lazy?

The way adults treat and educate a child during this stage of his development is critical. They can either accept the old beliefs about childhood and unknowingly interfere with their child's growth; or learn about the true nature of the child so that they can handle him in a way that will give him the best opportunity for success.

I hope that this book will do two things. First, I want parents to understand the Montessori Method better so that they are more able to enjoy and participate in their child's learning process. Second, I want to help adults see the world from the child's point of view, so that they understand him during the most serious period of his life, the time when he is in the process of creating the only thing that can bring him success and happiness—his mind.

---

2 To avoid confusion, I generally refer to the child as "he" and adults as "she" except when I cite a specific incident where the child is female or the adult is male.

Acknowledgements

I must first and foremost express my gratitude towards my husband, Dan Van Bogart, for his constant and unflagging willingness to help me with this project. He is a good editor and a great, methodical thinker.

I am indebted to my father, who was an excellent writer and inspired me to put my thoughts onto paper.

I am also grateful to Leonard Peikoff, who taught me a great deal about how to write in his lecture "Writing, A Mini-Course."

I am deeply indebted to Miss Lena Wikramaratne, friend and colleague of Maria Montessori, who gave me my training in the Montessori Method. I didn't appreciate her then, but I sure do now.

Harry Binswanger's course "Logical Thinking" at the Objectivist Conference in Virginia in 1992 helped me to understand the thinking process.

Carol Landkamer is my colleague and best friend, co-owner of our former school, Independence Montessori, and an excellent writer and editor. We wrote "Apologizing" together and this was originally published in the journal *Montessori Education*[1] under the title "Say You Are Sorry."[2] We also wrote a slightly different version of "Humor in the Montessori Classroom" which was originally published as "A Place for Laughter"[3] in the *Journal*. Carol taught me how to understand issues from the parent's point of view and how to tie my paragraphs together. She also helped me with a few sections of this book.

I thank my sister, Marilyn George, for co-writing the articles on "Sharing" and "Repetition" though I have since changed them. A different version of "Repetition" was originally published in the *Constructive*

---

1 (Note: This journal became *Montessori International* in the winter of 1999, and is now published by the Montessori St. Nicholas Charity).

2 "Say Your Are Sorry," by Charlotte Cushman, *Montessori Education* , volume 8 number 6, (United Kingdom: Montessori International Publishing Ltd., Summer 1998), page 8.

3 "A Place for Laughter," by Charlotte Cushman and Carol Landkamer, *Montessori Education*, volume 7 number 3, (United Kingdom: Montessori International Publishing Ltd., December 1995), page 44.

Triangle magazine.[4] Marilyn contributed to the articles "Ages and Stages" and "To Think or Not to Think," and wrote much of the article on "The Child's Concept of Time." She also taught me a great deal about the importance of the child's sense of touch.

Mary Anne Weninger, a friend and former parent at our school, taught me to be more aware of logical sequencing when listing a series of ideas.

I also thank my friend and colleague, Laura Hilse, my sister-in-law, Catherine Lamers, and my friend, Charles George, for their corrections, suggestions and helpful criticisms while I wrote this book.

Many thanks to Valda Redfern for her line by line editing and to Carol Landkamer and Jackie Lehman for taking the time to proofread the final copy.

I want to thank all the families at Minnesota Renaissance School for allowing me to take photos of their children for this book. Thanks also to Gay Hartfiel of Portraits from the Heart, who took some wonderful photos, one of which is on the back of the book. And many thanks to Desiree Van Bogart for convincing her daughter (my grand-daughter) to build the tower just one more time so she could take a picture which is now on the cover.

I was also fortunate to have the help of Mark Van Horne who prepared the text and cover design. His knowledge plus unfailing patience with our seemingly endless changes of design and illustrations was remarkable and greatly appreciated.

A huge thank you to Michael Berliner, whose critique greatly improved this book—I mean greatly! His attention to detail and accuracy was invaluable. He spent hours helping me and I just can't say enough about how much I appreciate it.

And lastly, I thank Fred Weiss of the Paper Tiger, the publisher, for giving me this opportunity to publish my observations, thoughts and ideas about children.

---

4 *Constructive Triangle*, Volume 10, #3, (American Montessori Society: Summer 1983).

If, in any two years of adult life, men could learn as much as an infant learns in his first two years, they would have the capacity of genius. To focus his eyes (which is not an innate, but an acquired skill), to perceive the things around him by integrating his sensations into percepts (which is not an innate, but an acquired skill), to coordinate his muscles for the task of crawling, then standing upright, then walking—and, ultimately, to grasp the process of concept formation and learn to speak—these are some of the infant's tasks and achievements whose magnitude is not equaled by most men in the rest of their lives.

These achievements are not conscious and volitional in the adult sense of the terms: an infant is not aware, in advance, of the processes he has to perform in order to acquire these skills, and the processes are largely automatic. But they are acquired skills, nevertheless, and the enormous effort expended by an infant to acquire them can be easily observed. Observe also the intensity, the austere, unsmiling seriousness with which an infant watches the world around him. (If you ever find, in an adult, that degree of seriousness about reality, you will have found a great man.)

AYN RAND

Chapter One
The Montessori Method

I watched them, seeking to understand the secret of these souls, of whose greatness I had been so ignorant! As I stood in meditation among the eager children, the discovery that it was knowledge they loved...filled me with wonder and made me think of the greatness of the human soul![1]

MARIA MONTESSORI

The Purpose of Education

The proper role of education is to prepare children for adulthood. When a child grows up, he will need to know how to live on his own. He must be able to identify the facts of reality and determine the appropriate actions to take in order to live a successful and fulfilling life. He will need to know how to make choices, good choices.

But knowing how to live is not something that "just happens." Man does not have any instincts that tell him which choices he should make. He doesn't automatically know which berries in the forest are poisonous and which are not. He does not automatically know which doctor he should see or which school his children should attend. And since some of these choices can make the difference between life and death, ultimately what he has to know is how to survive.

When a child goes to a conventional school he is taught to memorize a series of unrelated facts. Each child is given individual concretes and abstractions with no tie to a unifying principle. Because of this disconnectedness, the child has a more difficult time understanding the concepts being presented. He becomes confused and bored. Thinking is too hard.

1 Rita Kramer, *Maria Montessori,* (New York: Capricorn Books, 1977), p. 131–132.

He may "know" what he has been taught, but he cannot draw any conclusions, make any logical connections from one concept to another, or figure out the answer to a problem. Yet this process of thinking is what is needed in adulthood—this is what is needed for man's survival.

Thinking is essentially an issue of intellectual independence.

> Montessori wrote that an independent person is one who has within himself "the means of existence."... To be equipped for independent living means to be able to rely on one's own thinking. Consequently, Montessori education is directed toward developing the child's capacity for rational thought, his reason.
>
> ...
>
> Montessori education offers a child cognitive guidance, so that he may strengthen and develop his reasoning capacity. The Montessori Method helps a child develop "an ordered mind," a mind with a system for organizing facts.... An ordered mind is like a file cabinet whose papers are arranged logically; or, to use Maria Montessori's favorite analogy, it is like a library, as opposed to a mass of books piled up at random. Helping a child build an ordered mind is the main business of a Montessori classroom.
>
> ...
>
> The ability to reason is developed by basically the same means as any other ability. To learn the piano, for instance, one begins by learning to play three or four keys, then adds more keys, then builds combinations of keys into chords, etc. In Montessori schools, a child's intellect is developed by a similar method. Intellectual tasks are broken down into simple steps so that a child can concentrate on these steps one at a time and master them. After integrating what he has learned, he is ready to advance to more difficult tasks that he will use and build upon the earlier knowledge. [2]

Montessori education described in one word is "Independence." This does not mean that a child enrolled in Montessori is allowed to roam wild and do whatever he pleases. This also does not mean that there is no socialization with others. The independent individual, according to Montessori, is one who "through his own efforts is able to perform the actions necessary for his own comfort and development in life, conquers himself, and in so doing, multiplies his abilities and perfects himself as an

---

2 Michael Berliner and Harry Binswanger, "Answers to Common Questions about Montessori Education," *The Objectivist Forum,* Vol. 5, June & August 1984.

individual."[3] The Montessori child is taken by the hand and led, gently but firmly, through a system that allows him to develop his mind as an individual with very specific guidelines for his development.

Montessori education does not teach the child what to think, but how to think. This is done because the child is able to discover and verify answers on his own by working with concrete, sequential materials, rather than just memorizing unconnected facts. And in doing so, the child learns that his mind is competent and able to deal with reality. A person who can do this has self-confidence and independence rather than feelings of insecurity and dependence. When looking out at the world, his first thought is not, "What do others think is true?" His first thought is, "What *is* true?"

There is an ocean of difference between independent thinking and dependency. The dependent person thinks, "I'm not going to steal that car because I don't want people to be mad at me." The independent person thinks, "I'm not going to steal that car because it is the wrong thing to do."

It is man's mind that can observe which berries make one sick; it his mind that can use logic to figure out which doctors are competent, which schools are good. Man can even discover medical cures and launch rockets into space; and he can do all this because his mind is unique in the animal world—it can reason: "Reason is man's faculty for understanding reality and for guiding his actions on the basis of that understanding."[4] It is reason that man needs in order to survive and live happily, but reason doesn't happen automatically. A child has to learn how to think and thinking takes effort. This is why a proper education is critical.

Who Was Maria Montessori?

Montessori education was started and developed during the late nineteenth century by Dr. Maria Montessori. She was a physician and educator who experimented with the developmental and educational needs of the very young child. The results of her experimentation are widely used throughout the world and have been scientifically supported by research.

---

3 Maria Montessori, *The Montessori Method,* (New York: Schocken Books, 1965), p. 101.

4 Michael Berliner and Harry Binswanger, "Answers to Common Questions about Montessori Education," *The Objectivist Forum,* Vol. 5, June & August 1984.

As a child she was fiercely independent and persuaded her parents to let her continue with her own education even though she was a girl. Then she decided she wanted to become a doctor and went to medical school despite the disapproval of her friends and father. She was so determined to learn, that on snow days it was not unusual for her to be the only student who showed up to class. When she went on to become the first woman doctor in Italy, she received the pride and approval of her father.

After she began practicing medicine, she became intrigued by the problem of how to educate mentally delayed children. Through her work, she found that she could raise their school entrance scores to a level above that of the average child. This caused her to ask what could be achieved with normal children. A group of businessmen asked her to open a preschool daycare facility in the middle of Rome's slums. She called this school the "Children's House." It was here that she made most of her discoveries about children—what they are really like and how they really learn.

By observing the children, she discovered that they preferred her equipment to their own toys. As they worked with her specially designed materials, their attention spans and knowledge increased. Since it was the child's development that dictated her choice of materials, she continued to test them, keeping only those that held the child's attention and provided learning experiences. She prepared and re-prepared the classroom environment until she developed the basic materials still used in Montessori schools today. Montessori learned something else very important about children: they have sensitive periods for learning. She structured her entire method around meeting those sensitivities. Therefore, in her schools, children learn in a natural, spontaneous way. Her first school was so successful that interest in her method sprang up all over the world and many more schools were established.

At the start of World War II, Maria Montessori was exiled from Italy because she refused to brainwash the children in her schools and turn them into soldiers for Mussolini. During the war she spent most of her time in India, opening more "Children's Houses," developing her philosophy and materials, and training adults to be Montessori teachers. Recognizing that the child, by nature, requires a more abstract environment as he matures, she had many ideas about the child's educational needs beyond elementary school, and went on to develop her methods for children up to age twelve.

Montessori died in 1952 in Holland. Her method of education has become popular in many parts of the world, and her schools can now be found in six continents and throughout the United States.

What Is the Montessori Method?

You have enrolled your child in a Montessori school. You are excited. Maybe you have read about the method and like the idea of children learning independently and being respected as individuals. Perhaps your child's pediatrician recommended it. Or maybe you have observed the children of your friends who attend Montessori schools. They exhibit self-control and confidence and are eager to learn. They appear mature and advanced. You like what you have read, heard and observed, but what exactly is Montessori and how does it work?

The Montessori Method is an educational system based on how children actually learn, not how most adults think they learn. Many people suppose that children think like adults. They do not. A child is in the process of creating his mind. He is in the process of creating the adult he will become and he needs assistance, but a certain kind of assistance.

The Montessori Method starts the child with the concrete perceptions that he is already receiving in reality and guides him in a step-by-step manner towards abstract concepts. This is done in a carefully thought out, logical manner so that the child's mind is not confused with random or non-essential details. He can then file information in his mind in an orderly way so that he can easily retrieve it later. This is essential for efficient thinking.

Montessori education is a highly specialized, integrated methodology. The critical components of the Montessori Method are:

Order. Children need to establish a view of the world that is stable, and since the child forms himself from his environment, order is a major component of Montessori classrooms. Everything in the classroom is in order. The classroom as a whole is in order, organized into designated areas, each of which is part of a sequence. The materials on the shelves are in order, and each activity is displayed properly arranged in its container. Concepts are presented in a logical order and there is order in how they are taught. Order is part of the daily routine.

When the children finish their work, they return it to its proper spot on the shelf. When something gets out of order, the children help to put it back correctly, and at the end of the school day the children return the room to its original arrangement.

Classroom community. The classrooms have mixed age groups. The children are in each classroom (if possible) for three years. This gives the teacher an opportunity to closely watch a child's progress as well as get to know each child and his family on a personal level.

Children teach themselves. Children learn from observing, exploring and touching their environment and from the conclusions that they draw on their own from these experiences.

Educator. The adult is focused on the development of each and every child as an individual and is the link between the child and his environment, presenting him with materials for learning when he is ready.

Concentration. The child's ability to focus increases because the child is presented with materials during the proper sensitive period and then is allowed to practice.

Self-discipline. The child develops self-discipline through his work.

Discipline. Until the child achieves self-discipline, the teacher needs to firmly guide the child in order to correct, strengthen and improve his behavior.

Individuality. The children are treated and regarded as individuals. They are allowed, even expected, to be different—there is no requirement that everyone be the same. Each child learns at his own pace.

Social Development. Because of the emphasis on individuality, the children accept each other for who they are and find individual differences interesting rather than abnormal.

Independence. The children are taught self-responsibility from their first day in class.

Work and reality based. Montessori discovered that children prefer work over play, that what adults call play is actually the child's work. Children are given real activities to do rather than pretend activities.

Curriculum. The classroom is a prepared environment, geared to cater to all the sensitive periods for learning. It has specific areas, and, in each, the materials are arranged on shelves in the same order as that in which the child will learn them. For example, there are four main areas in the Children's House: Practical Life, Sensorial, Mathematics and Language. The Children's House also includes areas for geography, science, geometry, botany, history, music and art. In the elementary classrooms for the older children, certain areas contain many of the same materials as the Children's House, because the child re-visits these materials and uses them in a more advanced, abstract way.

Sequenced, hands-on materials. The children learn from using materials that progress from simple activities to more and more challenging ones, guiding the child from concrete to abstract ideas. These materials are presented to the children individually or in groups, depending on the material and the academic level of the child.

Repetition. The child is allowed to practice his work as many times as he needs until he learns the concept or skill and feels satisfied that he understands it.

Initiative. The child can choose to do any work that has previously been presented to him.

Records of the child's progress. The teacher observes the child and keeps records of his progress, so that when he masters a concept, she knows that he is ready to move on to the next one.

Structured Freedom. The child in the classroom is granted freedom, provided he takes responsibility for following class rules and uses his time productively.

Respect for rights. The children are allowed to work alone, undisturbed. If they interact with others they must treat them with respect. Abuse of self, others or property is not allowed.

Movement. Rather than sitting still in a desk all day feeling squirmy, the children are allowed to move about the classroom as long as their movements are purposeful and constructive.

Rewards and praise. Rewards and praise are not used as a means to motivate the child because those techniques keep the child dependent on the adult. The child's reward is his own satisfaction.

Beautiful environment. The classroom is attractive and the objects are well-maintained.

The Montessori Materials

A primary way children learn is with their hands. They cannot think abstractly, as adults can, by shifting thoughts around in their heads, so they need physical objects in order to figure things out. Therefore, rather than learning through lectures, worksheets, textbooks, television or computers, Montessori children learn by using scientifically designed materials. The children are drawn to them because of their precision and manner of presentation, which fulfill their inner desire to know. Here is a brief explanation of those materials:

Materials have a function. Each material has a specific purpose and is to be used for that particular purpose. The long rods are for the accurate perception of length, the color tablets for visual perception of color, the geometric solids for the identification of shapes, and so on.

Presentations. Before a child is allowed to work with a material, he has to be developmentally ready for it and be given a demonstration on how to use it.

Analysis of Movement. Before the teacher makes a presentation she analyzes all the movements involved, step-by-step, so that her demonstrations are accurate and clear. (During Montessori training I spent many hours practicing the presentations of all the materials.) As an example, say you want to learn how to play tennis. First you have to learn how to hold the tennis racket, then how to hit the ball, then how to hit it over the net, then how to hit it back and forth over the net with a partner, and then how to actually play a game. You take it a step at a time. This is the same way a child needs to learn.

Slow Presentations. We adults already know how to do things and have had lots of experience, so we can make a sequence of movements quickly without thinking about it. Our movements look very fast to children, however, and they find it difficult to catch all the steps and details involved in an activity. The Montessori teacher therefore slows down her movements when demonstrating the materials. Children love to watch these presentations. "Watch!" is almost like a magic word to them. They all stop dead in their tracks, eyes intently on the adult, waiting to see what will be shown to them.

Silent presentations. At the pre-elementary level, we make silent presentations to the children. Talk is limited to only the few words necessary to draw attention to the activity. This is because the child is so sensitive to language at this period of his life that too many words distract him; he will focus on what the adult is saying rather than pay attention to how to do the activity.

Isolation of the difficulty. The materials separate each concept from different, unrelated concepts. This makes learning clear and understandable because the child focuses on only one concept at a time. Other concepts are not included because they confuse and can frustrate the child. (Complications are fine for older children, but not when a child is first learning.)

Control of Error. Most of the materials are self-correcting, so that the child can see for himself if he made a mistake. If the child doesn't walk slowly enough and is not careful about how he holds a tray, the contents on the tray fall to the floor. If he doesn't pay enough attention to how he is pouring, the water spills. When doing the spindle boxes, if he doesn't count out the quantities accurately, he will end up with either too many or too few spindles when he is done. The only direct way the teacher corrects the child is to simply re-present the material later. Often this isn't necessary, however, because the child gets plenty of presentations by watching the older children who already know how to do it.

Montessori has sometimes been criticized for using these educational materials. Critics claim that it places too much emphasis on the concrete and that the child will be hindered in his abstract thinking, but when ready, children leave these materials. E. M. Standing explains this in his book, *The Montessori Method, A Revolution in Education:*

> This spontaneous ascent from the concrete to the abstract occurs when two factors are present: *First*, a certain general maturity of mind, and *second*, a great clarity with regard to the particular concrete process in question.....It is interesting to note that children often feel, inwardly, that it is quite an event when they discover that they can do their sums without the help of the material. Sometimes they will come up to the teacher and say with evident pride: "I did my sums today without using the frame!" [5]

Indeed, I have observed the same phenomenon. Children are happy and delighted to discover that they no longer need a material because they can work out a problem in their head. E. M. Standing continues:

> The child's mind whether he ever goes to school or not, will develop and will build up a system of its own. What we aim at, through the materials, is to assist this natural tendency. We should regard the materials then, not so much as difficulties to be overcome as helps to a development which is going on by its own energy, independently of us; one which will and must go on in any case. The materials help this spontaneous mental energy which, if left to itself in an unprepared environment, would find the struggle to create an orderly mental system beyond its strength. [6]

5 E.M. Standing, *The Montessori Method, A Revolution in Education,* (Fresno, California: Academy Library Guild, 1962), pp. 52–53.

6 E.M. Standing, *The Montessori Method, A Revolution in Education,* (Fresno, California: Academy Library Guild, 1962), p. 82.

The Individual Montessori Child

The children at Montessori's first schools, it was said, were amazingly independent and learned advanced skills at young ages. Their good manners, when they spoke to each other or to visitors who came to see their classrooms, were notable. Young children could take on the roles of hosts and hostesses as they set tables and served meals to their classmates. They were proficient at learning academic subjects previously thought to be too hard for children of that age. Much was said about the calm, peaceful classrooms, filled with students who actually enjoyed their work. People flocked to her schools from all over the world in order to see these children. Famous persons like Thomas Edison, Anne Sullivan and Alexander Graham Bell supported Montessori's early childhood learning method, and women's magazines featured articles about it. Virtually everyone knew who Montessori was because they had heard about her schools. In the 1920s, Montessori schools started to spring up in the northeastern part of the United States.

This new method had a very promising start. But then something killed the Montessori movement for about forty years. What was it?

The answer is philosophy. Ideas are what move the world, and the ideas that people accept or reject have consequences. John Dewey, the father of "progressive education," and his followers fought the Montessori movement. Among their criticisms were that the children were taught to read too early (they thought children shouldn't read until age 8), taught to read using phonics (they thought teachers should use the look-say method), and prevented from doing whatever they wanted with the learning materials (they thought this stifled creativity). But their greatest objection to Montessori was that the Montessori child focuses on developing his own individual mind.

In 1899, in *The School and Society*, John Dewey had written, "The mere absorbing of facts and truths is so exclusively individual an affair that it tends very naturally to pass into selfishness. There is no obvious social motive for the acquirement of mere learning, there is no clear social gain in success thereat."[7] The Montessori Method did not even exist at that time, but the book's dominant premise—that the individual should be subordinated to the group—gradually came to be accepted.

---

7 John Dewey, "The School and Social Progress," *The School and Society.* (Chicago: University of Chicago Press (1907), p. 29.

A philosophical principle like this does not jibe with the idea that the individual has a right to develop his own mind first and foremost. Therefore, the Montessori Method did not begin to take hold again in this country until the 1960s, as competency in academics deteriorated and people began to see the devastating effects of the progressive movement. Even so, we still hear the criticism that Montessori children are not group-oriented enough because they are allowed to work alone. Sadly, even some Montessori organizations have caved in, claiming that Montessori does center on developing the social side of the child. But this isn't true.

The fact of the matter is that the Montessori Method does focus on the individual rather than the group. Its unique characteristic is that it focuses on developing the child's cognitive faculty, his reasoning mind. It centers on the development of his brain, because everything comes from his brain. The brain needs development in thinking, and thinking is necessary for the proper development of self-esteem, intelligence, emotions, socialization, and physical movement and coordination. In order to learn, the child has to learn how to concentrate and think. This doesn't originate from a group, it happens inside him. He has to be allowed to do it and he has to be allowed to do it alone. He has to learn how to use his mind *now*, when his brain is developing its means of functioning.

Instead, most children are flung into progressive educational environments that don't take this need seriously. Because the progressive method is to focus on social relationships, children are expected to learn the same things at the same time, do their work as part of the group, progress with the group and conform to the group. Since their knowledge has not been acquired first hand, most children become dependent on others to tell them what the truth is and grow to rely on others for their opinions. A child who doesn't conform to the dynamics of the group, because he cares more about learning than social relationships, is often ostracized, bullied and humiliated by his peers because he doesn't fit the mold. So the child gets the message that the quest for knowledge isn't as important as "getting along with others," and he begins to live in fear of rejection. If other children do not accept him, the child wonders why and feels anxious. If he is accepted, he still feels that he could be rejected at any time. Children who have graduated from schools practicing John Dewey's philosophy, or have been raised on those principles at home, tend to suffer from insecurity.

Contrast that to the Montessori Method, which does take seriously the child's need to learn, and allows the child to continue the natural process that he started at birth: the process of pursuing knowledge. The child focuses on acquiring the facts about reality and then learns how to think by making connections between those facts and by figuring out solutions to problems. He learns how to use his mind competently. He knows what he thinks and is confident in what he knows. Feeling secure within himself, he is now ready for social relationships. Because he has been learning at his own rate and has not been expected to keep up with the group, he views himself and others as individuals. He is not obsessed by what others think of him because he is already self-assured. He does not worry about being accepted into a group but feels free to have friends. Instead of being pressured to conform to social norms, he is expected to adhere to objective rules where he must respect the individual rights of others. And look at the results: the children in the Montessori system are confident and happy.

The Montessori approach works because its fundamental principle of individualism is correct. The child needs to be left alone so that he can learn how to think; yet the Progressives hold that "truth" emerges from social interaction. That kind of socialization sabotages the child's efforts at thinking for himself, and his mind spins in confusion as he grasps at the opinions of the people around him, hoping to learn the truth from them instead of from his own observations. Children need to feel secure in what they know and comfortable in being alone with their own thoughts and conclusions.

It isn't that socialization isn't important. It is. Good social relationships are one of the essential joys in life. It's just that socialization should not be the main focus of education. Successful social interaction is a by-product of good cognitive development. We can't reverse cause and effect. The basis of good relationships is an inner security in knowing who you are and what you think, but a group-based educational method does not provide for that. (It is ironic, actually, that the Montessori Method is criticized for allowing children to work alone: Montessori children have more opportunities during the day to interact with their classmates than do their peers in the Progressive schools, who have to wait for recess or lunch to socialize. For more information on how the Montessori child socializes, see "Social Interaction in a Montessori School," Chapter 9.)

Fortunately, the Montessori movement is on the rise again because of its reputation for success. As in anything, in order to understand the reason for that success, one needs to understand the underlying principles that are responsible for it. In this case, one of those principles is that the Montessori Method is based on the cognitive development of the individual mind. This is what needs to be understood and defended over time. If we truly respect and love the child, we need to respect his right to his own life and his own happiness. He won't get the ability to live his life and achieve happiness from others—he will get it when he learns how to use his own mind.

How the Montessori Classroom Evolves Throughout the Year

Often when a child starts school for the first time the parents escort their child to the classroom, say goodbye, and then wonder, "What are they doing in there?"

On the child's first day of school he will be introduced to the other children and to the rules of the classroom. Then he will be given lessons that will increase his attention span, body control and independence, such as how to sit with his legs folded, carry a chair, roll a rug, fold a mat, walk around a rug or mat, walk, talk softly, stop when the bell is rung, carry a tray and push a chair under a table. Self-responsibility starts immediately. Children are shown how to take care of themselves and encouraged to participate right away in getting dressed, going to the toilet, feeding themselves, cleaning up after themselves, putting their own work away and so on. It is quite a struggle for children to learn to do the things that we take for granted. Learning how to sit on the line, fold their legs and sit still can take weeks or months. When they are finally able to do these activities they are very proud of themselves.

At the beginning of the year, the Montessori classroom is chaos. There are often many new young children getting into things, knocking over the pink tower, running, shouting, refusing to put their work away, crying, taking someone else's work, slamming doors, taking out work they are not ready for, and so on. Now is the time to set out the rules and make sure they're followed, because if this isn't done, the rest of the year will not go well. Therefore, in the beginning the teachers concentrate most of their time on these new students.

Once children have been shown how to do work, they are expected to find their own things to do. We don't entertain them; they are expected to keep themselves busy by choosing from the activities that they have been shown. It is not uncommon for some children to wait for the teacher to tell them what to do, and it can be concerning when they wander around aimlessly for a while. But learning how to be independent takes time.

Unlike in traditional schools, the children do not all learn the same things at the same time. They do not all do math together and then all do an art project together. In a Montessori classroom different activities are going on simultaneously all over the room. In one corner there may be a child practicing rolling up a rug or sweeping the floor (large motor activities), in another a child working on letter sounds (language), in another a child adding with the short bead stair (mathematics) and in yet another, a child at a table polishing a mirror (practical life). This variety of work provides lots of opportunities for integration, as children observe and absorb information from the activities of other children as well as their own.

Eventually, after the first month or so, the children abide by the rules, and the work becomes their main focus. They then go about their activities or observations independently. When this happens, the classroom has reached the stage of normalization and now the adults and children can relax. In contrast to traditional schools, where the teacher is the main focus and learning centers on what she says or does, the Montessori teacher knows she's doing her job when she can do *nothing* and the children continue to work. A sign of a good teacher is what happens when she leaves the room—her students do not even notice that she is gone and keep right on working.

Next, the holidays such as Halloween, Thanksgiving and Christmas get the children all stirred up (just when we thought we had them normalized), but January makes up for it when the children come back from vacation anxious to work. At that time, in many schools, the Montessori teacher brings in different work and unit studies, such as zoology, botany, geography, inventors, explorers, history, astronomy and the human body, begin. (Work is routinely rotated in and out of the classroom as children show a need or interest.)

As the year progresses, many positive changes appear in the children. By the time spring arrives, the children are so independent that the teacher is now spending most of her time observing the children rather than giving them presentations. An outside observer may misunderstand

and think that she isn't paying any attention to the children, but actually this is a wonderful sign. She knows she has done her job and that she did it well—the children are now working independently.

The Role of the Montessori Educator

When you enter a Montessori classroom during work time, it may be hard to find the teacher. She isn't standing at the front of the class, she usually isn't instructing all of the children at the same time, she isn't sitting behind a large adult size desk, she isn't the center of attention. She is most likely sitting with a student or small group giving a lesson or helping someone with his work. She may be sitting on the floor or at a small table, but she is probably with the students at their eye level, speaking with them individually. There might be one or even two children sitting on her lap, but it is evident that the activity of the children and not the teacher is the focus. This may seem unusual, and it is, because the Montessori teacher's role is completely different from that of conventional teachers. Her role is that of observer and guide, but with a firm vision of the end goal for the child—independence.

She presents students with activities that prepare for and promote this independence, such as how to control and coordinate one's body, how to take care of oneself, how to follow a sequence of steps and how to care for the classroom environment. The child is naturally drawn to these lessons, as it is independence that he wants to achieve. He then needs opportunities to select and practice these activities on his own. The Montessori classroom provides those opportunities because it allows children the freedom to make choices. The child can choose work that he wants to do provided he is ready for it and has had a preparatory lesson. The teacher then observes the child, in order to make sure he is making good choices.

Because of this freedom to make choices, it is often thought that the children can do whatever they want, but Montessori is not a free-for-all. The freedom is within a specific structure that is maintained by the teacher. We teachers observe the children and make assessments about their intellectual, emotional and physical development, and their behavior and social relationships (and keep records of those assessments). We watch, and when the child has mastered one material, we know he is ready to move on to the next step in the hierarchy and present him with the appropriate lesson. The advanced children are not held back, and those who are struggling are not forced to move ahead. We take the child down the path that he needs to tread, but only when he is ready. If he resists, we encourage. If he refuses, we insist. If he tries to go too fast, before he understands, we tell him he needs to practice what we have shown him before he moves on. If he wanders around the room disrupting the class, we make him stop.

Montessori is structured so that the opportunity for independence is incorporated into the child's day at every turn. The Montessori teacher leaves the children free to work without her. The fact that most of the materials are self-correcting regularly eliminates the need for her to point out the child's mistakes. Therefore, the child can figure out problems on his own. Praise is also limited so that the child does not become dependent on the teacher for his evaluation, and this leaves him free to evaluate his own progress. The child is expected to be responsible for taking care of himself. He is expected to put his work away, clean up his own messes, dress himself and so on, and he is given help only if he needs it.

The atmosphere in a Montessori classroom is very relaxed. Children are free to observe or work, but they are not allowed to be disruptive. The teacher maintains discipline by establishing clear rules and then enforces consequences if the rules are not followed. The goal, however, is for the children to become self-disciplined, which is a consequence of the self-control developed from their work. Once that has happened, the teacher disciplines less and less.

The Montessori structure gives the teacher an opportunity to get to know the children in a deep, comprehensive way. Since she has the children for three years instead of one, she gets to watch their development over a period of time, and knowing their history, she is better equipped to give them the correct assistance when necessary. Since each child's program is individualized, the teacher has plenty of time during the day to interact with him personally and listen to what is on his mind. The children soon discover that the teacher is the link to the materials, those wonderful materials that provide them with the information about the world that they seek. They are excited by her presentations of those materials and when they are left to practice with them alone, they notice things. So they rush to the teacher to tell her their latest intellectual discovery. And the bond forms.

The teacher makes a presentation to a child and then observes.

When I was a student, the atmosphere was completely different. I did not get to sit on my teacher's lap or give her hugs on a daily basis. There was no opportunity to share with her my dreams, thoughts and feelings whenever I wanted. Laughter was a rare occurrence and learning wasn't fun. Yet in the Montessori classroom there is plenty of time for work, the joy it brings and a special closeness with the teacher.

The reason this happens is that the development of the child's mind is taken seriously here. The teacher understands that independence is a requirement for the development of the child's reasoning process. When children are allowed to pursue knowledge on their own and figure out solutions to problems by themselves, they learn how to think. She knows that it is competence in this thinking that is required for his self-confidence and happiness and she provides the environment for that to happen. And look at the results.

The Very Young Child in Montessori

Often when we have observers in the classroom they are impressed by the independence and initiative that the children display. We sometimes get questions, however, about the youngest children. Aren't we concerned that they aren't "doing anything?" Is it ok that they spend most of their time observing? Aren't they wasting their time?

While it is true that many two- and three-year-olds spend a lot of time observing, it is not true that it is a waste of time. Before the baby learned how to talk and walk he spent most of his time observing his parents and other adults. Was that a waste of time? No, he was absorbing the information he needed so that he could eventually imitate us. This process does not stop just because he grows into a walking, talking being. Observation indirectly prepares the child for work that he will be ready for later. Would we withhold all conversation at home until the child is two years old, and then expect him to speak with ease? No. For the same reason, we need to allow him as much time as he needs to observe the older children in the Montessori classroom. The two-year-old is often not nearly ready for the activity, but he is soaking it in. The baby listens before he understands, and understands before he speaks, just as the very young child observes the older children doing their work before he is able to actually do it. These same children, when ready, learn much more

A two-year-old watches an older child do some math work.

easily than a new four-year-old just entering the Montessori classroom without this experience. Exposure is very important, and the young child is accumulating information for processing later. Montessori's response to visitors who inquired as to why all the children were not kept busy every minute: "Let them meditate." [8]

Another comment that parents make about their two- or three-year-old is the lack of concentration and restlessness he displays, and they worry that their child is too young to start school. "My child would never be able to behave like the rest of the class." But now is precisely the time for children to learn these skills. The longer we wait, the harder we make it for them.

Don't let the young child fool you. He is capable of doing many of the things that we see in the Montessori classroom. He can learn to take care of himself and attempts to button, snap and dress himself. He attempts to follow steps and organize things. He begins to display the ability to make his own decisions and choices. He becomes more coordinated as he becomes more aware of bodily movements by carrying and working with glass. He begins to think before he acts and displays more self-control as his actions become more purposeful. His attention span and absorption in work lengthen as he works towards independence.

Through this process the young child is taking the first steps towards his most important goal—the development of his own, most precious self.

---

8 Rita Kramer, *Maria Montessori,* (New York: Capricorn Books, 1977), p. 195.

Chapter Two
The Four Main Areas
of the Pre-elementary Classroom

These lessons, exact and fascinating, given in an intimate way to each child separately, are the teacher's offering to the depths of the child's soul. [1]

MARIA MONTESSORI

Practical Life

Of the four main areas of the Montessori classroom, Practical Life is probably the least understood. I have heard people call it the "kitchen" or "baby area." Yet Practical Life, the first area of the Montessori classroom that the child is introduced to, is a fundamental and crucial step in the child's learning experience. It is here that he learns how to concentrate. Practical Life prepares the child for the real world in which he will live, because he is provided with real life experiences rather than play. There are no toys in Practical Life (or anywhere in the classroom). Children prefer the real world and want to learn how to do real things. They would rather learn how to prepare real food and serve it than pretend to do it. Children are also attracted to the work in Practical Life because they want to do what they see adults do.

There are four main areas of Practical Life:

1. **Grace and Courtesy.** "Long ago Maria Montessori recognized that good manners lubricate social life and make it roll smoothly along the road of established custom. What is more, she found that children aged 2½–6 are in a 'sensitive period' perfectly adapted to

---

1 Maria Montessori, *The Absorbent Mind*, (New York: Dell Publishing 1967), p. 271.

Rolling up an oil cloth.

Learning how to tie a bow.

learning good manners. If we leave these things to be taught at a later age, the special and spontaneous interest will not be there..." [2] Thus Montessori included the area of Grace and Courtesy where the children are presented with formal lessons on manners. These lessons include: saying "please" and "thank you," saying "excuse me," opening and closing a door quietly, getting someone's attention without interrupting, resolving conflicts, waiting patiently and talking softly.

2. **Care of Person**. This area stresses independence and includes activities such as how to button, snap, zip, hook, buckle, tie, lace and pin; how to dress oneself, how to sew a button, how to polish shoes, how to prepare and serve food and how to wash hands.

3. **Care of Classroom Environment.** The child learns how to take care of his environment, with activities such as washing cloths, sweeping, mopping, washing tables, cleaning up one's own messes, polishing, table crumbing (using a small brush and dust pan to clean small particles off a table), washing dishes and taking care of plants and animals. With these exercises the child learns how to follow a sequence of steps.

4. **Control and Coordination of Body**. The child's dexterity is developed with the large and small motor activities in this area. Some examples are rolling a rug, folding a mat and manipulating small objects such as clothespins. (For more information see "Movement" in Chapter 5.)

Practical Life also prepares the child for:

- Mathematics. The child learns how to follow a sequence of steps, calculating distance by sweeping, and calculating quantity by pouring.
- Geometry. The child experiences shapes by folding.
- Reading. The child learns left to right orientation with polishing and top to bottom orientation with the dressing frames.

---

2 E.M. Standing, *Maria Montessori: Her Life and Work*, (New York: New American Library, 1957), Chapter 5.

- Writing. The child's wrist and fingers are strengthened, and eye-hand coordination is enhanced by all the fine motor activities. The pincer grip is also practiced in many of these activities.

Practical Life is hardly a "baby area." Babies are not ready to cut up apples, take care of animals, sweep the floor, dress themselves and so on. And while it is understandable that some people call it a kitchen, since children learn how to prepare food, wash dishes and clean there, it is much more than that. It is in this area that children learn the practical skills that they will need to know in order to take care of themselves when they grow up. In essence, they will need independence—and the foundation for it is established in Practical Life.

Sensorial

Sensory training is very significant in the preparation for academic learning. Everything that we perceive about reality must first come to us through our senses, but these sensory inputs do not constitute knowledge. Our brain must interpret and integrate these sensations, which is the starting point of all knowledge. Our senses tell us that something exists, but what that is must be learned by the mind. Humans and animals are alike in that they receive perceptions (sensations automatically organized by the brain), but humans are unique from all other creatures because we are able to conceptualize or reason. A concept is a mental integration of two or more concretes which are different, but with important attributes in common. Humans isolate the differences in similar things and then integrate them into one group, which gives them the ability to form a concept. In the process of conceptualizing, we separate out attributes (an aspect of an object that can be separated conceptually but not in actuality. For example, we can isolate the concept red in our minds, but it can't be separated from the material object.) This process is called abstraction.

The baby starts at the perceptual level. He grasps that something exists, but he does not yet know what it is. His brain is inundated with a tremendous number of sensations and they are all coming in haphazardly. By the time he reaches age two he needs to start putting all this confusion in order in his mind, making sense of what he has been perceiving. The purpose of the Sensorial Area is to assist him in this process. We do not present him with new impressions but help him to put into order the ones that he is already receiving.[3] By doing this, the child is able to abstract more easily and accurately.

What is noteworthy about how this is done in Montessori is that each concept that the child learns is isolated in such a way that it becomes clear and distinct from other concepts that often confuse him. For example, children can confuse texture and color. Sometimes when a three-year-old is asked what color his shirt is, he answers "soft." With the Montessori color tablets, the only way each tablet differs from another is just in color, not in texture, size, shape or anything else. That way, when the adult talks about color to the child or teaches him the names, the child knows exactly what concept is being addressed. This holds true for everything the child learns in this area, as well as in the rest of the classroom. Montessori called it the "isolation of the difficulty."

A child needs to learn concepts in a logical and orderly manner because knowledge progresses hierarchically. A child has to have a concept of "tree" before he can conceptualize "forest." As the child gets older he adds more and more information to his earlier concepts. He learns that some trees have leaves and others have needles. He learns the names for different kinds of leaves and parts of a leaf, kinds of roots, how a tree grows, what it needs to live, the process of photosynthesis, and so on. As the child moves forward to learn higher abstractions, any new information must be consistent with what he has learned before. If it isn't, he needs to rectify his errors. Contradictions left uncorrected confuse the child and undercut his self-confidence.

The Montessori Method presents concepts to the child in a systematic manner to help the process of abstraction. For example, with the Geometric Cabinet, first the child sees and feels the material object "triangle" and learns the word in the Three Period Lesson (See "The Three Period Lesson" in Chapter 3). Secondly, the child is given a card with the same size and shape of a triangle drawn on it, fully colored in. Third, the child is given a card on which the same triangle is drawn in thick outline. Fourth, the child is given a card showing a thin outline of the same triangle. Last, the definition of a triangle is given. The child's

---

3 E.M. Standing, *The Montessori Method, A Revolution in Education*, (Fresno, California: Academy Library Guild, 1962), p. 30.

Figuring out size using the
knobless cylinders.

Discriminating size from large to
small with the tower of cubes.

Building a tower with the broad
stair and tower of cubes. "Don't
make it taller than me," he said.

Distinguishing length with the
long rods.

abstraction is done in a logical way: gradual elimination of the object so that the child can visualize and consider the one idea—triangle. To mix these steps or to go backwards makes learning more difficult. It is much harder to try to visualize something when you have never seen it. You can try to conceive or guess what an object would look like if you had the definition, but understanding would take much longer.

Here is a list of equipment and some activities in the Sensorial Area:

- Knobbed cylinders, knob-less cylinders, tower of cubes, broad stair and long rods. The child learns size, width, length, depth and their gradations. This indirectly prepares the child for the concept of "ten" in mathematics, as each material has ten pieces.
- Color tablets. The child learns the primary, secondary, tertiary colors and their gradations. This prepares the child for art.
- Geometric Solids. The child learns sphere, cube, cone, cylinder, ovoid, ellipsoid, rectangular prism, triangular prism, square based pyramid, triangular based pyramid. This prepares the child for geometry.
- Geometric Cabinet. The child learns rectangle, triangles (isosceles, equilateral, scalene), polygons (pentagon, hexagon, heptagon, octagon, nonagon, decagon), parallelogram, rhombus, trapezoid, oval, ellipse, curved sided triangle and quatrefoil. This work prepares the child for geometry.
- Auditory materials such as the sound cylinders. The child learns loud and soft sounds and gradations.
- Music materials such as the Montessori bells. The child experiences the musical scale by playing and listening to the scale. He also learns to match the tones and grade them.
- Olfactory materials. The child learns how to match and identify odors.
- Touch materials. The child learns how to distinguish, sort and grade objects that are rough, smooth, soft, hard, heavy and light, cold, warm and so on.
- Sorting materials. The children sort objects by color, visual intensity (i.e. brightness), texture, size, weight, shape, intrinsic construction (e.g. glass, plastic, metal, wood) and so on. Once a child has sorted something, we will ask him if he can think of another way to sort it.

Matching colors of objects to
color tablets.

Grading shades of colors.

Matching fabrics.

Distinguishing different odors.

Using the constructive triangles.

The binomial cube.

Combining the tower, broad stair and knobless cylinders.

- Binomial and Trinomial cubes. These cubes are the concrete cubes that prepare the child for the algebraic equations of the binomial and trinomial theorems. As the child works with these he learns how a cube is constructed.
- Some classrooms have the cubing and Pythagoras materials, which prepare the child for algebra.
- Once children understand the basic concepts, they are allowed to combine the materials to create new patterns and ideas. This often includes using more than one sense.

The child is in the process of setting up a structure by which his mind will operate for the rest of his life. He will create the foundation for his thinking process which can't be changed later on without great difficulty. The question is, will he organize his mind like a filing cabinet or a dumpster? Montessori helps the child create an orderly filing cabinet, because the materials and methods help him to distinguish and classify his impressions logically, thereby reducing his confusion about reality. His brain then becomes uncluttered and clear. This is a necessity for a mature, reasoning mind.

Mathematics

Mathematics, the science of measurement, is crucial in the reasoning process.[4] Man uses mathematics when he identifies relationships between concretes and abstractions and forms concepts. When he forms the concept "table," for example, he notes that all tables have legs but that one table can have shorter or longer legs than another table, or that all tables have tops, but the tops can be of different shapes and sizes. He sees that tables have certain characteristics in common but that he can omit the particular measurements of those characteristics because they vary from table to table. Since forming concepts must be done without contradictions, there is a method the child must use to arrive at the right conclusions. This method is called logic. Logic is the non-contradictory identification of the facts of reality.

---

4 For more information read Ayn Rand's chapter on Cognition and Measurement, *Introduction to Objectivist Epistemology*, (New York: Penguin Group, 1979).

In mathematics the child learns actual logic through the manipulation of objects. As he moves objects around, he can see for himself the nature of reality and why something is or isn't logical. In doing this, the child is preparing his mind for abstract thought—he solves problems using objects at first and as he grows he gradually replaces those objects with abstract concepts.

Maria Montessori was aware of the importance of mathematics in the development of the intellect. She called it the Mathematical Mind.

Here is the general progression of math in the pre-elementary classroom:

1. Practical Life lays the foundation for order, sequencing, problem solving, and concentration.
2. The Sensorial Area lays the groundwork for organizing the facts of reality. The child also learns about the number ten (there are ten cubes to the tower of cubes, ten prisms to the broad stair, ten rods to the long rods and so on). As he works with those materials he sees that a whole is made up of many parts. In order to do the exercises, he has to estimate relationships—to figure out: Which is the biggest? Which comes next? Which is smallest? How much can I fit in that box?
3. Observation. The child is further prepared as he watches the older children do math in the classroom.
4. Long rods. The child works with the long rods sensorially, placing them in order and noting relationships of length (that one rod added to each progressive rod in sequence is the same length as the next rod in sequence).
5. Number rods. He sees the same rods, but each section is divided and alternately colored with two different colors. Previously, the child judged graduated lengths; now, he sees that units make up the whole. As he learns to count the units, he learns the concept of quantity.
6. Sandpaper numbers. Using the sandpaper numbers, he learns the symbols for these quantities (the sandpaper numbers also prepare him for writing).
7. Association of number rods and symbols. The child counts the rods and matches the numbers he counts to their corresponding symbols.

8. Spindle boxes. The symbols are in sequence but now the quantities are separated. The concept of zero is introduced.
9. Counters game. The child must put the number symbols in sequential order and associate the correct quantities with them.
10. Teens. The child learns the quantities, symbols and associates them.

From this point the child can work on linear and skip counting, the decimal system, fractions and telling time.

- Linear and skip counting. Using the Bead Cabinet, the child discovers the relationship between linear, square and cube quantities. He also learns to count in sets.
- Decimal System. The child learns quantities (one unit, one ten, one hundred, one thousand), then the symbols and then their association. He learns the relationship of units to tens, tens to hundreds and hundreds to thousands.
- One hundred board. The child puts the symbols 1 to 100 in order.
- Lay Out. The child learns the sequence of quantities and symbols for 1 to 9,000.
- Bank game. The child learns how to exchange ten units for one ten, ten tens for one hundred and ten hundreds for one thousand. After he has done much practicing and has associated quantity and symbols, he learns how to compose and read a number.
- The child learns the operations of addition, subtraction, multiplication and division. In the beginning we do not care about correct answers, because we want the child to understand the process involved in each operation. Each step in learning these operations gradually becomes more abstract and eventually leads him to memorize the combinations.
- Stamp Game, Dot game and Abacus. These are abstract materials for performing the math operations.
- Skittles. The child is introduced to fractions.
- Fraction circles. The child works on fraction equivalencies and some simple math operations.
- Time. The child learns to tell time with the hours. Some children go on to learn more.

The child needs to form his concepts through the use of logic. With the

Counting the number rods.

Tracing over a sandpaper number.

Associating quantities and their symbols.

The Counters Game.

The Lay Out.

Using the golden beads to figure out 10 x4.

The Division Board.

Working on fraction equivalencies.

Montessori math materials, the child learns logic as he gradually works toward abstractions. He becomes familiar with quantity perceptually before he learns symbols, association of symbols and quantities, sequencing of numbers and mathematical operations. By learning relationships between quantities and symbols; between squares and cubes; between units, tens, hundreds and thousands, the child forms concepts and expands his mind. "The purpose of measurement is to expand the range of man's consciousness, of his knowledge, beyond the perceptual level: beyond the direct power of his senses and the immediate concretes of any given moment. Man can perceive the length of one foot directly; he cannot perceive ten miles. By establishing the relationship of feet to miles, he can grasp and know any distance of earth; by establishing the relationship of miles to light-years, he can know the distance of galaxies."

Language

Humans are cognitively superior to all other animals because they can reason (and can thus control their environment and their own lives). A person uses mathematics in the process of forming concepts. He forms a concept for a given kind of thing when he has integrated the appropriate number of abstractions from real instances of it, and he then labels that concept with a word, which is a symbol for the concept. Language is a systematic combination of such symbols that arranges concepts in a logical sequence and is, therefore, primarily a tool of cognition. "The primary purpose of concepts and of language is to provide man with a system of cognitive classification and organization, which enables him to acquire knowledge on an unlimited scale; this means: to keep order in man's mind and enable him to think." [5]

It is essential that the child create a logical system of classifying concepts in his mind so that he can think efficiently. The Montessori Method is an invaluable aid to the child in this process because of its emphasis on order. Children are, however, prepared for language years before they come to school.

The child is sensitive to human speech even before he knows who is speaking. By the time the baby is four months old his eyes are focused on the mouth of the speaker and he can be seen making little motions

---

5　Ayn Rand, "The Cognitive Role of Concepts," *Introduction to Objectivist Epistemology*, (New York: Penguin Group, 1979).

with his lips as though he were making silent words. At six months the child begins to babble, imitating the sounds of human speech, and by the time he is eight or nine months old, he has uttered every sound in the alphabet of his native language. It is interesting to note that the child does not utter and imitate *every* sound in his environment, but is drawn towards language. Now the child begins to utter sounds, but they are no longer an imitation in preparation for speech—he begins to speak with meaning. He knows what he is saying and with one word he can mean a whole sentence (e.g. a child may say, "Cookie" and put his hand out, meaning, "I want a cookie.").

By the time the child is one and a half years old he is trying to form phrases and sentences, and at age two he knows many words. At age two and a half he can speak very well. All this takes place in his subconscious, absorbent mind.

Between the ages of 2½ and 3½ he is still very sensitive to language and is now ready for the Montessori activities that will prepare him for higher level linguistic skills. There are three main sections in the Language area of the classroom: vocabulary and speech, reading and writing, and grammar.

Vocabulary and Speech.

- Vocabulary. When the young child enters Montessori school he will encounter a language- rich environment. The children are constantly chattering with each other, talking about their work and how it should be done. They teach each other vocabulary with the nomenclature material, such as kinds of airplanes or parts of a flower. I have even seen children teach concepts to others by using the Three Period Lesson (see "The Three Period Lesson" in Chapter 3). They will discuss solutions to puzzles and why this or that won't work. I have also heard them have intellectual discussions as to whether there is such a thing as Santa Claus or God. They talk to each other about the stories we have read or sing the songs we have taught them. The children also routinely converse with their teachers, because the teachers are always accessible. All this discussion takes place as they do their work throughout the day. Conversations help children expand their vocabulary and give them plenty of time to practice their speech.

- Speech. A Montessori school education helps all children with their speech development because of this language-rich environment. Every time we introduce a new concept to the children we tell them the word and ask everyone to repeat it. During the Three Period Lesson the child also repeats a lot of words. In addition, sound analysis and the sandpaper letters (the two major preparatory steps for learning how to read) help with speech, because the child hears and repeats sounds in isolation.

Reading and Writing. From about age 2½ to 5 the child is going through his sensitive period for learning how to read and write.

Preparation for reading and writing:

- Picture Matching. This prepares the child to recognize symbols.
- Visualization. The child learns how to make pictures in his mind from his experience with the concrete materials and through abstraction games (hiding an object and asking the child to find it or to name what is missing).
- Sound or word analysis. The child learns to analyze the sounds in words by breaking them down into their component parts.
- Sandpaper letters. At age 2½ the child is introduced to the phonetic sounds of the letters. The child says the letter's sound as he traces the shape with two fingers. This prepares him for writing, because, as he traces the letter, he develops his muscular memory (recalling the motions necessary to make the symbol).

Preparation for writing:

- Metal Insets. At age 3 the child is presented with the metal insets, which also prepare him for writing. (There are other materials in the classroom which prepare the child for writing, such as the fine motor work in Practical Life, the knobbed cylinders and moving the fingers and wrist around the geometric forms from the geometric cabinet.)
- Nomenclature material. Between ages 3½ and 4½ children may spontaneously begin to write, being at first interested only in the sensorial aspects of writing.

- Movable alphabet. From age 3½ to 5 the child learns how to build phonetic words.

Reading:

- (See "Teach Me to Read" in Chapter 3.)

Grammar. After the sensitive period for reading and writing, the child is sensitive to learning grammar. The children love grammar because the manner in which it is presented is clear and fun. The child plays simple games that teach him the meaning of a given part of speech. Then he is presented with a symbol for that part of speech. When he reads sentences, he symbolizes the parts of speech and can see the pattern in language. He can see that every sentence has a noun and a verb; that prepositional phrases have a preposition, article and noun; and so on. For this there are the following exercises:

- introduction to the verb, logical verb game
- introduction to the noun, noun family game
- article introduction—definite and indefinite, singular and plural
- adjective introduction, logical adjective game, detective adjective game
- conjunction introduction
- introduction to the preposition, preposition game
- adverb introduction, logical adverb game
- pronoun introduction
- interjection introduction
- reading commands—simple
- interpretive reading
- sentence analysis

Language allows the mind to retain concepts. The Montessori classroom is a tremendous aid to the child in the process of learning and storing concepts because it provides the necessary structure for the child to logically classify words in his mind. The young child is extremely sensitive to language. There is an explanation for it—he is forming his early concepts. He is learning how to reason.

In addition to the fine motor work in Practical Life and the sandpaper letters and numbers, these activities also prepare the child for writing.

Learning how to use the metal insets.

The sandpaper letters prepare the child for reading and writing.

These children are looking at a painting and writing down their observations.

Here the children have just learned about verbs. They are writing them down and symbolizing them with a round, red circle.

Chapter Three
A Few Montessori Lessons

*An interesting piece of work, freely chosen, which has the virtue of inducing
concentration rather than fatigue, adds to the child's energies and mental
capacities, and leads him to self-mastery.* [1]

MARIA MONTESSORI

The Three Period Lesson

The Three Period Lesson is the foremost Montessori lesson used to
teach vocabulary, letters and number symbols. In this lesson the child
experiences the sensory data necessary to understand the concept. When
learning the geometric solids, for example, the child feels each individual
shape with his hands as he says its name.

Adults may think a child knows a concept if he can point to the object when he hears the name, but that isn't the case. The child does not
really know a concept until he can tell you the name when you point to
the object.

The Three Period Lesson is a lesson that parents can easily do at home.
Here is an example of how to present it with the geometric solids:

1. Take out the sphere. Carefully roll it in your hand and say, "sphere."
   Then hand it to the child and invite him to repeat what you did. He
   should roll it gently in his hand and say, "sphere." Then pick up the
   cube. Slowly feel each side and say, "cube." Hand it to the child and
   invite him to repeat. Last, pick up the cone. Again, feel it with your
   hands and say, "cone." Do this several times.

---

1 Maria Montessori, *The Absorbent Mind*, (New York: Dell Publishing, 1967), p. 207.

Naming the geometric shapes with eyes closed.

2. Place the three shapes in front of you. Ask, "Where is the cone?" The child then points to the cone; he can feel it again and say, "cone." Then ask, "Where is the cube?" The child feels the cube and says, "cube." Do this for each of the shapes many, many times. The second period is the longest period of the lesson. If at any time the child makes an error, take him back to the first period: "No, that is the sphere. Where is the cone?"

The second period can be varied in many ways to make it more interesting. You can place the shapes around the room and have the child go find them. Or you could close your eyes and ask him to place a particular shape in your hands. When the child is successful in this period, you can move on to the last period.

3. You will now see if the child does indeed know the names of the shapes. Point to a shape and ask, "What is this?" or "This is the _____?" If the child makes errors, go back to period one and start all over.

The Nomenclature Material

In Montessori the children learn how to make booklets, and in doing so, write long before they read.

It is very important that, before a child learns to read, he understands that concepts are named by words and that written words are not just scribbles, but symbols for concepts. With the nomenclature material, the child sees a picture (a symbol for a concept) and also a word (another symbol for the concept). This helps him to isolate in his mind the idea that each concept has a written symbol. (The child does not fully grasp pictorial symbolism until his elementary school years.)

The child has been prepared for the idea of conceptual symbols in other areas of the classroom. He first experienced a concept sensorially and later learned the name, then the symbol. He felt and counted a number rod, then learned the name and learned to recognize the written symbol "10." He felt and experienced an actual hexagon, then learned the name and learned to recognize a picture of a hexagon. When he sees the written word next to a concept, it reinforces the idea that everything in reality has a name (symbol). This inspires the child's curiosity and he wants further information, more names for more things.

Parts of a fish booklet.

As he explores the nomenclature materials, his concepts go beyond first level concepts. For example, most children already know the concept "airplane" before they enter school. From the nomenclature material he can expand that knowledge and learn more and higher-level concepts such as parts of an airplane or kinds of airplanes. This motivates the child to learn how to read, because he comes to realize that if he can read he will learn more concepts.

Before children are ready to do booklets, they must have adequate fine motor control (prepared for in Practical Life) and be able to learn the names for concepts (prepared for in Sensorial). When a child wants to make a booklet, he must learn the names first, using the Three Period Lesson. Then he must reproduce the booklet by writing or tracing the written word and, in most cases, by also coloring the appropriate parts. In addition to refining pencil control, this also reinforces the newly learned information. The children can now recall new concepts more easily because they can refer to their booklets.

Children are very attracted to this work and enjoy it very much. They love the thrill of accomplishment when they complete a booklet and are often motivated to do more. Some children like to see how many they can make in a day or a week. The more children do this work, the more quickly they learn new words, and their conceptual framework expands dramatically.

Teach Me to Read

(Please note: The purpose of this section is to explain what needs to be done to enrich a child's environment so that he can learn how to read. This is not meant to be an all-inclusive essay on reading. I am not a reading specialist and there are many important and worthwhile books that have already been written on this subject. If a child does not learn how to read within his sensitive period, he needs to be seen by a reading specialist for an evaluation.)

Sometimes, when new Kindergarten students without any previous Montessori experience enter school in the fall, one of them will ask me, "Miss Char, when are you going to teach me how to read?" Parents of these children occasionally tell me that their child expected me to do this right away. Parents, too, may have this expectation and may ask, "When will my child read?"

There is a time range during which children are most sensitive to learning how to read (see "Sensitive Periods" in Chapter 4). However, just as we cannot predict the exact day when a child will take his first step or utter his first word, we also cannot predict the precise time that a child will read. The process of learning how to read is very much the same as that of learning how to walk. Before he can walk, the child goes through a long period of preparation for walking. He observes us and figures out how to imitate our movements and how to strengthen and coordinate his body. Over time he learns how to sit upright and crawl, then to support his leg muscles by pulling himself up on furniture. Eventually he pulls himself all the way up to a standing position, lets go of the furniture, and takes his first step. All this is done without formal instruction.

The same process happens in learning how to read—preparation begins years before the child even enters school and then by the time he starts Montessori school, at about 2½ to 3 years of age, he needs even more preparation before he is ready to read such as:

- **Books.** Children need to be read to every day. This is one of the most important ways to prepare a child to read.
- **Picture Matching.** Picture matching prepares the child to recognize the letter symbols. Picture matching includes many activities such as matching identical pictures, sorting pictures by category or function, finding hidden pictures, finding what is missing in a picture, matching objects to pictures, matching a picture to its outline, matching one half of a picture to the other half, and so on.
- **Visualization.** Children need to learn how to visualize so that when they read they can picture the events in their mind. Abstraction games such as hide and seek help with this.
- **Word or sound analysis.** The child learns to analyze the sounds in words by breaking them down into their component parts. Take out a set of objects or pictures, say the sounds of the word for one of them, and let the child try to figure out which one it is (e.g. "cuh-a-tuh" for "cat"). Don't worry about how the word is spelled, only how it *sounds*. You may need to practice this a bit at first until you feel comfortable with it. "I Spy" games are also great at this age: "I spy with my little eye something that begins with 'buh.'"
- **Letter sounds.** Children need to learn the sounds the letters make instead of the names of the letters, because this prepares them for reading.

Sounding out short phonetic words.

Building words with the
moveable alphabet.

Children often choose to read during work time.

- **Word building.** Once the child is successful with word analysis and knows ten to twelve letter sounds, he can begin to build phonetic words with a moveable alphabet. At this stage we do not correct his spelling, just as we did not correct him when he took his first steps. He is in the process of learning how to put sounds and letters together, so spelling isn't important yet.
- **First reading lesson.** (Sensitive period 4 to 4½ years of age) The child learns how to sound out three letter phonetic words. Some children may remain at this level for a year or longer.
- **Simple Phonetic Words.** The child sounds out one-syllable phonetic words longer than three letters such as "twin," "swam" or "scrub."
- **Phonetic Blends.** The child sounds out phonetic words with more than one syllable and more than one vowel such as "dentist," "picnic" or "continent."
- **Second Reading Lesson.** The child is introduced to the phonograms. He learns that some letters go together to make a different sound such as "sh," "th," "ing" and "ch."
- **Puzzle Words.** The child is introduced to words that do not follow any rules and need to be memorized such as "two," "the" and "I."
- **Simple Phonetic Books.** The child reads books that have short phonetic words with a few puzzle words in them.

Children may go through all these steps and still not actually be reading; they may still be sounding out each word individually. Then all of a sudden, as Montessori observed, they "explode" into reading. It almost seems as if it happened overnight, but it didn't. The preparation took a long time. The child put a lot together and figured it out. Other children do not experience an explosion but, rather, go through a more gradual reading process. Adults assume that early readers are more intelligent than children who explode into it later, but this assumption isn't true. The child who reads later, providing there is no undue delay, may be thinking about the various inconsistencies in the English language and once he does explode, he is often a strong reader.

There is no reason children should have trouble learning how to read unless they have a learning delay, but even most children with delays can at least sound out three-letter phonetic words if they start with us at 2½ to 3 years of age and stay with us for at least three to four years before moving on to first grade. When children are prepared for reading properly, they usually flow right into it. For most children, learning how to read is as natural as learning how to walk.

The Silence Game

The Silence Game is an excellent exercise in which silence is used to draw attention to movement. The children try to be as quiet as possible and in so doing learn how to control their bodies. This game was developed by Maria Montessori when she discovered that children really do like peace and serenity. She found this out by accident when she came into the classroom holding a four-month-old baby. Montessori relates:

> (The baby) was so still that her silence impressed me greatly and I wanted the children to share my feelings. "She is not making a sound," I told them. And jokingly I added, "None of you could do so well." To my great surprise I saw that the children were looking at me with an extraordinary intensity. They seemed to be hanging on my lips and to be feeling keenly what I was saying. "Notice," I continued, "how soft her breath is. None of you could breathe as silently as she." Surprised and motionless, the children began to hold their breath. At that moment there was an impressive silence. The tick-tock of the clock, which was not usually heard, began to become audible....No one made the least perceptible movement. They are intent upon experiencing the silence and reproducing it....The children all sat perfectly still breathing as quietly as possible, having on their faces a serene and intent expression like those who are meditating. Little by little in the midst of this impressive silence we could all hear the lightest sounds like that of a drop of water falling in the distance and the far-off chirp of a bird.

> That was the origin of our exercise of silence. [2]

During the Silence Game, the children work to make silence. They understand that silence means there will not be any noise. The children try to be very, very quiet, but they soon discover that if they move, it breaks

2 Maria Montessori, *The Secret of Childhood*, (New York: Ballantine Books, 1966), p. 123–124.

The Silence Game.

When a child is sitting quietly, the teacher calls his name to blow out
the candle and go to work.

the silence. The turn of a foot or the twist of a leg can make noise, so the child's total attention becomes focused on his body as he plays the game. As he develops self-control over his body, he also becomes aware of sounds in his environment, and because the room is so quiet he learns how to get inside his head and think.

There are different versions of how the Silence Game is played. Here are a few:

- The teacher plays soft music and lights a candle. She then whispers one by one the names of those children who are sitting quietly, and they can come forward to blow out the candle and then go to work.
- The teacher leaves the room and calls the names of the children who are sitting quietly to join her in the hallway.
- After the period of silence is over, the teacher asks the children what they heard during the game.

While many children initially have trouble sitting still, they all make progress by the end of the year. The Silence Game can be a good indicator of how well the children are advancing overall. The absence of movement indicates good self-control and self-awareness. Chances are, if a child does well playing this game, he is mature and progressing well academically. The children love this game and often request it.

Chapter Four
Child Development

The essence of independence is to be able to do something for oneself. [1]

MARIA MONTESSORI

Sensitive Periods
What are they and why are they critical to a child's development?

A sensitive period is a time when the brain is at its peak for optimal learning of a specific skill without formal training. There is a time range during which most children, regardless of race or gender, learn how to crawl, walk and talk. This is universal world-wide. Some children do it a little earlier and some a little later, but if they don't learn it when that part of the brain is most active, it becomes harder to learn later.

No one sits a child down and says, "Today I'm going to teach you how to talk." In the first two years of life, a child learns to speak, without formal instruction, by absorbing his environment. Yet an adult would not be able to do the same thing were he to visit a foreign country for two years. If a child has the right exposure while his sensitive period for a specific skill is at its peak, he will flow right into learning it with ease.

When a sensitive period closes down, the next area of the brain opens up for development, as the child enters into another sensitive period. Pathways in the brain develop in a certain sequential order, and each stage lays the foundation for the next one. The child must take his time at each point so that he can fully absorb what he needs for the next period.

---

1 Maria Montessori, *The Absorbent Mind*, (New York: Dell Publishing, 1967), p.155.

The brain has its own timetable for development, so the length of time it takes to learn a skill varies from child to child. This is why putting undue pressure on a child to excel or holding him back in his development is harmful. Our goal as educators is to enrich each stage of development as much as possible in order to strengthen the brain.

Montessori learned about sensitive periods from the writings of Jean Itard (1774–1838), a French physician who stressed that in order to grow up normally a child must experience the proper stimulation during these developmental stages. Montessori expanded on his work and observed that children have sensitive periods not only for crawling, walking and talking, but also for order, concentration, sight, reading, grammar, addition, and so on. In the Montessori classroom there are materials and/ or lessons designed specifically to meet all these sensitive periods; but in traditional and modern classrooms, sensitive periods are not even acknowledged, let alone satisfied. It is important to note that when a sensitive period is missed, succeeding periods become much harder because of the hierarchal structure of acquiring knowledge. If a child misses his sensitive period for fine motor control, writing will be difficult; if he misses his sensitive period for learning the letter sounds, reading will take more effort; and so on.

While Montessori gave the ages for the sensitive periods in her training courses (they are not listed in her books), she stressed that the teacher must properly observe a child to figure out what sensitive period he is experiencing.

Here are some examples of sensitive periods:

- Sight: 0–4 months
- Touch: 0–4 years
- Concentration: 2–4 years
- Order: 2–2½ years
- Control and coordination of body: 2–5 years
- Language of native tongue: 0–5 years
- Speech: 0–6 years
- Preparation for writing with the metal insets and sandpaper letters: 3 years
- Preparation for reading with word analysis: 2½–4 years
- Preparation for reading with letter sounds: 2½ to 4 years (Age 2½ is the critical age and with some children even earlier)

- Reading short phonetic words: 4–4½ years
- Reading sentences: 5–6 years
- Building words: 3½–4½ years
- Grammar: 6–9 years
- Basic mathematical operations: 4–5 years
- Social skills: 2–5 years
- Morality: 2–6 years
- Brain's method of functioning: 0–6 years

If the sensitive periods are missed, can they be made up? No. The child's cognitive development will fall behind what it otherwise could have been. Can the damage be corrected later? This is a good question. While the brain can create new neural pathways, the effort required to do so is immense, and in some cases, corrections may not be possible. When we adults try to learn how to speak a foreign language, we find that some sounds now seem impossible to make. A sensitive period, when gone, is gone forever. This is why meeting a child's sensitive periods for learning is critical.

Reality

I was sitting on the floor of the classroom presenting the cubed tower to a three-year-old student. It was the first time she had seen this material and I needed her full concentration. Then I felt someone standing next to me, bending his body into mine, nudging me, trying to get my immediate attention.

"Just a minute," I said.

The little person did not want to wait, and leaned in against me again, "Miss Char."

"Just a minute, I'm almost done," I reiterated, hoping it would ease his impatience. But he would not leave.

Feeling his sense of urgency, I finished presenting the tower, and turned to see who was the source of the interruption. It was Joey, another three-year-old, cute as a button. "Miss Char."

"Yes?" I said.

"Have you ever been a purse?"

"A *what?*"

"A purse. Have you ever been a purse?"

I looked directly into the big brown eyes staring intently into mine. I glanced across the room and saw my assistant watching with her hand on her mouth, making a valiant attempt to hold back rolls of laughter. Inside myself, I could feel a geyser of giggles start to erupt but successfully pushed them down. I looked back at Joey, his eyes still locked on my face.

"Why no, Joey. I can't say as I've ever been a purse."

Without missing a beat, he turned right around and walked directly over to another child. "Hey Josh, have you ever been a purse?"

I looked at my assistant and could feel the laughter returning; the question he was asking was hilarious. It was when I saw him go to each and every child in the room with his question that the thought struck me—he was deadly serious. I had learned when I took the Montessori training that the child's relationship with reality was precarious, but I had no idea—I mean really, no idea—that it was like *this*.

Some years later another incident got my attention. Our youngest daughter, then three years old, was curled up on my lap listening to me read a story. When I was done reading, she pointed to a picture of a character in the book and said, "Mommy, I am afraid that witch will come out of the book and get me." When I assured her that could not happen, she said, "I know, but I'm still scared." I stopped, looked at her and thought about Joey. It was then that I decided to take a deeper look at the child's mind and his view of reality.

I thought about a book at school that shows all kinds of goofy things going on: a man mowing a carpet with grass coming out of it, an object coming out of a painting on a wall, fish swimming in a bird cage, and so on. I remembered that it was only the five- and six-year-olds who found the book humorous. The two- and three-year-olds just looked at the older children dazedly, as if to say, "What's so funny?" The younger children did not know yet that these things can't really happen, or why they do not make sense.

I started to pay much closer attention to things that frightened children. I noticed that when I read books to the children in my class, the two- and three-year-olds would sometimes slightly cower at certain pictures. I have a real, stuffed owl that is mounted on the wall. Even though it is obviously dead, younger children thought it might come alive and fly around the room. Then there were the fears of animals, sounds, separation from parents, and other anxieties. The fear of monsters seems to be pretty universal, but fears came in all shapes and sizes, some predicable and some not.

Why can learning about the world be so scary for the young child? The baby has to learn everything from the beginning and, for the very first time, as he faces a whirling chaos of sensory data. He needs to put it all together to figure it out and it is a daunting task. We may think that Joey's question was unusual for a child to ask, and it was. But it was a question that clearly illustrates just how confusing reality is at this time in his life and that, for the child, learning about the world is serious business.

We know when we are safe but how would a child know that? He hasn't been alive long enough to observe or experience very much yet. We can tell him that, no, the witch will not come out of the book. We can tell him with our arms opened wide that we will catch him when he jumps into the swimming pool. We can tell him that the puppy will not hurt him, or that the dog is in his pen with a lock on the gate, and we can even show him the lock. We can tell him over and over that the sound he hears outside his window at night is nothing to worry about. Yet he still worries. He worries because he does not have enough information to know that what we are telling him is true. He cannot take us on faith; he has to know it for himself.

Children ask all kinds of questions about the nature of reality. They want to know if reality is what they perceive it to be. Children constantly watch me perform a task that they have seen me do many times and then ask me what I am doing, even though they can see very clearly what I am doing. Children will ask, "If you show me work, then I've been shown it, right?" They will do an addition problem and count, "One, two, three, four, five, six, seven…is the answer seven?" Children want verification that reality is what it is. If they could ask it philosophically they would say, "Is A, A?"

Children want to know if reality is unwavering or if it will change. Objects themselves are unstable to them; they cannot foresee what objects will do because they don't have enough knowledge about their identity and don't understand that causality depends on that identity. What an object can do or have done to it, depends on what it is. People and animals are even harder to predict because they are moving objects. Can people fly like birds? Can birds turn into chocolate? Are cars and trucks alive? (Three-year-olds have the misconception that anything that moves is alive.) Will something that doesn't move come alive? This is why order is so important to them. Once they figure something out, they become upset if something changes. They want reality to stay the same and remain constant—to be something they can rely on—or they feel insecure.

At the same time, if something happens that they do not like, they can literally try to change reality. Children think that if they tell a lie enough times, it will change what happened, even if they are caught red handed. "I didn't do it. I didn't do it. I didn't do it." "But I watched you do it." "But I didn't do it!" People think that children say this to avoid getting into trouble, which is true, but there can be more going on. I recall an incident when I was five years old and did something wrong. My brother and sister immediately climbed on my case, reporting my dastardly deed to our parents. But being the youngest, I was fed up with always being blamed for every wrongdoing, so I thought I would try a new strategy. I was sure it would work; just keep denying that I did it and it would change what had actually happened. I remember lowering my eyes when I didn't get by with that.

Children have a very hard time with cause and effect. "I didn't break it, it was an accident." Translation: "It was an accident, I didn't mean to drop it so I couldn't have broken it." They live in the immediate range of the moment, the here and now. They have very little concept of time. This leads to an inability to see consequences or think long range, and also leads to many other misconceptions (e.g. that death is not permanent).

Children are like little philosophers and will argue with each other about facts, trying to figure out how they are determined. "My dad says…" "Well *my* dad says…" They think that if someone says something, that makes it true. "She says I'm mean. Am I?" "Emily said I don't have a baby sister and I do. Do I?" They want to know, what is the truth? And is it true because someone said it is true?

So how does a child determine what is true? The primary way the young child learns in the beginning is through touch and experience with concrete objects. The child is like a little scientist—testing, testing, testing. Babies will drop items from their high chairs over and over and then look down and watch intently to see what happens. Will it go down each and every time? That is what they want to know. They are experiencing their very first lesson in the principle of gravity. Children also test cause and effect. Before I was two years of age I remember crawling around on the floor and noticing an outlet. Being curious, I plunged my finger into it. I learned the consequence of my action and so did my mother when she heard my wails. But some time later, when I was crawling around on the floor, I saw another outlet and without hesitation plunged my finger in again, wondering if the same thing would happen. I found out! Another time, I was with my father in the front seat when he was driving. I must have been about five years old. I remember thinking, "I wonder what would happen if I grabbed the steering wheel and gave it a yank." I did it and found out from the immediate and voluble reaction of my dad that it was a very dangerous thing to do. Then I thought, "I wonder if dad will react the same way if I do it again. I bet he will." So I grabbed the steering wheel and gave it another tug. My dad was very, very upset with me and his reaction matched my prediction and confirmed my thoughts about safety in the car.

Children are hindered in their view of reality when they are not told the truth. Adults often lie to children in the hope of avoiding conflict. When the child wants a cookie and his parents do not want him to have one, in order to avoid the child's tears, some parents tell him there are no cookies. The child wonders about this. He thought he saw cookies in that cookie jar, but now he is told there are none, so he begins to doubt himself. The same thing happens when a parent lies about the child's age to get a cheaper admittance fee to a movie, or when a child hears his parent call in sick though the parent is clearly fine, and so on. Lying to a child, or in the presence of a child, undercuts his confidence in his ability to figure out reality. The solution? Be honest.

There are times when adults do not want to lie, but do so because they want to spare the child sadness. I once heard a young girl state that her mother was scared of her father (the parents were in the process of separating and it was an abusive relationship). The mother immediately denied it, making all kinds of excuses to smooth the accusation over. The child's body shrank and her face clouded over: "But Mommy..." The mother continued to deny it and the child grew sadder and then withdrew. The mother's intentions were to protect the child from fear, but what happened instead was that the child felt insecure in what she perceived to be true. Children think, "What's wrong with me?" In these situations it is best just to tell the truth. It does not mean that all the details need to be told to the child (yes, he beats me every night and I have black and blue marks, etc.), but verifying what the child knows to be a fact is crucial for his confidence in his mind. The truth is a lot less scary than the unknown or the feeling that one is incompetent to know reality.

Adults will also lie to children for the purpose of having fun—for example, telling them that certain fantasy characters exist such as Santa Claus, the tooth fairy and the Easter bunny. For the same reasons, lying is wrong. It only adds to the child's confusion about reality and his fear of the unknown. If Santa is real, then why are monsters not real? Why are only the good fantasy characters real, but not the bad ones? This does not make sense to children. Parents rationalize lying by saying that the child will figure it out when he gets older. This is true, but the question is, what is happening to him in the meantime? He has accepted a contradiction between what he has been told and what he has observed. What other inconsistencies will he accept because of it? When a child finally learns the truth about Santa, he can be angry at his parents initially and feel a sense of betrayal that his parents lied to him. As he grows up, he realizes that these are just games that parents enjoy playing with their children, and that no harm was intended; so they usually do not harm the child-parent relationship in the long run, but they can still harm the child's development. Adults will say that their belief in Santa did not hurt them as a child, but most adults cannot recall much, if anything, from the time when their minds were forming their basic mode of functioning in determining the facts of reality. (Adults have a hard time swallowing this idea of letting children in on the truth about Santa because they really love playing these games; but the games can still be played as long as children are told that the games are pretend. And, as a matter of fact, the Santa game can be even more fun when children are allowed to participate, for example by helping to stuff the stockings.)

What about the child's misconceptions, things he doesn't know enough about yet to be able to form the right conclusions, such as the dangers of the dark or monsters? Handling a child's fears is a judgment call and depends on what the child is afraid of and why. For some fears, such as a fear of monsters, all one can do is wait it out until he is old enough to understand that they aren't real. In the meantime, the adult can comfort the child, let him use a night light in his room, and at the same time assure him that these things do not exist. For other fears, it is best to give him a gentle nudge so that he can learn from experience that he doesn't need to be afraid. The child may cry at the thought of going into the wading pool, but holding him and slowly easing him into the water and staying right there with him is a good way of helping him overcome that fear. The goal is for the child to understand that he cannot expect to know everything about the world yet, but that he can still deal with it as he learns about it.

It can be shocking to find out just how unstable reality is to the young child. If he does not have a firm grasp of what exists, how can he go on to think, to reason, and to make connections from one idea to the next when he is an adult? The ability to think clearly is a person's only means of dealing with the world and his life. We have no automatic way of knowing answers to problems; we have to figure them out logically. Thoughts and ideas are based on concretes, on a foundation of facts. If the foundation is corrupt, all that follows is mush.

When children grow up, they will be citizens of a country. What happens then, when the majority of the citizens have inept brains and are faced with something ominous, such as a dictatorship? People often refer to this as a political crisis, but it is much more fundamental than that. It is a war of ideas over whether someone else has a right to control your life or whether you have the right and responsibility to control your own. If Joey thinks reality is too confusing and overwhelming, he can go no further. He will take the word of others for what is true and become a follower. Since he does not think for himself, he will feel helpless and conclude that someone else might as well take care of him, so let family, friends, neighbors or the government do it. This is not the road to productivity and happiness. The way a person learns about and deals with reality in childhood directly affects what he becomes as an adult.

Many modern-day philosophers state that there is no such thing as objective reality, that reality is whatever you want it to be, that no one can know anything for sure, and that there are no absolutes. Evidently, living in a state of confusion, fear and dependence is acceptable to them. Not to me. The value of learning about the nature of existence cannot be overstated. When Joey looks in your eyes with all the innocence that a child can bring and says, "Have you ever been a purse?" give him what he needs—a stable, guiding hand towards his quest to understand reality.

Order

The two-year-old has an unmistakable need for order. He asks for the same dinner plate or glass or blanket. He wants to kiss his mother goodbye in the exact same spot every day before going to school. He wants his routines to remain intact and needs forewarning when they are changed. It is fortunate that the child is drawn to order so naturally, as it is order that is needed to learn. Some of these routines seem pretty silly from an adult perspective, but they are the start of logic and very necessary for the child to establish the stability of his world. Will a rock stay a rock? When I can't see it? When someone throws it over the fence?

Order is a sensitive period that peaks at age two and gradually decreases as the child gets older. Maria Montessori discovered this sensitivity through incidents such as the following: A young girl was crying uncontrollably and no matter what the adults did, she continued to have a tantrum and was inconsolable. Someone picked up a wet umbrella which had been set down opened up so it would dry, and she closed it. Immediately the child stopped crying. Montessori re-opened the umbrella to see if that was what was bothering the child. Sure enough, the tantrum resumed. Once closed, the crying again stopped. It bothered the girl that the umbrella was opened up inside the house. In the child's mind, umbrellas were to be open only outside, where it was raining.

For the two- and three-year-old, things *must* remain the same. The child is learning simply that they *are*—not yet that they exist independent of his consciousness. He is learning the nature of reality. And in learning this, if the carpet gets pulled out from under him, it causes internal bewilderment and unhappiness. The morning after a wind storm, the light switch doesn't turn the light on. The child flicks the switch over and over. Later the child refuses to eat breakfast, or go to school, or to put on his coat. The security of permanence is gone. The more intelligent the child, the more upset he will be. Even the changing of seasons can be upsetting. Remember that to a child of this age, it's all magic: snow, leaves falling, flowers blooming—all magic.

What would happen if you were in a huge hurry and rushed into the grocery store to buy some milk only to find that everything had been changed around? Nothing was where it used to be. The meat department was now over by the pharmacy and the bread was in the fresh produce department. Not only that, but everything else was disorganized as well. All the cheeses weren't together, some cereal was in every aisle, the bananas were in with the potatoes and so on. Can you imagine your frustration? This is exactly the type of frustration a child feels when order is changed for him. The difference is that the adult has life experiences and knows this is a temporary situation. He knows, for example, that the milk is in the grocery store somewhere, even though he doesn't know precisely where. The child, on the other hand, has a problem. He doesn't even know whether or not the milk is in the store, because he hasn't had the experience needed to put his mind in order.

Jossie, age two, was standing near her slipper drawer at school, close to tears. "Now, Jossie, don't be difficult," her teacher said. "Put your gym shoes in your drawer. Do it right now or you will be in big trouble." Reluctantly, Jossie put the shoes into the drawer, but looked back angrily. The teacher remarked to the other adults standing nearby that Jossie was very stubborn and unreasonable, and commented, "At least this time she didn't throw one of her temper tantrums."

The child's sensitivity to order is probably one of the most frequently misunderstood aspects about children. They are often shamed, scolded or punished when adults don't understand that their sense of order is upset. We need to be aware that their understanding of the world is extremely limited. They are learning the facts of reality for the very first time and since they do not yet know what is and isn't real, what can and can't happen, they don't want anything to change. Change upsets the very world they have been trying so hard to sort out. In Jossie's case, she thought that only her *slippers* were supposed to go in the drawer, and she was very upset at the change.

The father of one of my students told me that of all the things I told him about children, their sensitivity to order helped him the most in understanding his child. Order is the starting point of logic as the child seeks knowledge about reality. And because of that, children have not just a desire for order, but a *need* for order.

Concentration

Mark loved school and could hardly wait to arrive every day. He came into the classroom, sat on the line quietly, and paid attention during circle time. During work time he took out activities one after another, occasionally socializing with his friends. He was working on higher math skills and had a reading workbook. When his teacher showed him a lesson, he always took it out on succeeding days to practice it. Sometimes he would observe rather than work, but rarely disrupted the other students. He seldom had to be directed towards work; he was independently motivated.

Mark knew how to take the initiative in learning—he knew how to get started all by himself and he did it every day.

Johnny, on the other hand, complained that there was nothing to do at school and that he would much rather play with toys. During first circle he had a hard time sitting still and paying attention. During work time, when his teacher showed him a lesson, he did it only once and then waited for her to tell him what to do next. He would wander around the room, unable to decide what to do, and often ended up getting into trouble. His teachers were constantly telling him to find something to do, but Johnny wouldn't work unless someone was sitting right next to him, working with him. He told his parents that the teacher never showed him any work, and said he wanted to do the bank game and a reading workbook.

At conferences, Mark's parents were glad that he was learning how to think for himself. They were eager to hear about his behavior, and his choice-making and problem-solving skills. They viewed his self-motivation as success. Johnny's parents, on the other hand, wanted their son to excel academically. They asked lots of questions about how Johnny was doing in math and reading, but they never once asked the teacher the most important question of all.

Before a child can advance, there is something fundamental that he needs to learn. Dr. Montessori wrote, "The first essential for the child's development is concentration. It lays the whole basis for his character and social behavior."[2] Concentration is the starting point for academics, character, social skills, morality, intelligence, body coordination—everything. Most children at ages 2–3 begin with very short concentration spans, because they are bombarded with so much information that it is difficult for them to focus. Montessori helps them to sort out the essentials of reality, and it is amazing how quickly their concentration improves. In addition, Montessori schools are ideal for fostering the child's attention span, because his sensitive periods are met, and because the child is allowed to practice his work *without interruption*. This is vital. Montessori observed:

> Praise, help, or even a look, may be enough to interrupt him, or destroy the activity. It seems a strange thing to say, but this can happen even if the child merely becomes aware of being watched.

2 Maria Montessori, *The Absorbent Mind*, (New York: Dell Publishing Co., 1967), p. 222.

> After all, we too sometimes feel unable to go on working if some-
> one comes to see what we are doing. The great principle which
> brings success to the teacher is this: *as soon as concentration has
> begun, act as if the child does not exist.*[3]

The whole idea is for the adult to fade into the background so the child can concentrate.

The child is also allowed to repeat his work as often as he likes, as repetition is exactly what he needs; he must practice what he is learning until he has mastered it before he can go on to the next step. No one would expect a classical pianist to be able to play a complex piece like Rachmaninoff's second piano concerto without having mastered, through constant repetition, all the many steps required to achieve musical compe-tence; yet some adults expect a child to function in a classroom without mastering each of the steps required for competence in *his* endeavors. Sometimes people worry that their child is bored because he does the same work over and over, but the work he has chosen has grabbed his attention and he is learning a very important skill—how to concentrate. (See next section on "Repetition.")

Montessori had this to say about the child who can focus his mind:

> The child who concentrates is immensely happy; he ignores his
> neighbors or the visitors circulating about him. For the time being
> his spirit is like that of a hermit in the desert: a new consciousness
> has been born in him, that of his own individuality. When he
> comes out of his concentration, he seems to perceive the world
> anew as a boundless field for fresh discoveries. He also becomes
> aware of his classmates in whom he takes an affectionate inter-
> est. Love awakens in him for people and for things. He becomes
> friendly to everyone, ready to admire all that is beautiful. The
> spiritual process is plain: he detaches himself from the world in
> order to attain the power to unite himself with it.[4]

If you are Johnny's parents, what can you do to help him concentrate? Here are some of my suggestions:

• Let the child initiate his own activities, then don't interrupt him

---

3 Maria Montessori, *The Absorbent Mind*, (New York: Dell Publishing Co., 1967), p. 280.
4 Maria Montessori, *The Absorbent Mind*, (New York: Dell Publishing Co., 1967), pp. 272–278.

while he is engaged in them. However, the activities must be purposeful. He can't be allowed to run around being destructive.

- Purchase materials that he is interested in, show him how to use them and then let him work on them independently. If a child refuses to work on something by himself without you there, you need to work on getting him to feel comfortable without you. Otherwise, when he goes to school, he won't work unless another child or the teacher is working with him.
- Provide "alone" time for your child every day. If he isn't used to being alone, start out with a short amount of time and increase it as he gets used to it.
- Create a calm, quiet environment. Too much noise and commotion overwhelm the child and can cause attention difficulties.
- Make sure your child gets enough sleep. Lack of rest affects attention and mood.
- Make sure your child eats nutritious food.
- Do not tell your child he is smart. Instead, encourage him to try hard. (See "Praise" in Chapter 7.)
- Turn off the television. (See "Television" in Chapter 6.)
- Do not let your child spend time on the computer. (See "Computers" in Chapter 6.)
- Send your child outside to play. It is remarkable how much this can help. He has to pay attention to his environment and invent his own things to do.
- There are times when children need to be required to sit still and listen, as when reading a book. Toddlers may be able to sit for only a very short time and that's okay. Just go with what they are capable of and try to encourage them to gradually increase their attention span.
- Enroll your child in Montessori school when he is most sensitive to learning how to concentrate (age 2 to 3).
- If a child starts Montessori by age 3½ and concentration does not improve by the time he is 5, there is probably something wrong, such as health issues with vision, hearing, allergies, etc. Have your child examined by a physician.

It isn't that Johnny's parents don't care about him or don't love him. They do. Johnny's parents didn't ask the teacher if Johnny could concentrate, because they didn't know that concentration is something Johnny needs to learn before he can progress in his development.

Repetition

One Monday morning I received a phone call from Billy's parents. They wanted to talk to me as soon as possible. Could they meet with me after school? Sure. Billy was a perky, cheerful five-year-old whom I adored. I wondered what they wanted to talk to me about.

After school, Billy's parents arrived right on time, but as they walked down the hallway towards the classroom I could tell they were upset— very upset. I felt awful. They came into the classroom and sat down silently. Then they began to ask questions. Why was I so mean to Billy? Was I angry with him? Didn't I like their son?

Huh?

I thought back to Friday. Billy's aunt had come to observe. Billy had taken out the cloth-washing work. He'd washed the cloths again and again and again until he was done, then carried the wash basin back over to the sink to dump the water out. As he'd lifted it to pour, it slipped out of his hands and the water spilled all over the floor. The tile floor was no longer a floor, it was a lake. Billy had immediately gone to get the mop to clean it up. He had mopped and mopped and mopped. He'd mopped so long and so hard that before I knew it, the afternoon was over; but the lake had gone and the tile floor had been returned to its normal dry state. He'd done a great job. He hadn't asked for any help. Once or twice he'd started chatting with his friends and I'd reminded him to finish, but he'd seemed happy. If he'd felt frustrated, I hadn't noticed it. I was impressed that he had stuck with it and got it done.

I could understand why the observer had been upset. She'd probably come expecting to see Billy working on math problems or reading and been shocked to see him cleaning instead. Since many adults do not like to clean, she had viewed Billy's task as onerous. She probably hadn't known that washing the cloths had been his choice. She most likely hadn't realized that he'd experienced a lesson in persistence and responsibility that day. She had not understood that through the repetition of his work he had been learning how to be successful, and that his pride in this success was what had mattered.

The child develops concentration from doing a chosen
purposeful activity over and over.

Children like to practice, and it doesn't bother them how long they do it. If it had taken me all afternoon to wash cloths and clean up a water mess, it would have upset me, because I have other things I want to do; but I'm an adult, and adults shouldn't view these events in children's lives from an adult's perspective.

This is a hard concept for parents to understand. We get lots of questions about children who practice the same thing over and over, and bring home the same work day after day. "Why does he cut paper every day?" "He cut up apples all day long? (sigh) Really?" "How many continent maps will he do before he does something new?" "Another Columbus booklet? Again?" "Doesn't he ever learn anything else?" "Doesn't he ever *do* anything else?"

Children learn from repetition, the act of going through a chosen activity over and over again. And there is something fundamental about it that is crucial for their development. Montessori discovered this when she observed a three-year-old girl working on the knobbed cylinders:

> I then decided to see how concentrated she was in her strange employment. I told the teacher to (have) the other children sing and (march around). But this did not disturb the child at all in her labors. I then gently picked up the (little) chair she was sitting and set it on top of a small table.
>
> As I lifted the chair she clutched the objects with which she was working and placed them on her knees, but then continued with the same task. From the time I began to count, she repeated the exercise forty-two times. Then she stopped as if coming out of a dream and smiled happily. Her eyes shone brightly and she looked about. She had not even noticed what we had done to disturb her. And now, for no apparent reason, her task was finished. But what was finished and why?
>
> This gave us our first insight into the unexplored depths of the child's mind. This little girl was at an age when attention was fickle, when the mind skips from one thing to another without being able to stop. And yet she had become so absorbed in what she was doing that her ego became insensible to external stimuli. Her concentration had been accompanied by a rhythmical movement of her hands as she lifted the different objects together.[5]

---

5 Maria Montessori, *The Secret of Childhood*, (New York: Ballantine Books, 1966), p. 119–120.

Once children learn how to concentrate, they don't learn from doing something only once, or by doing it quickly so they can move to the next activity. It is from practice that proficiency is attained. How many of us learned where all the keys on the computer keyboard are by pressing each of them only once? How many of us can read a book only once and remember everything about it? Or listen to a philosophical lecture once and recall all the important points? Or learn how to sew or do wood-working in a single lesson? Or learn any new skill by trying it only once?

It is important to remember that the practice a child does in the Montessori classroom is not the same thing as drill. Drill is imposed on a child, an exercise requiring him to repeat something over and over in order to learn it by rote. Usually drill is boring and uninteresting to the child, who does it only to please the adult. In contrast, repetition chosen by the child meets his needs and therefore is very interesting to him. The older baby chooses to pull himself up and walk around the table for long periods of time and at frequent intervals during the day. No one questions this kind of repetition. Everyone knows he's practicing for walking, and it is always clear that the baby is enjoying himself.

In the Montessori classroom, the activity that a child repeats is chosen by the child and is done because he wants to do it. *The child makes the choice.* The young child repeats because he is learning how to do the activity; he strives to accomplish it and feels good when he succeeds: "I did it all by myself." The older child repeats in order to perfect his movements and to make them more precise. It is very important that we do not continually disturb the child during these times of practice. We don't want him to conclude that he is "not good enough." This is why the Montessori environment is ideal for the child: it allows a child to repeat activities as much as he desires, without drill.

Evidently when I explained all this to Billy's parents, it satisfied them, because they did not withdraw him from school. Learning through repetition is important. Some work, such as cleaning, may be mundane to the adult; but it is significant to the child and that is why he does it over and over.

Choice Making

When children were babies, they crawled around everywhere, exploring and putting objects into their mouths. It seemed as though they were constantly on the move, and they were. They were gathering information for the next stage of development, when the brain's way of functioning changes. At this point the child's subconscious can no longer drive his actions, so he must learn how to direct them by making conscious choices.

Parents can prepare their children for this stage by beginning to offer them a few choices when they are in the high chair:

"Do you want this cracker or that one?"

"Do you want this plate or that one?"

When the child gets a little older, "Do you want to wear this outfit or that one?" Simple choices like this are helpful in preparing them for the stage when they start putting together all the information they have gathered and choose what to focus their minds on as they form concepts.

The choices offered to children should be only choices that they are ready to make. They cannot be allowed to decide whether or not to take medicine, brush their teeth, or take a bath; or choose what school to attend; or misbehave or do things that are unsafe. I once had a student, Kayla, who wore her swimming suit to school in January when it was -30° F. When I questioned the father about it he looked at me oddly and said, "Well, you said we needed to let our children make choices and this is what Kayla wanted to wear." The choices allowed have to be safe, age appropriate and commonsensical.

The challenge comes in deciding what to do when the child doesn't want to make a choice. It is not uncommon for children to refuse disciplinary choices. "You can either stop screaming or go to your room." The child may continue to scream without going to his room, in which case the adult has to follow through with the choices that were given and escort the child to his room. Sometimes the child will reject the choices we give him and insist on one that is unacceptable. If the child continues to defy the adult, then he needs to be told that if he doesn't choose one of the options he was given, the adult will choose one for him.

If children make the wrong choices, they need to be allowed to feel the consequences so that they will think before acting and see the connection between what they think and what they do. If a child carries a glass of water carelessly, it may fall and make a mess. The consequence is that he needs to clean up the mess. If he spends all his money on candy, he won't have enough money to go to a movie. The consequence is that he doesn't get to go to the movie. By experiencing consequences, children learn to think ahead.

Some children have a hard time making choices. This can happen when adults do too much for them, when they are constantly told what to do, when they lack self-confidence, or when they are used to being entertained (e.g. by TV, video games and computers). Children need to take care of themselves, make their own decisions and create their own activities to keep themselves busy. They won't learn how to make choices if someone is already doing it for them. Later, when they go to school, they may stand around waiting for the teachers to tell them what to do. Some children just take a little time to figure out that they are expected to find their own work. With others, we may make a work choice for them, remind them of what work they have been shown, give them suggestions, tell them they must work alone, or give them a time limit for making a choice. But ultimately it is the child's responsibility to start making choices on his own.

I detest books like "101 Ways to Keep Your Child Busy," because their message is that it is the parent's responsibility to find things for the child to do. It is not. In conventional schools, the teacher also takes responsibility for keeping children busy by telling them exactly what they must do, almost from moment to moment. If a child doesn't learn how to make choices, there will be negative consequences. The child might be afraid of making the wrong choices and feel insecure. If he is constantly told what to do and when to do it, he will learn to follow someone else's directions, instead of doing his own thinking and following his own conscience. And guess where that leads when he becomes a teenager—Barbara Coloroso explains in her book *Kids are Worth It*:

> The major problems arise when the teen decides he doesn't want to please his parents anymore. More than once, (controlling) parents have said to me, "Would you look at this kid. He was such a good kid, so well behaved, so well mannered, so well dressed. Now look at him!" I say, "You know what? He hasn't changed. From the time he was young, he dressed the way you told him to dress; he acted the way you told him to act; he said the things you told him to say. He's been listening to somebody else tell him what to do. He's been doing it. He hasn't changed. He is still listening to somebody else tell him what to do. The problem is, it isn't you anymore; it's his peers."[6]

---

6 Barbara Coloroso, *Kids are Worth It: Giving Your Child the Gift of Inner Discipline* (New York, Harper Collins Publishers, 1994).

A child like this is at risk of caving in to peer group pressure and falling into all kinds of trouble and unhappiness. What will the dependent child do when his friends command that he do something illegal or immoral? If a child doesn't learn how to make simple choices, he will have a hard time making more complicated ones later, such as choosing between good and bad, choosing between right and wrong, taking the initiative, making friends, and so on. Choice making is the starting point of independence. When the child makes a choice he is saying, "I want." He is asserting himself as an individual; it is what *he* wants, not what someone else wants. He is starting to exercise his free will. By making choices, he starts to evaluate, and he begins to form values—his own values, which are essential in the child's steps toward autonomy.

Independence

Charles refuses to steal because he is afraid that his father will get mad at him; but his friend, Karl, refuses to do it because he thinks stealing is wrong. James, age five, has behavior problems, refuses to do his work and disrupts the class. His mother thinks he is exhibiting independence. A teenager, Lisa, thinks she is exercising her independence when she defies her parents' values and takes on the values of the crowd at school. But who is being independent? What exactly is independence and why is it important?

Independence is the recognition that you are responsible for yourself and therefore must do your own thinking, and make your own judgments, decisions and choices based on this thinking. Because the correctness of your thinking is not guaranteed, you can make errors; but thinking and making mistakes is far preferable to unthinking memorization of facts. The independent mind can correct honest mistakes; it can go back to reality for the answer. But a mind that knows only how to memorize has been seriously hampered because it doesn't know how to distinguish truth from error, and cannot even begin to figure out if what it believes *is* an error.

> No matter how vast your knowledge or how modest, it is your own mind that has to acquire it. It is only with your own knowledge that you can deal. It is only your own knowledge that you can

claim to possess or ask others to consider. Your mind is your only judge of truth—and if others dissent from your verdict, reality is the court of final appeal. Nothing but a man's mind can perform that complex, delicate, crucial process of identification which is thinking. Nothing can direct the process but his own judgment. Nothing can direct his judgment but his moral integrity. [7]

Self-reliance and self-sufficiency are vital for survival and crucial to the happiness of every human being. Consequently, independence should be the primary aim of a proper education. When people hear that Montessori's goal for the child is independence, they often raise their eyebrows, thinking that Montessori children do whatever they want, whenever they want; but this is due to a misunderstanding of the meaning and end result of independence.

When I had my own children, I felt well prepared because of my Montessori training, but there was one aspect that totally shocked me—how early the child strives for independence. Before our children were a year old they held their own bottles and attempted to put on their own socks. I watched in total awe as they tried and tried to put on their own socks over and over and over. Often they would concentrate on their goal for twenty minutes, sometimes longer, and they did not get discouraged or frustrated even though they were not successful. This convinced me more than anything that striving for independence is a natural and normal objective for the child.

In order for a young child to become independent, he needs muscular skill and coordination (how to zip, tie, etc.) and knowledge so that he can make decisions with meaning ("What should I make for lunch?"). While he is learning, he needs to be left to practice by himself without directions from the adult, so that he can focus on what he is doing rather than on what someone else is saying.

The Montessori rule of thumb: We try to *never* do for the child what he can do for himself. Think of this from the adult point of view. You just purchased a brand new computer and are eager to learn how to use it, but every time you sit down to try, instead of showing you how to use it and then giving you a turn, another adult swoops in and takes over. When the adult keeps doing things for the child, the child hears this message, "I can do it better than you and you're incompetent." Is this the message you want to give your child? Think about your interaction

7 Ayn Rand, *For the New Intellectual,* (New York: Random House, 1961), p. 126.

with him throughout the day. How many times do you do for your child what he could and should be doing for himself? Do you put on his shoes for him? Put on his coat?

Watch your child carefully. If he is struggling while trying to do something, ask him if he wants your assistance rather than assume he can't do it. Try to provide time for your child to dress himself. This may mean you will be inconvenienced—you may have to get up earlier in the morning.

> (Montessori) knew it was harder to teach a child to feed, wash, and dress himself than to do those things for him, "but the former is the work of an educator, the latter is the easy and inferior work of a servant." It hindered the child's development rather than fostered it. [8]

Letting a younger child be independent takes more of your time—but trust me, when he gets older and can do things on his own, it will be well worth it. You won't have to be watching his every move, making sure he has done what he is supposed to do. You will feel freer and he will feel capable. In Montessori we want to hear a child say, "I can do it all by myself!" Then we know his self-esteem is building.

Here are some milestones for independence. Pre-elementary children should be demonstrating competency in these skills:

- Bathing—age 3 (although help may be needed to rinse soap out of the hair). The child should begin to participate in his own bathing as soon as he is interested, which is usually before age one.
- Feeding himself—should begin as soon as the child shows an interest. Should be competent by age 2.
- Fixing own lunch—can begin simple tasks at age 2 (such as buttering toast). Should be competent to fix an easy meal by age 5 with adult supervision.
- Putting on own coat—17–18 months
- Dressing—ages 3–4

In the development of a healthy independence the child must be allowed to make choices (see "Choice Making" in Chapter 4), but within a proper framework; as he gets older, you expand this framework, allowing him to make more choices with more complications.

---

8 Rita Kramer, *Maria Montessori*, (New York: Capricorn Books, 1977), p. 120.

My mother did what many mothers did when I was growing up—she did *everything* for me. I grew up feeling insecure. I felt inept. When I was a teenager I was afraid to do many things that my peers weren't afraid to do, such as riding a bus. My sister talked about being afraid to answer the telephone. Can you imagine that? Most children rush to answer the phone. They think it's fun. Not us. We were totally dependent on our mother to do everything for us.

There are times, however, when it is okay to do things for the child that he usually does for himself. For example, you are late for an appointment. Explain to your child that you know he can do it himself, but you are late and so in this instance you will help him. That way you are acknowledging his competence and giving him a logical reason for doing it for him this time.

Conventional education sets the child up to be dependent on his peers. Often the whole group is punished for what one child does, so the group then puts pressure on the child to conform. Then is it any wonder that as an adolescent, he doesn't have a mind of his own or any confidence to say "No" when his peers do something wrong? He has been taught blind conformity instead of reason, instead of independence.

I'm not saying that the child be allowed to do whatever he wants to do: he still needs adult guidance, but you must keep in mind that it is normal that he wants independence, and you must give it to him as he shows you that he can handle it. When the adult does not allow independence, the child becomes angry, demanding, withdrawn. I have even seen it in toddlers and babies.

Have you ever thought about the most dreaded aspects of old age—not being able to read; losing your hearing; not being able to go where you want; needing help getting dressed; not being able to move? What is it that we are most afraid to lose? It's our independence. Without it, in essence, there is no life. Give life to your child—give him the gift of independence.

Work and the Child

TGIF is an acronym that stands for "Thank God It's Friday." It expresses relief that the work week is over and now the fun can begin, because the weekend is finally here. It has become a popular expression and when someone says it, it is assumed that everyone within earshot agrees and is looking forward to two days off. Yet my father didn't feel that way about Fridays. His favorite day of the week was Monday. "I just love looking forward to a whole week of work," he often told me as I was growing up.

I have often thought about my father's attitude toward work, especially after becoming a Montessori educator and observing the joy that children express over their work. "I got so much work done today!" I often hear a child say with open pride; or, "Look! I did it all by myself!"

During party days, we always have children who take out work, or come up to us and ask, "Would it be okay if I worked today?" We not uncommonly hear about children who can hardly wait until the weekend is over so they can go back to school. From time to time parents even tell me that their child wanted to move into the classroom so he could work all the time. I'll never forget the time I was having lunch with my colleagues and there came a knock at the door. On the other side were three elementary students who asked, "Could we please, *please*, finish our algebra instead of going outside for recess?" This same attitude occurred in the early Montessori schools. Rita Kramer, in her biography of Maria Montessori, wrote:

> When (Maria) Montessori found the teacher had made medals to give the children as rewards for good work she watched to see what would happen. The children accepted them politely but with little interest; they were more interested in being allowed to get on with the work itself... [9]

And Montessori relates that she was astonished when this incident happened:

> ...the Argentinian ambassador, hearing it said that in our schools children of four and five worked entirely on their own, read and wrote spontaneously, and had an excellent discipline not imposed by authority, found himself unable to believe this. So he thought he would pay a surprise visit. Unfortunately, it happened to be a holiday, so he found the school shut. This was a school called "The Children's House" in a block of working men's flats where the children lived with their parents. Just by chance, one of the children was in the courtyard and heard the ambassador's expres-

9 Rita Kramer, *Maria Montessori*, (New York: Capricorn Books, 1977), p. 120.

At the end of the day the children enjoy taking
responsibility for cleaning the classroom.

sion of annoyance. Guessing he was a visitor, the child said, "Don't worry about the school being shut. The caretaker has the key and we are all here." The door was soon opened and all the children went in and began to work...Only on the following day did the teacher hear what had happened. [10]

Children do love to work. They may have differences as to what kind of work they prefer (some love to prepare food and others to clean), but it isn't the specific kind of work that matters—it is the love of work itself. They feel an excitement about learning, the same kind of excitement as at Christmas, when they can hardly wait to open all the unknown boxes and find out what is inside. It is fascinating and fun because they are discovering the contents of the boxes for the very first time. This learning is work and this work is what children want to do.

So what has happened to most people between childhood and adulthood that has killed that love of work? Just exactly when did children cross the line from wanting to work to not wanting to work? When exactly did work become a negative? What changed?

Sadly, many adults misunderstand the child. When they see him work, they think it is play. When they see him pretend, they think he prefers the unreal world. They don't understand that when a child pretends to make cookies, he would actually prefer to be making real ones. So, many adults steer children in the direction of play rather than work, implying that work is tedious rather than pleasurable (forgetting that even hobbies and other relaxing activities such as reading involve work). To stifle the child's love of work is to suppress the deepest need of his nature. Children like to learn; and the work they go through in the process is the way that they develop their inner spirit; it gives them a feeling of accomplishment. They feel that they are capable of handling themselves in the world and that gives them a sense of pride and joy. And it's fun!

Once, when I was ill, I went to the clinic, which was located in a nearby store. Sitting close by was a mother and her young daughter. The mother got up and purchased some lottery tickets. When she sat back down, she said, "I sure hope I win." Her daughter asked, "Win what, Mommy?" The mom replied, "The lottery. If I win the lottery I will *never* have to work again." I was flabbergasted. Is that really the message that we want children to receive, that work is so awful it is to be avoided at all

---

10 Maria Montessori, *The Absorbent Mind*, (New York: Dell Publishing Co., 1967), p. 233.

costs? Any desire in that young girl to learn, accomplish, produce, think, achieve or create was brutally slapped down at that moment.

The period when children are uncorrupted by evil and wrongdoing is called childhood innocence. Let's not corrupt the minds of children by teaching them that something is bad when it is actually good. It is gratifying to me to know that my dad never lost an important part of his childhood innocence—he kept his work ethic. Let's help all children keep theirs.

Imagination

Ashley, age two, a perky, happy, bright child, loves to do things that seem out of the ordinary. She uses objects in a curious way, like pretending to paint or pretending to pour with empty containers. I often hear people say, "Ashley has such an imagination!" I commonly get remarks like this about young children. But is it really true that this represents an active imagination?

Imagination is the act of forming mental images of what is not actually present, or the act of creating mental images of what has never been directly experienced (a new mental image). Forming mental images is not something that automatically happens—it is something that is learned over time, in conjunction with the child's experiences. Young children go through a process of integrating their sensory information—what they see, touch, smell and hear. They need a lot of sensory input before they can make the integrations needed to visualize something (i.e. use their imagination). For example, before they can visualize a chair, they have to have experienced many chairs—their different shapes, sizes, colors, textures, weights, temperatures, sounds, smells, tastes and so on. It takes a long time, often years, before all this information is integrated and a visual symbol for it formed in their minds.

Most misconceptions about children arise because people falsely assume that the child's mind is like the adult's. We can visualize things, so when we see a young child "pretending," we think he too can visualize what isn't there. We think that when he is pouring from one empty container into another, this must come from his imagination. It isn't something he has observed from us, so we think he has thought of it on his own; but this is incorrect.

The young child is still learning about the differences between real and pretend. When Cassie, our oldest daughter, was little, she had a toy kitchen set in her room. When she turned two years old, she seemed very confused by it; she would take my hand, place it on the kitchen set, and then look at me as if to say, "Show me how it works." (Being the child of a Montessori teacher, she was used to my showing her work.) I myself was confused while showing her, because it wasn't real, it was pretend. She figured out that water didn't really come out of the faucet, the food couldn't be eaten, the stove couldn't be used for cooking, etc. Nothing happened and she lost interest in it. She started using it to store her books in, so we got rid of the kitchen set. In retrospect it was a mistake to have had it in the first place.

Are children attracted to fake kitchen sets? Yes. Why? Because they see adults in kitchens and they want to learn about them. They eventually lose interest *because* fake kitchens aren't real. The children who don't lose interest often have issues with concentration, behavior and maturity.

When a child pretends to paint or to pour, he isn't using his imagination. In order to imagine, one first has to know what reality is. The young child is in the process of figuring out reality. For example, when he "pretends" to pour, he would like really to be pouring. He wants to know if anything will come out of that container. We know it won't, because of our experience; he doesn't. When boys play with trucks, they are trying to figure out what it would be like to drive a real truck. When girls play with dolls, they are trying to figure out what it is really like to be a mommy (or in the case of Barbie dolls, what it would be like to be a grown-up woman). When children pretend to be a puppy, they really want to know what it would be like to be a puppy. We call it "play" but it is actually the child's work. It is work he must do in order to grow up.

Will older children pretend? Yes. When the five-year-old goes home and plays school, he is reliving it. He is learning from the repetition. Children will relive and act out real life scenarios as they continue to figure out the adult world. But if you give a child a choice between pretending and doing the real thing, he will choose the real thing.

Parents ask, "When I see my child doing these things, is it a problem? And what should I do?" No, it's not a problem. It is normal at first. Just give your child plenty of experience with real objects so that reality comes more clearly into focus. When a child "pretends" to pour, bring him something real to pour. Give him real paints (not a computer painting program). Let him help you take care of a baby or help you bake a real cake. Give him opportunities to do real things.

When two-year-olds start school, we see them do things like Ashley did (when she tried to pour with the bottles), but it usually doesn't last long because they start to figure out reality pretty quickly. We don't have any traditional toys in the classroom because such toys can be confusing. In rare cases a child will continue to misuse the classroom materials, and those who don't leave the world of non-reality are the ones we worry about. Parents sometimes tell me that they never did leave it until adulthood. Childhood for them was, understandably, extremely difficult.

Ashley's strength isn't that she has a vivid imagination; it's that she is very persistent in her quest to figure out the real world.

How the Young Child Communicates

A teacher receives a telephone call at home, late at night. It is from an upset parent. She is frantic. Her four-year-old son, Jake, has told her that his classmate, Stephen, said that he hated Jake and was going to kill him. The mother is worried that her son has been threatened and is concerned about his physical and psychological safety at school. The teacher tells the parent that she will speak with the children the next day, get to the bottom of what happened, and report back. The following day the teacher finds out that Jake had taken some of Stephen's work, and Stephen, not knowing what to do, did indeed say that he hated Jake and wanted to kill him. The teacher talks to the boys about better ways to handle the problem. Though the parent is informed of the discussion and told there is nothing to worry about, she is unconvinced and withdraws her child from school.

That was unfortunate. Young children do not know how to handle social situations. Stephen was angry and wanted Jake to give him his work back, but he didn't know what to do. The night before, Stephen had heard someone on TV use the words "hate" and "kill" and that person had also been very angry. So, Stephen repeated what he had heard, hoping those words would resolve his difficulty. Stephen had no intention of killing Jake. He had only a very vague understanding of what killing meant and did not even know that death is permanent—in his mind, it was like going to sleep.

Had Jake and Stephen been sixteen instead of four or five, and assuming Stephen had been serious, Jake's mother would have been correct in her assessment and in her action. But as things are, she has caused her child undue harm. Jake will have learned that it is not okay to be angry, and if the mother continues to overreact in this manner, Jake may learn to provoke people's anger to get what he wants from his mother. Or he may become so embarrassed at his mother's overreactions that he becomes afraid to share information with her.

On Monday Susan, age four, comes home and announces to her parents that she never gets to feed the fish at school. She is very upset. Upon further investigation, the parents find out that Susan fed the fish every day the previous week. Thinking that Susan is lying, they punish her. Was it okay to punish her? No. Susan was just expressing her disappointment that she didn't get to feed the fish that particular day. Children have a lot of trouble understanding time concepts, hence the misuse of the word "never." From the child's point of view, the word is not being misused, and Susan really thought she "never" got to feed the fish.

Sometimes, if you ask a child what a word means, you can have a very enlightening experience. Anna, a four-year-old, was upset because Alan, age five, said he wasn't her friend. So I called Alan over and he confirmed that he had said that. I asked him, "Do you know what the word 'friend' means?" "No," he replied. So I asked him if he had any friends in the class and he named three boys. Then I said, "Why are they your friends? What does friend mean?" He said, "If you just want to play, or do something, or do a booklet, or that stuff." Then I explained that you can have a friend and not see him or work with him, and he said, "Oh yeah, like Jim. I'm not with him all the time." So I said, "Do you think you could be friends with Anna?" He said that yes, she could be his friend, but he didn't want to work with her that day.

The child's understanding of words and concepts is incomplete at this age. When we think of a friend, we think of someone who shares our values: and the more values that are shared, the closer the friendship. We like to spend time with and share our thoughts and feelings with this person. We understand that our friend can have other friends, and that doesn't affect *our* friendship. We also understand that we can be apart from each other and still be friends. Children, on the other hand, are in the process of figuring out what words mean. Perhaps a friend is someone who's nice to him, or someone he likes to run around the room with. As the child grows, he will add more and more to concepts until he reaches adult understandings. In the meantime he may have lots of misconceptions.

These examples illustrate how important it is to understand how young children communicate. Without an adequate knowledge of how the child's mind operates, serious errors can be made. Below is a list of principles to keep in mind when your child communicates with you:

1. **Just because a child uses a word, he does not necessarily have the full adult, conceptual understanding of the meaning of that word.**
   - His concepts are very limited, so he may have only a vague idea of what the word means.
   - Children will use a word when they haven't a clue as to its meaning. They are experimenting with different words in different contexts and will try them out to see what happens. Or perhaps they are simply parroting back what they have heard.
   - Children will use words to get their way, or as an avoidance technique. "I can't" often means "I don't want to." "I'm bored" can mean "I'm tired" or "Entertain me."
2. **Children have a hard time distinguishing the difference between reality and fantasy. Therefore, they will tell stories.**
   - A child may want something, so he pretends he has it (a new puppy or an imaginary playmate).
   - A child may be trying to figure out something in reality (what dialing 911 means), so he tells a whopper (paramedics came to the school).
   - Children will imitate and repeat what they've heard others say. This is common with two-year-olds.
3. **Sometimes children lie.**
   - A child wants his way, so tries to manipulate others (e.g. Jake knows he left the mess on the floor, but lies in order to get someone else to clean it up).
   - A child *literally* thinks the lie will *change reality*.
   - A child wants to avoid reality—he knows he left the mess on the floor, but doesn't want to admit it. Maybe he is afraid of getting into trouble, or maybe he is ashamed.
4. **Children will ask the same question over and over.**
   - They don't know how to ask what they want to know and so therefore the adult isn't answering the real question.

- They are figuring out the concept of object permanence (e.g. the two-year-old child who asks every day, several times a day, "Where's Daddy?" The child hopes he's out there somewhere, but isn't sure).
- They are trying to verify reality. Will it change or stay the same? Maybe in time it will change.

5. **Children don't know how to communicate their feelings.**
   - They may be sick, frustrated, angry or tired, but they have a hard time figuring out how they feel and how to express it. They need help from adults with this.
   - They may say something that is false because they don't know how else to communicate what they are feeling. For example, "I don't like school," can actually mean, "I love you Mom. I miss you when I am at school. Therefore, I don't want to go to school."

6. **Children do not understand the concept of time.**
   - "Yesterday" means any time in the past and "tomorrow" means any time in the future.
   - They will misuse words like "new," "never," "before," "after," etc.

7. **Children will say things to get attention.**
   - Child may copy another child. (John saw Miranda get attention when she showed the teacher her loose tooth, so he pretends to have one.)
   - Child makes up lots of stories because he loves the reactions he gets from adults.
   - Child uses certain words because of the reactions he gets from adults.

8. **Children "tattle" because they are in the process of forming their own moral code.** They judge from the adult reaction whether the offense they are reporting is serious or not.

9. **Children do not understand cause and effect, so will attempt to control others.**
   - They often do this through words: "You will be my best friend if…" or "I won't invite you to my birthday party if you don't…" This is more common in girls. Other common phrases: "I'm going to run away from home." "My mommy would let me do that." "My dad says I'm old enough."
   - If a child has trouble communicating what he wants to say, he will frequently hit, push or shove to get his way. This is more common in boys, toddlers, or children with a history of ear problems.

10. **Children base what they say on perceptual data.** For example, the teacher wants to find out who ate the cheese and crackers and looks in the garbage. She finds the plastic wrapper and holds it up, asking, "Who ate this?" Child admits it was his. Child announces to parent at dismissal time that he ate plastic for snack.

11. **Children have a very hard time forming visualizations in their minds and therefore have a difficult time recounting events.** That is why, if you ask a child what happened, he will look away from you in the direction of the event.

12. **Children cannot reason with the use of words as adults can.** Children learn how to reason through the manipulation of objects and through real life experiences. Therefore, a child may tell you he understands something you just explained to him, when in fact he does not.

Since the child's mind is vastly different from ours and he has no way of grasping how *we* think, we have no choice but to try to understand the way *he* thinks. When in doubt as to what is going on with your child, gather more information to find out the facts. Consult his teacher or anyone else who can give you some insight. Think about the personality of your child, his age, and the principles of how children communicate. By doing so, you will know better how to respond to what has been said and will gain a greater understanding of your child. He, in turn, will feel freer to talk to you openly because he will know that you are truly trying to understand what he has to say. You will also enjoy and take delight in the mind of the child.

The Child's Concept of Time

Parents can become very frustrated when their child dawdles instead of completing a task such as getting dressed in the morning. "Hurry up! You'll be late for school!" But the child continues to linger. Why?

The concept of time is very difficult for young children to understand. Which sense directly perceives time? How many seasons change before a year has gone? And twenty-four hours—where are they? Why is an hour divided into sixty minutes? What does "half past" mean? What is the difference between "quarter past four" and "four fifteen"? And so on. It is often difficult for adults to remember that a vast ocean lies between our understanding of time and the child's.

- The two-year-old has no sense of time at all. This is why he is often so slow and dawdles so much. "Yesterday" and "tomorrow" are often confused, and "today" is not always clear. Therefore, a period of waiting often seems like an eternity to the two-year-old. Even the terms "before" and "after" are unclear. A Montessori teacher told his 2½-year-old that he would postpone diaper change until after story time. When the book had ended, and the father began to gather the diapers and rubber pants, the child cried defiantly and refused to cooperate. Although the child could say the word "after," he had not absorbed its meaning.

- The three-year-old relates time to very concrete experiences. "It will be as long as it takes to eat lunch" or "as long as it takes to get to the neighbor's house." Anything in the past is "yesterday" and anything in the future is "tomorrow."

- At four, the child understands past and future in the most vague of terms. He may ask things like, "When will I be a baby again?" or, "Is this the morning?" or, "Is today now?" He knows there is a difference between one day and many days. He knows vaguely that "a few minutes" means something shorter than "a few hours."

- At five, the child understands that the clock is used to measure time, even though he cannot use it that way himself yet. However, he understands that school begins at 9 o'clock, and he can watch for the hands to get there.

- Some six-year-olds can tell time to the minute and seem to have a good sense of time passing, and how long it has been, by other significant events such as hunger, parent's arrival home from work, etc.

Jean Piaget (1896–1980), was a developmental psychologist who is known for his theory of cognitive development in children. He argued that the mind develops in biologically programmed ways and that there is no way to speed up the biological program (for learning how to read, tell time, etc.). What Piaget and Montessori both tell us, though, is that a child's mind is like a fertile field beneath a vibrant sun: if we regularly throw seeds its way, it will in time produce a crop. In the spirit of cultivation, then, here are some suggestions for language development and the kinds of activities that can foster the growth of a child's conceptualization of time.

- **Age 2.** Because the two-year-old feels as if time (and hence wait-ing) is forever, prepare him for events soon before they are due to start, rather than telling him what will happen "next month" or "next week."

- **Ages 3–6.** Be very precise in the language you use about time with the three- to six-year-olds. Instead of saying, "Tomorrow is your birthday," say "When you go to sleep and wake up, it will be tomorrow and your birthday." Children can also be encouraged to think about time with comments such as, "In five minutes it will be time for dinner" and "What did you do last night before dinner?"

- **Age 4.** It is wise to expose the child to the seasons, months, days of the week, hours and minutes. The telling of time is not necessary here, but rather the sequencing of events. It is even more helpful at this age to teach fractions and their names (what is it that a quarter and a half hour represent?), and to count by fives (only after the child can count to a hundred by ones).

- **Ages 4–6.** The child of this age could be presented with a sand timer right next to a clock with a minute hand. Explain that it takes one minute for the sand to fall, which is as long as it takes the second hand to go once around the circle face. If you purchase a toy clock, try to find one with detachable numerals so that the child can assemble the clock face. Digital watches and clocks are not a good idea at this age, as they are much too abstract. The very young child cannot see the relationships of hours to minutes. The older child can make wrong connections—for example, a first grader told a Montessori teacher, "It will be 3 o'clock when the digital clock says 3:12, because the hour hand will be on '3' and the minute hand on '12.'"

- **Time lines** are beneficial for both the younger and older child. You could make a time line of one day, one week, one year, or the child's life. Draw a horizontal line on a long piece of paper or scroll and divide it into equal parts. On this time line you could place pictures of events that have already happened. In this kind of activity your child's study of human history is beginning.

- **Calendars** are also a good idea. When each month ends, detach that page and tape it to the preceding one. Do this each month, and your child will begin to see a linear representation of the passage and measurement of time. You could highlight the *seasons* of the year on this time line, too. It would be appropriate for the child to have his own calendar on the wall under the family's calendar, which he could use whenever he wanted. You will probably find your child imitating you by writing on his calendar. As your child gets older he can begin to record events or schedules for each day. Look for children's calendars that are sold with stickers representing holidays, birthdays, etc., because a young child can use these easily even if he can't read or write yet.

Looking over a time line of his life or of the family tree, a child can begin to have the experience of thinking backwards and forward in time. The seeds for the future can be planted: What would it be like to grasp the technology of a culture different from our own? Or what was it like to live before there was a light bulb? The growth in the child's conceptualization of time, then, becomes the pathway that opens him to the awareness of human history and culture.

Separation Anxiety[11]

When a young child begins school, it is normal for both child and parent to experience mixed feelings. They are often excited, knowing that the school will provide social and intellectual stimulation, but at the same time feel anxiety over leaving each other. This anxiety is normal, but when and how it is dealt with is crucial.

Typically, the two- to three-year-old child goes through an identity crisis when separating from the parent. Because he needs to become independent, yet knows that he is still dependent, a conflict arises. His independence is evolving simply because his maturity is also evolving.

1. He is now physically separate from his parents. He can walk and move around well.
2. He has acquired a language that he can now use to communicate.
3. He reads body language extremely well. He will look at the eyes to see if the adult is wavering, knows if the adult is unsure, and may decide to throw a temper tantrum in order to get his own way.

11 Portions of this section were reprinted from "A Periodical Publication for Parents" Westminister Day School.

During this time of identity development, the child needs to establish some separation.

The child is making his own separate identity ("Let me do it myself!") and wants to feel understood by his parents. If his parents attempt to delay his striving for independence, the child will have repressed anger. The longer his independence is delayed, the worse the anger and the more traumatic the eventual break. Another risk of delayed separation is that the child will feel as if the world is a big, scary place, where he can't handle being on his own, away from his parents. He may also have trouble forming attachments to people other than his parents.

Once the child begins school, he may be frightened by his new surroundings, maybe even wondering if his parents still love him. He may even feel anger about this, which can explode at home moments after expressions of excitement about school. The parent may worry: Is he too young? Do the teachers really know what they are doing? Will my child behave in school? Have I raised my child right so far? Will I still be needed by my child?

Resolving the feelings of fear, anger and sadness associated with separation may be one of the most important steps in his development. If this is the first separation, the way these feelings are resolved now could be the prototype for all the separations that follow. Handling the emotions of separation early in life has an impact on how your child will handle these same emotions later in life.

Some possible signs of separation anxiety:

In the child—
- Resistance to going to school: says he doesn't want to, resists getting ready for school, complains of tummy ache before school.
- Complains of lack of friends or mistreatment by others at school.
- Cries and clings when parent tries to leave.
- Refuses to leave at pick-up time when parent arrives (I've waited for you, now it's time for you to wait for me).
- Resistance to participating when at school: refuses to take off coat or leave boots in the hall, hovers near the classroom door or one of the teachers, wanders around to avoid involvement with learning materials, withdraws into thumb sucking, has regular toileting "accidents," avoids teachers.

In the parent—
- Finds reasons or excuses to bring the child late.
- Prolongs the moment of parting: says goodbye more than once each day (hidden message: child not really safe here without me).
- Needs to "explain" the child to the teachers.
- Tries to leave school without saying goodbye (I don't want to have to deal with this).
- Feels ashamed or angry if the child cries.
- Feels overly critical of the teachers.
- Wants a detailed report from the teachers each day.

Suggestions about what to do:

1. Be prepared. Know in advance that some of these feelings are normal, and know their signs. If you decided your child was ready to go to school, and chose a school you could trust, then relax and rely on the judgment you made at a less trying time to carry you through the separation period.
2. Emphasize to your child the time when you will pick him up and what you may do together after that.
3. Be honest about your feelings. If it is hard to say goodbye, then let it be hard; phony cheerfulness will not fool your child or make the anxiety disappear faster.
4. Let your child have his feelings. If he feels sad or mad or scared, let him know it is still okay to go to school.
5. Give support with positive expectations. Remember that you are happy that your child can go to school, that he will have other friends to play with and that you expect him to like it as you do. If you convey to your child, with or without words, that you are sure he will enjoy himself at school, you encourage him to feel secure, comfortable and free.
6. Give additional attention at home for a while by setting aside time together every day so that your child can count on it.
7. VERY IMPORTANT—make sure your child is in the care of one of the teachers, say goodbye, and then leave promptly. Lingering increases the child's anxiety. The teachers know how to handle this and the child normally stops crying shortly after you are out of eyesight.

Usually the anxiety associated with separation passes with the opening weeks of school. It is not uncommon, however, for it to appear again later in the year, or even the next year. If you become concerned, a conference with your child's teacher can be very helpful.

Chapter Five
The Learning Process

It is not the accumulation of a direct knowledge of things which forms the man of letters, the scientist, and the connoisseur; it is the prepared order established in the mind which is to receive such knowledge. [1]

MARIA MONTESSORI

Touch

After you read this paragraph, take a look around the room. As your eyes scan the objects around you, think about what they would feel like if you put them into your mouth. What would they feel like to touch with your fingers? What would they sound like if you hit them with your hand? Are they rough or smooth, hot or cold, soft or hard? Do they have a smell? Note how you already know the answer to those questions as soon as you look at something. Have you ever thought about this? How do you know this and when did you learn it?

You learned this when you were a baby, crawling around, putting things into your mouth (the most sensitive touch organ) and pounding your fist on objects. Babies and toddlers are absolutely dependent on their sense of touch. If the baby had no sense of touch, he wouldn't survive. He wouldn't feel hungry or know when he had eaten enough—he wouldn't be able to eat. But even assuming he could live, reality would have no meaning to him: he'd feel no weight when lifting, no textures when touching, no hot, no cold—nothing. It is because of our sense of touch that we, as adults, need only look at an object to immediately know a lot about it. We have fully integrated all the information we

1 Maria Montessori, *The Advanced Montessori Method*,(New York: Frederick A. Stokes Company, 1917) p. 206.

acquired as babies, so now we take what we know for granted. It is for this reason that people think our most important sense is sight; but sight gives us only light and dark and color. Our eyes now tell us what we learned as babies through touch. Here are some examples:

- Studies have been done with babies who had begun to crawl. In one room a piece of glass was placed over a hole in the floor. It was observed that only after having crawled all over the room for a period of time did babies suddenly stop at the glass and hesitate. Why? They had been developing depth perception by crawling, touching and climbing; *then* they sensed a change. Sight hadn't given them depth perception—if it had, they would have stopped at the glass right away. [2]
- When babies who are born blind at birth grow up and gain sight as teens or young adults, it takes time before they can distinguish by sight alone objects they have previously touched. [3]
- I once saw a girl 15 months of age in a shopping mall bend down and touch each floor tile before crossing it. Her eyes didn't tell her it was okay to walk to a different tile; the information came from her fingers.
- Children at 18 months, when walking out of a garage, often walk to the crack between the garage and driveway, crawl over it, then stand up and walk. Sight doesn't tell them that it is okay to walk over the crack.
- I have seen children at 18 months of age try to sit in 3-inch miniature playhouse chairs. Their eyes are not telling them the tiny chairs are too small.

It seems pretty obvious that a child needs to use his hands to feel the difference between rough and smooth, light and heavy, soft and hard; but a child also needs to touch to discriminate length, size, width, depth, and so on. I have seen children feel cubes in order to figure out if they are tall or short enough or trace over the shape of a letter before they can identify it. I have also watched young children trying to figure out quantities. If

---

2 Jan Faull, *Your Brilliant Baby in Week 25: Crawling and Judging Depth Perception*, http://www.babyzone.com/baby/baby-week-by-week/week-25-baby_65860

3 Valarie Ross, *When the Blind Can Suddenly See, Do They Know What They're Looking At?*, http://blogs.discovermagazine.com/80beats/2011/04/11/when-the-blind-suddenly-see-do-they-know-what-theyre-looking-at/(April 11, 2011)

they have too much, they don't automatically know that they need to take some away. Conversely, if they don't have enough they have to figure out that they need to add some. They have to actually have their hands on the quantities and move them around in order to figure this out.

Working with objects helps the child to establish stability in what seems to him to be an unstable world. He doesn't yet know that inanimate objects don't change. When doing an addition problem such as "7 + 3," children will count both quantities and get ten. After doing this a few times, rather than just starting at the seven and then counting the quantity of three, "seven, eight, nine, ten," they will continue to count both quantities. Children will keep counting the first quantity over and over for months in order to confirm that it remains the same amount and won't change. It does no good to tell them to stop counting on their fingers: they need to count this way in order to confirm reality.

The child also needs to sort physical objects in as many different ways as possible. He needs to handle, identify and classify identical and opposite things, and be able to grade them. The older child will then use more abstract materials to identify and classify concepts in science, geography, geometry and so on. All this work prepares his mind to think and make connections later on.

The child cannot be educated simply by verbal lectures or visual images. According to Dr. Steve Hughes, a neuropsychologist in the Twin Cities, the pre-frontal cortex—the reasoning part of the brain—must be developed by the child's using his hands to interact with his environment in order to get all the sensory information he needs.[4] Maria Montessori was way ahead of her time when she said, "The hands are the instruments to man's intelligence."[5] And while the young child needs to touch with his hands in order to learn, it is important to note that even older children need a certain amount of touch in exploring the world. And not only that, they like sensory input from other parts of their bodies. I'll never forget when our 13-year-old wanted to take off her socks, get out of the car and walk on newly poured pavement so she could feel the squishiness beneath her bare feet.

So the next time you see a child giggling as he stomps his feet in a mud puddle or making snow angels in the snow, you will understand that there

4 Dr. Steve Hughes, "Good at Doing Things: Montessori Education and Higher Order Cognitive Functions," (paper presented at Bergamo Montessori School, Sacramento, California), http://www.goodatdoingthings.com/, September 1, 2012.

5 Maria Montessori, *The Absorbent Mind*, (New York: Dell Publishing Co., 1967), p. 27.

is more to these kinds of activities than meets the eye. There is a reason why he is having so much fun: he is connecting with his world—and he is doing it through touch.

Taking the Initiative in Learning

One of the most impressive things about Montessori children is their self-confidence. In the classroom they go about their business independently by choosing their own work throughout the day, moving from activity to activity. They don't wait for us to tell them what to do; they just take the initiative and do it.

Observers see children reading, or doing math problems that require addition, subtraction, multiplication and division. They see them working on the concrete understandings of the binomial and trinomial theorems, squaring and cubing numbers, algebra, the theorem of Pythagoras, and fractions. The children pursue their quests, searching out a triangular-based pyramid or a scalene triangle. They parse sentences, finding the verbs, nouns and articles and labeling them with grammar symbols. At circle time they raise their hands to relate what they know about Chopin or Beethoven. They may even be able to tell the story of the Boston Tea Party. All this they do independently, and with great enthusiasm.

When parents visit they remark, "Wow, the children are learning so many advanced concepts so young!" But while concluding that it is wonderful that Montessori children do so well, a parent sometimes thinks that since his own child isn't as self-motivated as the others, he needs a more traditional school where he is told what to do. "I just know that he would learn more then, because, after all, at circle time my child does not raise his hand to answer questions." But it is precisely the more traditional school that a child lacking in self-direction does *not* need.

In a traditional educational setting, the children are told what to do and when. Everyone is expected to learn the same thing at the same time and at the same pace. The child doesn't understand what he is being taught because he has no (or very little) hands-on equipment to use and doesn't learn in an organized manner. Often, information is just dictated to the child in a non-sequential way. Since he doesn't understand what is being taught to him, he may have a very hard time moving to the next level of human thought (that of conceptualization); he can only repeat what he's been told. Then, as a teenager, he waits for others to tell him what to do and does not see the need to initiate action. As an adult he can't make the connection between one piece of information and another—for example, he can't compare what a politician says this week to what he said two months earlier. Note that this individual still has no motivation, and now his ability to reason is greatly diminished.

But doesn't a baby come into the world with a natural desire to learn? And if this is true, what happened? Did he just lose it?

Barring developmental delays, learning does come naturally for the young child. By the time he is two to three years of age he still feels compelled to explore and move and touch, but now his thoughts and actions must be directed by conscious choice. He is ready to do what will make him fully human. He now has to use his free will to learn. This process requires effort, and the proper educational methods and environment are crucial in promoting this development. Prior to this, his mind was more or less pre-motivated; now, he has to direct and constantly reinforce the positive development of his learning. Before, his mind started automatically; now, he has to learn how to start and operate it all by himself. He has to learn how to think.

As the child grows into the next stage of development, his mind is in a state of confusion. He has taken in a lot of information. Now he needs to make sense out of it and put his mind in order. His body lacks control and he moves rapidly from one object to another, touching and grabbing, sometimes with jerky movements. He does this because he wants to know about reality and his relationship to it. At this point it is important to encourage the child to keep learning for himself by allowing him to make choices in a prepared environment that promotes the development of an orderly mind. He also needs limits so that he can develop self-control. If these are provided, the child's self-motivation continues to develop naturally by his own choice and he learns to concentrate at a conscious level.

Self-motivation, self-direction and concentration are learned. They aren't capacities that a child is either born with or will never have.

While it is impressive what Montessori children are capable of learning, their most fundamental and critical achievement is this: they have learned how to use their own minds. They know how to find their own work without being told what to do. Rather than just continuing to memorize information, they are processing it, thinking it through, understanding it. They are using their minds in a systematic way. But this didn't happen overnight. It took two to four years in a Montessori school where they were encouraged to find their own work. They were carefully presented with sequential activities that met their sensitive periods for learning. They were allowed to repeat these activities as often as necessary to gain a complete understanding of the material. They were guided in a step-by-step manner, each step getting a little more challenging, becoming a little more abstract. They learned how to connect the facts of reality using the concrete materials provided for them. What happened is that they learned to have confidence in the efficacy of their own minds, and they are now using them accordingly.

What happens when a child doesn't learn how to use his own mind? Is the damage done to a child's mind irreparable? The time wasted cannot be made up. As adults we can learn foreign languages but we speak them with an accent. This is an example of how the growing brain has optimum times for its development. Similarly, older children can learn how to concentrate and take action, but not without great effort. The middle school teachers at our school have told us countless times that they can see a *huge* difference between the children who started Montessori during their pre-elementary years and those who did not.

"They lack independence. They wait for us to tell them every little thing to do."

"They aren't self-motivated."

"They don't get their work done."

These children improve in time, but only when consistent effort is made toward independence. And even though they can improve, precious time has still been lost. At this age they should be focusing on different things; they should already have learned how to get their work done. Because the optimum time for development of independence was missed, their full development was impeded and slowed down, made much harder.

The problem is that the brain's general mode of functioning is established by age six and it takes great effort to change it afterwards. Just as a building's foundation will determine its strength and success, the foundation of the brain will determine a person's ability to think and,

This is what a typical day looks like in the classroom when the children take out their chosen work.

therefore his success. We spend much more time worrying about how much exercise our body gets than how well our minds are developed.

While all children are different, the vast majority don't come to us already self-directed *and* able to concentrate *and* persistent *and* self-confident *and* mature. Barring any maturational delays, this all comes together for them in their Kindergarten year. These self-motivated children are what we have been working so hard to achieve all these years. These children, whom people are so impressed with now, also lacked independence when they started school. They weren't raising their hands three years ago either. But look at them now.

Does Speed Indicate Intelligence?

One morning I presented a math lesson to a small group of children; after the lesson they were to complete some work that went with it. One by one the children completed the work and walked away to go do something else. Elizabeth, a brilliant student, still hadn't finished. She sat alone with tears welling up in her eyes.

"What's wrong?" I said.

"My mommy said people who are last are losers."

I explained to her that for children who learn in school there is no such thing as winners and losers, because learning is not a race. It doesn't matter how fast you learn, because speed is not an indication of how smart you are. As a matter of fact, I liked that she wasn't in a hurry to finish.

Knowing Elizabeth's mother, I knew she would not have meant to give her child that message. She most likely had been talking about a sports game or a race; maybe she hadn't said anything like that at all (sometimes we never do figure out exactly how children arrive at their ideas). Nonetheless, this incident illustrates how children can take what we say literally and form misconceptions about what they hear. It is important to clear these up so that children don't form the wrong conclusions. It would have been tragic for Elizabeth to have concluded that she was a loser.

But, just for the sake of conjecture, what if Elizabeth really had understood her mother correctly? What if her mother really had said, and meant, that in order to be intelligent, she needed to learn quickly? Would her mother have been correct? No! Children need to take their time.

There are basically two ways to learn. Memorization is the first method and is associated with the perceptual level of functioning. Animals are at this level and stay there, never rising above it. Humans, however, though starting out at the perceptual level of learning, do rise above it when they form concepts. In order to form concepts, children cannot just memorize any more—they have to form abstractions, which is the process of isolating certain aspects of reality and then integrating them into concepts. A child can form the concept "two" as a quantity, but animals cannot, even though they can perceive two stones. To then take that a few steps further, a child can build on the concept of quantity to add, subtract, multiply and divide. Once the child understands whole quantities, he can move on to fractions and, through a series of steps, eventually to algebra. Animals cannot do this because they can only memorize; they can't think. You will not see a bunch of puppies gathering round to work on a math problem. This is why humans have launched spaceships but animals have not; humans can reason.

Understanding concepts and their relationships to one another takes effort—it takes thinking. That can't be done fast. I think this is one of the biggest misconceptions about learning: that speed indicates intelligence. A child can memorize lots of isolated data quickly, but when he does so he is functioning at the same learning level as the rest of the animal kingdom. He may, indeed, be smart just like a puppy, but this is not intelligence. (I am not, of course, referring in this discussion to children with learning delays, where speed *is* an issue. That is a different topic entirely.)

In the *Return of the Primitive: The Anti-Industrial Revolution*, Ayn Rand defines intelligence as "the ability to deal with a broad range of abstractions." [6] In order to deal with a broad range of abstractions, a child has to have an orderly mind, much like a filing cabinet. He needs to have the correct definitions for his concepts so he can file information in the appropriate file folder. As he goes up the ladder of knowledge, he needs to check to make sure that what he is learning now is consistent with what was learned before. When he learns something new that may contradict previous knowledge, he needs to know how to go back and check his premises so he can see whether the new item is true or false and, if need be, correct his earlier conclusions. This involves a process of thought and it doesn't happen automatically.

---

6 Ayn Rand, "The Comprachicos," *The New Left: The Anti-Industrial Revolution*, (New York: New American Library, 1971) p. 160.

It is damaging for a child to think that he should have quick and immediate answers for everything. For example, it takes time and experience for a child to learn good social skills. He has to figure out the right way to treat other people. Adults have a similar challenge. They also have to figure out the right way to treat other people which is reflected in philosophical questions such as "What is the proper social system for man's survival?" Note that this particular question has been debated for centuries. Deep questions in life take a lot of thought, often years of thought. It is unrealistic and even cruel to lead children to think otherwise.

There are certainly times when speed is important, such as in emergencies, debates and games, but the context here is learning. In school, when a child is learning something for the very first time, speed is not useful. Children who think they need to be fast will blast through things, miss steps and have a lot of trouble understanding more advanced concepts later on. They may feel that they need to "win," and this can cause anxiety and depression. Children who are pressured to go too fast will resort to memorization and can remain at the perceptual level and fall behind. Children need time to reflect and think about what they are taught, so that they develop understanding.

Jane Healy[7] is a learning specialist to whom I refer in the chapters on television and computers. She is concerned about the speed at which children are expected to learn:

> Children are not allowed to sit and think. They are constantly rammed through a curriculum to see how fast we can move them along. As they're marched from activity to activity, even the schedule of the school day doesn't allow time for anyone to reflect. ... The key word is 'understanding,' not just a forced march through a set body of subject matters. ... Children who can't reflect and who have never been able to pause long enough to be able to solve a difficult problem are going to be far down on the literacy scale.[8]

Innovative thinkers and creative individuals like Albert Einstein, Thomas Edison, Walt Disney and countless others were considered slow learners in school. Ask yourself how that could be true. Slowing down when trying to grasp new ideas actually improves one's thinking and leaves less

---

7 Jane Healy is an educational psychologist who has spent decades figuring out how the environment affects the developing brain. She has written several books on the topic such as *Endangered Minds: Why Children Don't Think and What We Can Do About It.*

8 Jane Healy, *Wild Duck Review* (Vol. IV, No.2) 1992.

room for error. Quick-minded people often trust the first idea that pops into their head, and it may not be a valid idea. In order to understand and integrate new knowledge, the child needs to take his time without pressure to be smart and quick.

The ironic thing about Elizabeth is that she was miles ahead in intelligence compared to most other five-year-olds, yet she was on the verge of tears thinking that because she wasn't fast, she wasn't good enough. We must not confuse smart puppies that learn tricks quickly with children who are in the process of learning how to reason. Intelligence is attributable to only humans because they can think, and thinking takes time. Allow Elizabeth to take her time and she will have a stronger mind, one that is more able to reason accurately. Now *that* is intelligence.

To Think or Not To Think

An experiment was done with two groups of two- and three-year-olds on the principle of conservation—in this case, the conservation of mass (i.e. the mass of an object remains the same regardless of changes in form). The experimenter showed the first group two balls of clay of equal size and the children agreed they were the same. Then he squashed one of the balls flat, explaining to the children that even though this one now looked like less clay, it was still the same amount as the other. The children accepted this explanation without question. With the second group of children, the experimenter again squashed one of the balls of clay flat, but offered no explanation. This group of children said there was less clay in the flattened ball (the two- or three-year-old is simply too young to understand the concept of conservation).

When the children were four and five years old, the experiment was repeated—with a variation. This time, when the children weren't looking, the instructor replaced one of the equally sized balls of clay with a bigger ball before flattening the other ball. The first group, who had been told two years earlier that mass was conserved, said the flattened ball was the same size as the other. The second group looked for the clay that "fell to the floor" and said, "Some must still be in your hand."

That experiment tells us that if you give the child information before he is developmentally ready, he will simply accept what you told him and give you the answer you want to hear.

Jean Piaget did an experiment with classification. He had a box of wooden beads, some of which were red. He asked children whether there were more wooden beads or red beads. The four-year-olds answered "red" even though all the beads, including the red ones, were wooden. Not until age five to eight would the child reverse his answer—if given experience and not told what the answer was. At age four the child still needs to practice looking at and sorting things in several different ways. The child must be left, however, to sort them *his* way. Giving him the answers at this stage will prevent him from reasoning them out by himself, and he may find no reason to think out answers to more abstract questions as he grows older.

At age four children enjoy problem solving, but the answers are not important to them at this time. If the problem is too easy, they quit; if the problem is too difficult, they quit; and if the adult tells them the answers, they quit. It is important that we match the problem to the child's experience and interest—making it difficult, but not too much so.

A few children at this age start to show poor responses to tasks requiring judging and thinking, such as: giving up, doing destructive acts, asking for too much help, prolonged crying, pouting, and other exaggerated behavior. It is of utmost importance that we notice these signs and correct the situation as soon as possible. What the child needs is encouragement to do it all by himself. Direct adult help at this point encourages the poor responses as the child learns to get attention, get sympathy, and get someone else to do it. If this situation is not resolved soon, the child will exhibit the following later on: short attention span, fear of trying, lack of confidence, lack of motivation and a lack of flexibility in considering alternatives. (Keep in mind that there is a big difference between poor responses to problem solving in general and poor responses to specific problems, which must be handled totally differently depending on the child. The way an adult knows the difference is by knowing the child and how well he is responding to problem solving now. For some suggestions that are useful in encouraging children to think, please see appendix.)

When a child asks a "why" question or wants the answer to a problem, the adult needs to stop. Is this something the child can figure out for himself, or does he need the answer now? It is okay to let him ponder some things even if he has to do it for a long time. When my siblings and I were growing up, our father would pose a different riddle for us to solve every Sunday at the dinner table. We had lots of discussions and roared with laughter as we figured out the solutions. The interesting thing was, our father never told us the answers no matter how we begged. He would only confirm the answer for us when we got it right, so we could go for weeks or months before figuring it out. The process of learning the logic in arriving at the answer was as pleasurable as knowing that we got the correct answer. I have also watched children in school reason something through from start to finish and then seen them jump up and down with delight because they were able to do it independently. Why deny children that fun and satisfaction?

At two years of age a child is capable of considering alternatives. He chooses, then acts. He plunges in "head first" less and less often. This is the beginning of free will and choosing "to think or not to think." At age five there is a shift from adult orientation to peer orientation. The more a child looked for answers from adults prior to age five, the more he will look for them now from his friends—even to the point of giving up his own judgment and viewpoint to agree with his peers, and even in the face of evidence that those friends are wrong. Children like this will learn not to question and usually continue to accept the wrong answers even when the facts show otherwise.

So the next time you are about to tell your child the answer to a puzzle or the solution to a problem, stop. Give him what he really needs instead—encourage him to think.

Creativity

Creativity is highly valued in our American culture. This shouldn't be surprising, particularly since America has been the world's leader in innovations since the founding of our country. Our lives have improved immensely because of the creative thinking of individuals, which has resulted in innumerable inventions such as the light bulb, the phonograph, the airplane, the smart phone, the refrigerator, medical advancements and on and on and on.

While creativity is highly esteemed, it is also, unfortunately, misunderstood. People think that it leaps out of nowhere without any connection to previous knowledge or skills and that it is possessed only by those who already have an innate creative potential. Conventional education, basing its methods on these misconceptions, views the ideal nursery school environment as a free-for-all, in which the child expresses himself by running around and doing whatever he wants. And in their view, you never know, he just might be one of the few with an innate creative potential and his creativity, fostered by this chaos, could spring forth at any time.

Creativity is not restricted to just a few people, nor is it fostered by an atmosphere of accepted turmoil, nor does it burst out of nowhere. Creativity comes from learning about reality, thinking about what you have learned, and applying it in some unique way. "'Creation' means the power to bring into existence an arrangement (or combination or integration) of natural elements that had not existed before." [9] Iron ore was rearranged with other elements to make steel; steel and aluminum were combined in new ways to make airplanes; from the idea of the airplane came jets; jets led to moon rockets. The rocket ship had to be invented, but its component parts already existed; it could not have been built without those, or in the absence of a body of knowledge about space travel and aeronautical construction. The rocket ship did not spring into existence like a ghost in the night.

Creation doesn't start with...creation. It starts with knowledge, and the primary focus of education in the beginning must be the *acquisition* of knowledge. Knowledge needs to be presented in an orderly way so that the mind can file information logically and retrieve it reliably; only then can the mind make the novel connections that are the essence of the creative process. Once knowledge and skills have been attained, freedom is necessary for the mind to bring innovations into existence.

The Montessori Method has been criticized for its supposed lack of creativity. This criticism comes from the progressive philosophy of education that permeates our schools today. Their position is that in order to be creative, a child must be unconstrained by reality. Montessori's position is the opposite. She thought that in order to invent, a child first needed to understand the facts of reality. "Yet no one can say that man creates artistic products out of nothing," she wrote. "What is called *creation* is in reality a composition, a construction raised upon a *primitive material* of the mind, which must be collected from the environment by

---

9 Ayn Rand, *Philosophy Who Needs It*, (Indianapolis/New York: Bobbs-Merrill Company, 1982), p. 31.

means of the senses." [10] "The mind that works by itself, independently of truth, works in a void." [11]

I list below the main criticisms of Montessori, with my rebuttal after each:

1. *It does not allow the child to do whatever he wants whenever he wants. It is not a free-for-all where anything goes—the children are required to follow rules and respect the rights of others. Stifling free spirits stifles creativity.* A child cannot concentrate and therefore cannot learn in an environment where individual rights are not respected. Chaos is not conducive to creativity. Period.

2. *Since Montessori is reality-based, the children do not get to use their imaginations, hence they can't be creative.* This statement presupposes that children start out with imaginations. They do not. Forming mental images is not something that automatically happens—it is something that is learned over time in conjunction with the child's experiences with the real world. Therefore a reality-based education provides the essential foundation for creating an imagination.

3. *But children need to pretend in order to be creative. They need to fantasize.* Pretending is not the same thing as creativity. What do children create when playing house? They are simply re-creating what they know about houses and how people live in a house. When children play pretend games, they are imitating. The key to creativity is not fantasizing; it is the preparation of the mind. Montessori stated:

> If, then, the true basis of the imagination is reality, and its perception is related to exactness of observation, it is necessary to prepare children to perceive the things in their environment exactly, in order to secure for them the material required for their imagination. Further, the exercise of the intelligence, reasoning within sharply defined limits, and distinguishing one thing from another, prepares a cement for imaginative constructions...The fantasy which exaggerates and invents coarsely does not put the child on the right road. [12]

---

10 Maria Montessori, *Spontaneous Activity in Education,* (New York: Frederick A. Stokes Co., 1917) p.245.

11 Maria Montessori, *The Advanced Montessori Method,* (New York: Frederick A. Stokes Company, 1917), p. 187.

12 Maria Montessori, *Spontaneous Activity in Education,* (New York: Frederick A. Stokes

Not only does exaggerated fantasy not put him on the right road, but it can have deadly consequences if a child is not grounded in reality. It is not creative when a child jumps off a building because he believes himself to be a superhero. It is tragic. Children cannot be left free to aimlessly wander around in Fantasy Land, all in the name of creativity.

4. *It is too rigid, too orderly. It isn't free enough.* Order is an essential component of creativity. How can you take knowledge and rearrange it in new, inventive ways if you don't have it in order in the first place? The child takes information from his environment to form his mind. If the environment is orderly, he will put his mind in order. If not, he won't, and he will be less likely to be creative later on. The pre-elementary Montessori classrooms have an entire area devoted to helping the child put into order the sensory perceptions that he is receiving. This is a fantastic foundation for creativity. In addition, the child is allowed freedom to pursue knowledge within a framework that leads him toward abstractions, and these abstractions are important in forming his imagination.

5. *The children acquire knowledge from the use of hands-on educational materials that are to be used only for their designated purpose. That stifles creativity.* Each material does have a designated purpose—to teach the child about a specific aspect of reality and to help him put his mind in order. E.M. Standing explains why Montessori always insisted that the materials be used correctly:

> It is, in fact, only another way of saying that the child must respect the principle of order which is inherent in each of the materials. By so doing, the principle of order in the child—which is the intellect—is strengthened. The more powerful an intellect, the more surely does it act like a light which illuminates and puts in order, making clear what was hitherto chaotic and unrelated. [13]

Knowledge about reality is what is needed for children to form their imaginations. Once the child has prepared his mind with the basic information, he is allowed to use the materials in creative ways within the parameters of their purpose. The child learns about

---

Co., 1917) p. 254.

13 E.M. Standing, *The Montessori Method, A Revolution in Education*, (Fresno, California: Academy Library Guild, 1962), p. 35.

length, width, depth and size with individual Sensorial materials. Once he understands the concepts, he can combine the Sensorial materials, putting them in order in different ways (i.e. creatively), as the long as the materials are not abused.

I don't think that the inventors who put so many hours of hard work into their creations would agree that creativity comes from nothing. Creativity is the "ability to produce something new through imaginative skill." [14] Imaginations are created during childhood from a basis of reality and order. Once the foundation is built, creativity can arise from it. It is ironic that Montessori, the educational system that stresses the essential components of creativity, is criticized for the very things that make creativity possible in the first place—reality, order, freedom and above all, reason.

In order to understand exactly what is needed for children to learn and create, Maria Montessori went straight to the source—the child. She observed facts about the nature of the child, logically arranged those facts and created an awesome educational system. And she did it by using her…imagination.

Movement

Movement is an integral part of the learning process. It is important not only for physical, social and emotional development, but also for intellectual development. There is a connection between the cerebellum (a part of the brain associated with motor control) and cognitive functions such as memory, spatial orientation, attention, language, decision-making, and more. Movement increases blood flow to the brain and this can't help but have a positive effect on its performance.

Unlike in Montessori schools, children in conventional schools are made to sit at a desk all day long. This is cruel, not only because their bodies are growing and need to move, but also because they are denied the opportunity to develop their full cognitive potential. Children who move as they learn remember their lessons much better than children who are immobile. If the name of the capital of Peru was told to you while

---

14 Merriam-Webster on line dictionary, http://www.merriam-webster.com/dictionary/creativity.

you sat on a chair, what would your chances be of remembering it four years from now? But if you were to learn the capital of Peru by repeatedly placing a pin into its location on a map of South America (as is done in the Montessori elementary classes), you would find it easier to recall.

When something is learned through movement, the information is better understood. Young children typically confuse "d" and "b." Being able to tell the difference between the two depends on an understanding of orientation (in this case, which side of the line the circle is on). A child has to understand the different orientations of his body and other objects in space (up, down, under, beside, etc.) before he can understand the orientation of shapes on a piece of paper.

Montessori also noted that in order to concentrate, children need to move as they work with the materials. This is even more important than a noiseless environment.

> Some visitors to Montessori schools, especially those accustomed to the rigid silence of the old order, imagine that it must be very hard—if not impossible—for children to concentrate on their work in the midst of all that coming and going and general stir in a Montessori classroom, which we have compared to the busy hum of a hive of bees. Yet experience shows the contrary. It is movement, through the point of contact, which ensures concentration—not silence. For we must remember that the child is not trying to concentrate on a person; nor yet on an idea in the abstract—which would be difficult. Given the material, however, with the movement it elicits, he can concentrate "even to isolation point" without absolute silence. [15]

In addition to moving so that they can concentrate and learn, children also need to learn how to coordinate their bodies. This is not a matter of physical fitness, however, because most children who come to us at 2½ to 3½ do not generally have motor problems. They are totally physically fit. They have plenty of physical stamina, as any adult knows who tries to keep up with his child as he moves about the house. The child's muscles are developed and being used. Therefore, when educators talk about motor development, what they mean is motor refinement—*control* of the use of muscles.

---

15 E.M. Standing, *Maria Montessori: Her Life and Work*, (New York: New American Library, 1957) p. 246.

The two-year-old has to pay attention to what her body is doing or the glass could drop and break.

Walking in the maze and keeping his balance.

The children carry the materials one at a time with both hands which enhances body awareness and control. Here, as the child stretches her arms out to carry each number rod to her rug, she also feels the differences in length.

Children have to learn self-control, and control of bodily movements is integral to control of the self. There are two types of muscle control: gross motor (use of the entire body) and fine motor (use of finger muscles). The advantage of the Montessori Method is that the activities are structured so that the child has to *think* about his movements. When he carries a tray, he has to pay attention to where his body is in space, and in relation to nearby objects and people, so that he doesn't spill the contents of the tray. He has to pay extra special attention if the tray contains glass, because if that falls, it could break. We show him how to set down objects gently, without making any noise, thereby using silence to draw his attention to his body and what it is doing.

Here are some examples of activities in our classrooms that refine gross motor movement:

- rolling rugs
- washing tables
- cleaning such as sweeping or mopping
- cloth washing
- carrying a tray
- walking on the line
- walking in a maze using the long rods
- carrying a chair or table
- folding a large cloth
- walking around rugs and mats
- stopping when the bell is rung
- setting objects down gently, without making a sound

Here are some examples of activities in our classrooms that refine fine motor movement:

- manipulating objects such as tongs, tweezers and pop beads
- opening and closing containers
- sewing
- folding
- practicing dressing skills with the dressing frames
- using puzzles with knobs
- spooning
- pouring

- using a baster or eye dropper
- crumbing a tray
- rolling an oil cloth

The young child does these activities to learn the movement: for example, he may sweep the floor in order to learn how to sweep. The older child does them to achieve a goal or to perfect his movements. He may sweep the floor in order to get it clean or to do it better than the last time. The older child may also do an activity in order to relax, or for the pure joy of doing it: for example, playing a song he likes on a musical instrument.

The ultimate Montessori exercise in the control and coordination of the body is a game called the Silence Game, during which the children try to be as quiet as possible (see "The Silence Game" in Chapter 3). This game is the consummation of the refinement of movement that the child has been working on all year. To be able to sit still and create silence, one must have achieved good self-control. To take total control of the body with movement is to have this much movement—none.

It is important to remember that mind and body are not separate entities; they are integrated and work together. The Montessori classroom is, likewise, integrated. The children do large motor activities in the same room in which they do all the rest of their learning, unlike some schools that have separate rooms for different activities. We integrate the body and the mind in the classroom because you can't have one without the other in the learning process.

Flashcards—Are They Okay?

Parents are often flabbergasted at how quickly their child learns when he is very young. Children have terrific memories and those as young as two years can seem to figure out difficult scenarios. They can often decipher what we are saying when we spell a word, or recognize travel routes when they are riding in the car. Maybe they already know their colors or shapes, or can count to forty or higher. When parents observe these things, they understandably conclude that their child is very bright and try to encourage the development of this intelligence—very often, by making the child memorize facts.

Flash cards are usually used for this. Children are taught to memorize the addition and subtraction facts with them. They are also taught how to recognize words on flash cards in the hopes that they will be early readers. Not only is this not beneficial, it is actually detrimental.

The two-year-old is at the perceptual level of learning. He perceives and memorizes things about the world around him, and he observes that things exist; but he needs to learn *what* these things are and how one relates to another. As he figures that out, by thinking and integrating, he forms concepts and rises to the next level—the conceptual level.

Our goal as parents and educators is to help the child rise from the perceptual to the conceptual level. However, when children are made to memorize at this age, they get into the habit of expecting an immediate answer. Then, when faced with a new problem, they shut down in frustration, or become angry, or conclude that something is wrong with them.

For example, the youngster who is made to memorize math facts will have a hard time when presented with the process of addition or subtraction later on. When he is shown how to take the beads and add them together, he won't make any effort to do the work, because he is used to spouting off an answer. Thus he will continue to have little or no understanding of what addition really is. The child who has learned to read through memorization will have similar difficulties. When faced with a new word, the flash card memorizer won't have any idea how to sound it out. Spelling will be even harder, because the child won't have a clue how to transform sounds into letters.

I have found it interesting to observe that even though most children can count to a high number when they are as young as two or three, they begin to stumble through the teens by the time they are four. The reason for this is that at the earlier age they were merely memorizing, in the same way as they memorized nursery rhymes. Now they are trying to logically understand quantities and their relationships and progressions. We know that they are reasoning this out because when they try to think what comes after a number such as 39, they say "thirty-ten," which is a logical conclusion.

Memorization has its place in the educational process and is of value—but only after understanding has been attained. Once the child has experienced and understood addition, and realized that numbers and quantities don't change when manipulated but remain constant (which he learns only through experience), he is ready to memorize the addition facts. When the child knows what sound each letter makes and can hear the individual sounds in words, and after he has had a lot of experience sounding out and building lots of phonetic words, then he can be introduced to memory words. Reversing this process only serves to confuse and delay the child.

If a child uses memorization as his main mode of learning, he will have a very hard time learning how to reason. Recall the children you knew when you went to school, specifically those who seemingly had photographic memories and could rattle off dates, names and places for memory based tests. Note that these were the same children who later struggled with and flunked the essay tests. I have also noticed from my personal experience that children, who had been considered brilliant and begun to read through memorization at age three, were seriously lacking in independence and reasoning skills by the time they were teenagers.

Whom do we consider brilliant—a person who can memorize an enormous number of unrelated facts and recite them, or a person who can figure out the relationships between one cell and another and discover the cure for cancer? To me the answer is obvious. Throw away the flash cards.

Chapter Six
Interference in the Learning Process

If your child never has a chance to be alone and quiet within his own mind, how can you expect him to learn to use it well?[1]

JANE HEALY

Let Your Child Fail

Occasionally, parents worry that their child may fail, so they rush in to take care of the problem or try to prevent it from happening. They over worry, from every wrong answer on his addition problems to his falls on the playground. They may hover over their child, worrying about this and worrying about that. They give him constant reminders so he won't forget what to do. They correct his every error. Why do they do this?

From what I have observed, most parents love their children and want them to be successful. As teachers, we want your children to be successful too. That is why we are here. But I think that sometimes adults have misconceptions about how success is achieved. They are afraid that if a child makes a mistake it will sadden him and harm his self-esteem. They don't want their child to experience negative feelings because, they think, that will stand in the way of his achieving success. They believe this because our culture tends in that direction.

This is what needs to be understood: it is important to let your child fail! Not only is it important, it is necessary. How will a child learn without making mistakes? If he encounters nothing but success, how will he experience achievement? How will he know the feeling of success if he has never known failure? In order to succeed, man must strive. Without goals there is no reason to move forward; but worthwhile goals can be

---

1 Jane Healy, *Different Learners: Identifying, Preventing, and Treating Your Child's Learning Problems*, (New York: Simon and Schuster Paperbacks, 2010), p. 344.

achieved only with effort. Success is earned, not inborn. The child needs to understand that mistakes and failures can happen as he works his way towards a goal.

As teachers, we see children fail every day. They work on puzzles and have trouble figuring them out. They forget the sounds of letters as they sound out words. They start running around the room and we put them in time out. This is a natural and normal part of childhood—making mistakes. We expect it. It is a normal part of learning. This is true not only in their academics and behavior, but also in their social relationships and physical development. I don't know of a single child who hasn't had a problem with a friend, fallen on the playground, or made math errors.

It's from making mistakes that we develop a fuller and deeper understanding of what we are trying to learn. While failure is not the same as knowledge, we can get knowledge from our failures if we think about what went wrong. If I am trying to make a raft and I am never successful at making it float, I can still learn something about flotation. If I try to bake bread and can't get the dough to rise, figuring out why makes me understand more about the baking process. If I run around out on the playground in my sandals instead of my tennis shoes and I fall because of it, I learn that I should wear my tennis shoes next time. If I count quantities too fast and make errors, I learn to slow down. If I want to do some advanced language games, maybe I should work harder to learn to read. If I get hungry during snack time, maybe I should remember to bring my snack into the classroom before class starts, like the other children.

Making mistakes won't harm a child's self-esteem, but being obsessed with failure will. If the child gets the message that it is wrong to fail and that he has to do everything perfectly at the first attempt, he will soon realize it is just not possible. He will conclude that the end result matters more than the process he uses to arrive at it. Without knowing the process, the child won't know how to get the correct result, so will resort to guessing and, ultimately, memorization. Failure happens along the way in life and we should not give our child the impression that it doesn't. If he accepts this misconception, then when he does encounter failure, he will be devastated because he will think something is wrong with him—and *that* would harm his self-esteem.

Don't get me wrong: we all want our children to be successful in the long run; but in order to be successful, the child has to experience some struggles along the way. He may feel sad at times, but feelings of sadness or discouragement can be motivating to try harder. If the child becomes overly discouraged, however, we do need to help him; but even then, in the end, *he* is the one who has to learn how to handle his problems. (Obviously, there are certain kinds of failure that we cannot allow: those involving safety issues, such as a child's crossing the street when a car is coming, or going into deep water when he doesn't know how to swim.) Nevertheless, I don't want to give parents the impression that they shouldn't contact the teacher for more information if they have some worries or questions about their child. We want to help you with your concerns and we don't want you to worry unnecessarily when your child's development is normal.

I hate to tell you how many times I fell before learning how to water ski. Thomas Edison failed one thousand times before successfully developing the light bulb. If he thought it was wrong to fail, we wouldn't have the light bulb today. The Wright Brothers had numerous failures before launching the Flyer at Kitty Hawk. It was their tenacity that gave us the airplane, not their fear of failing. We can't wrap our children in bubble wrap, nor should we. It isn't the end of the world when the child fails; he needs to learn how to stand up and keep going. Don't deny your child success by denying him failure.

The Helicopter Parent

Janeen, the mother of a three-year-old, had just enrolled her son, Corey, in school. Janeen was full of questions about the program and wanted to know if the staff would make sure that he ate during snack time, remind him to go to the bathroom at the same time every day, and encourage him to make friends. "At his old school, he played by himself," said Janeen. The new teacher explained that was typical behavior for a three-year-old. Then, at home that night, Corey told his mother that another child had said mean things to him. Instead of asking Corey what had happened and giving him ideas on how to handle it, Janeen called the school, demanding to know just who had done this to her child. The staff member assured her that they would try to find out what had happened. When Janeen brought Corey to school the next day, he pointed out another three-year-old in the hallway and said that was the child who had said mean things to him. Janeen, rather than taking this information to the teacher and letting her handle it, immediately scolded the child. Further investigation revealed that Corey had been sticking his tongue out at other children in class and they had told him to stop. This, he had thought, was mean. To top it all, the child Janeen had scolded in the hallway hadn't even been present on that day.

Three weeks later, Janeen was concerned that Corey wasn't reading yet. She wanted to know just exactly what was going on and why her child wasn't performing. The teacher tried to explain that, again, it was developmental; most three-year-olds aren't ready to read, and even those who are, don't do it in only three weeks. Janeen demanded a computer print-out of all the work that Corey did every day in school.

Janeen continued to monitor Corey's every move throughout childhood, wringing her hands every time he made a mistake, constantly calling the teacher with questions about his social behavior and school work, trying desperately to prevent him from experiencing anything uncomfortable. Some children act out when treated this way. Others turn into manipulators, enjoying the reactions and the drama that plays out among the adults in their lives, all because of them. Corey, however, withdrew. He felt anxious, wondering what he did that caused the latest uproar and when the next shoe would fall. Small decisions such as what to wear or eat were difficult as he was afraid of making a mistake. He started to feel as if nothing he did was good enough, so he eventually quit putting forth any effort in school. By the time he got to middle school, he was constantly behind in his work with his mother still swooping around him, interfering in his life and blaming others for his every mishap.

Helicopter parents pay extremely close attention to their child, especially in educational settings, to his detriment. They rush in to protect him from any harm or failure, preventing him from learning from his mistakes. They worry unnecessarily about their child's progress, even when the experts assure them that everything is fine. They are so named because, like helicopters, they hover closely overhead, monitoring their child's every move, whether they are needed or not. In Scandinavia, this phenomenon is known as "curling parenthood"—parents who run ahead of the child, sweeping friction from his path.

This is not the same thing as the involved parent. The involved parent wants to know what is going on, but still understands that the child is an independent being with a right to his own life. She knows that while it is her responsibility to raise the child to eventually become a moral, upstanding adult, he will make errors along the way. The involved parent attends parent conferences and parent information meetings, and observes her child in the classroom. She knows what is going on, but stands on the sidelines as a guide and mentor. This parent does not expect her child to "perform," but to develop at his own pace. This parent realizes that the child should be encouraged to learn how to deal with the outside world on his own and only steps in when absolutely necessary to protect her child from physical or emotional harm.

Children of helicopter parents have a hard time growing up. Children like this often lack self-confidence because they feel unable to fend for themselves. "As children become accustomed to having their parents take care of every aspect of their lives, they feel that this absolves them of all responsibility and expect their parents to continue taking care of them," says Jyoti Modak, operator of a weekend club for children in India. [2] When a child is raised to be dependent on his parents, he transfers that dependency to his peers during adolescence, and by the time he reaches adulthood, he bases all his conclusions about the world and life on what *others* think. Needless to say, this does not create a happy, self-assured, confident adult.

It has been my experience that parents—even helicopter parents—love their children and want the very best for them. Their intentions are good, but they need to relax. Fretting about incidents that are a normal part of childhood experience will make the child more anxious and put a damper on the joy of raising him. Competence and happiness don't come from helicopters; they come from the firm hand of support, love and guidance.

Pushing Children to Learn—Is It Okay?

When parents visit Montessori schools they are often impressed with the order and beauty of the classrooms, and amazed that children can learn advanced concepts independently and calmly. Since Montessori children often excel academically, some parents enroll their child expecting that they have "purchased a passport to academic excellence." Deborah Jackson, author of *Do Not Disturb—Benefits of Relaxed Parenting*, wrote, "...

---

2 Kanchan Maleskar, "Are You a 'helicopter' Parent?," Rediff News, India, February 22, 2007, http://www.rediff.com/getahead/2007/feb/23parent.htm

what I have found, in talking to parents and staff of Montessori schools around the country is that many parents have completely the wrong idea. The true spirit of a Montessori school has nothing to do with pre-set goals like learning to read by a certain age."[3]

Indeed. In 1912 Anne E. George reported:

> ... (Montessori) is always unresponsive if she suspects a visitor of being interested only in the fact that her children read and write at an early age. To take a superficial attitude toward her methods is to place a wall between your mind and hers.[4]

What, then, is the true aim of the Montessori Method? In a word—independence, and the result is the child's profound love of his work.

Adults do not have to prod babies to learn. Notice how much effort it takes for the baby to pull himself up on a chair for the first time as he prepares himself to walk. Notice also his intense concentration. This did not require adult interference. Montessori noted, "The only language men ever speak perfectly is the one they learn in babyhood, when no one can teach them anything!"[5]

When a child enters Montessori school between the ages of 2½ and 3½ he is presented with lots of choices so that his aspiration to progress can continue. The child finds some piece of work in the classroom that fascinates him, he repeats it over and over, and his concentration soars. The child eventually transfers this interest to another activity, then another, until he has felt the desire to learn everything in the room. An adult who does not understand this may step in and tell him he needs to do something more difficult, more exciting, more "academic." The child will think there is something wrong with this desire, and his drive to learn will be hampered.

When a child finds satisfaction in his choice of work, no matter how mundane that choice may seem to an adult, he finds satisfaction in *himself*. This is how self-esteem begins. If parents have enrolled their child expecting that he will excel, unrealistic expectations are then placed on him. He is pressured to do work he finds uninteresting or too difficult. Maybe he isn't even ready for it. Parents will make comments that un-

3 Deborah Jackson, "We Don't Push Children Here," *Montessori International* magazine, 18 Balderton Street, London, 2003.

4 Rita Kramer, *Maria Montessori,* (New York: Capricorn Books, 1977), p. 167.

5 Maria Montessori, *The Absorbent Mind*, (New York: Dell Publishing Co., 1967), p. 6.

knowingly crush the child such as, "You made that *again?*" Extremely bright and accomplished students are also pressured to read better or read more. Some parents will even require that their child accomplish certain work at school (without the teacher's knowledge or consent) or else get into trouble at home. Some parents of children who have been enrolled for only a few days or weeks will ask the teacher if they have been "challenged enough." Raising a star has become more important than raising a happy, well-balanced child.

The child may comply with his parents' wishes for a while but eventually will come to think that nothing he does is ever good enough and will feel unloved or become out of control. The child may withdraw, disrupt the class, lack initiative or revert to thumb sucking. He may also become bossy, depressed, nervous, fearful, or low in self-esteem. The teacher is also put in an uncomfortable position. She must defend this child without offending the parents who dearly love him. The teacher, parents and child play an equal role in the education of the child and they all need to be on the same team. Now they are at odds with each other.

Some parents wonder about children who "do nothing" and think these children should be pushed. But are children really doing "nothing" when they observe before doing? Are they really doing "nothing" before they learn to speak?

Okay then, what about disruptive children? Or lazy children? Or angry and fearful children? Don't *they* need a push? If a child's desire to learn stops, something is wrong (e.g. a physical ailment, unrealistic parental expectations, inconsistent discipline, emotional upset, too much TV or computer time, etc.). Children with deviations are handled on an individual basis in the Montessori school; some with firmness, others with gentle encouragement. If a child needs the former approach, the teacher should tell the parents. In this case, the parents and teacher may agree on a plan of action together. For example, if a child, typically third grade level, is not completing his work at school, the parent may impose a consequence at home, such as no telephone or not having friends over until the work is complete.

Pushing a child is an intrusion into his inner life and kills his spirit. A child needs an environment where he can feel joy from initiating his own work. Academic excellence is a by-product of working for inner satisfaction, and it is precisely because Montessori children are *not* pushed that they are free to excel.

A child will eventually grow up. He will not have an adult prodding him, pushing him, forcing him anymore. Who will make him perform then? And will he do it for self-satisfaction or for approval from others?

Peter Dixon, a senior lecturer in teacher training at King Alfred's College in Winchester, said, "People who work with children have to be able to stand up and speak for the three- and four-year-olds. They are not entertainers, they are educators. They have to say: 'This is who children are and this is what they need to be doing. We do not push children here.'" [6]

Over-Correction

When your child uttered his very first word, "baba," did you correct him and say, "No, it's not a 'baba,' it's a bottle?" When he was learning how to walk and he fell, did you say, "You fell?" No, of course not: you celebrated the fact that he was learning. You knew it was difficult for him, and instead of correcting his errors, you encouraged him. You were his biggest advocate. You clapped your hands with a big smile on your face and cheered him on.

But somehow, as the child gets older, adults feel the need to correct his every mistake. When a five-year-old brings home a four-digit addition problem with the wrong answer, the parent is quick to point it out to the child and his teacher. Children who work on puzzles are constantly corrected when they put pieces in the wrong places. When the child brings home twenty-five identical booklets about Tchaikovsky, the parent sternly points out to him that he needs to do something else.

Over-correction discourages the child. It seems obvious that it would dishearten the baby while he is learning, but adults seem to lose sight of the fact that the growing child needs the same kind of support and encouragement that he received when he was smaller. Correcting a child is certainly appropriate and necessary at the right time and for the right reasons (for example, improper behavior needs to be corrected, immediately and consistently); but knowing when mistakes are okay is difficult unless you understand the nature of the child and the learning process.

---

6 Deborah Jackson, "We Don't Push Children Here," *Montessori International* magazine, 18 Balderton Street, London, 2003.

One of the major differences between adults and children is the way they do their work. An adult does work for the sake of the end result; he wants it to look good and be without error, so that he can move onto the next project. This is not at all how a child approaches work. The child works because he is trying to figure out how adults do things so that he can get control of himself. How do they sweep the floor? How do they use a pencil? How do they wash clothes? What do they do in the kitchen? Unlike the adult, the child doesn't care about the end result at this time—he cares about learning how to do the activity. The difference between the child and the adult is this: *The adult works for the end product, the child does not.* The child works in order to learn *how* to do the activity. The adult is product oriented, the child is *process* oriented. (This process stage is temporary. The child eventually becomes focused on the product after he has practiced and has become successful with the process.)

The five-year-old who makes errors with his four-digit addition problem does not care about the answer yet and he will make lots of errors walking back and forth to the bank in the classroom where he works out his math problems. He drops beads, he grabs the wrong symbol for his answer, he confuses the hundreds and thousands—but it doesn't matter to him. He is having fun. The beads are beautiful and he is learning how to exchange ten units for one ten, ten tens for one hundred, and so on. He is also learning what addition means, and that when smaller quantities are put together they make larger quantities. Correction would crush his enthusiasm and excitement.

The same is true when a child is first learning how to put sounds together to make words. Children start out writing words phonetically (by the sounds of letters) and misspell them, and that is okay at first. Young children also make grammatical errors when they speak: "I goed to the store." "I didn't for a couple while." "That is more smaller." "I am getting very bigger." Children make these errors, not because they have heard someone speak this way, but because they are figuring out grammatical principles. Parents don't need to worry that if they aren't corrected now, their children will forever speak or spell this way (language skills are dealt with at the elementary school level); but they could easily stifle the child's thought process by telling him that he's doing it wrongly.

When the child is in the process stage, it is important that we do not correct him, but rather stand back and observe him. If he is showing frustration in what he is trying to do, ask, "Do you want some help?"

or "Would you like me to show you how to do it again?" And of course you always do it correctly to provide the example and inspiration for him. When the child moves into the product stage, he will bring your attention to it. When the child becomes aware that words have specific spellings, he will ask if he spelled a word correctly. After he understands the basic mathematical operations, he will ask you if he got the correct answer.

Answers do not become important until the child has reached a basic understanding of what he is trying to learn. When a child is corrected during his process stage he will simply accept what the adult has said, and if this goes on long enough, the child will quit thinking. We don't want this. When the child is trying to figure it out, let him.

Late to School....Again?

John was getting extremely frustrated with his four-year-old daughter, Rachel. No matter how hard he tried, he just couldn't get her to school on time. She dawdled getting dressed, she took her time while eating, and she got distracted while putting on her coat. He found himself constantly telling her to hurry, so much so that he felt like a nag. He tried explaining to her the importance of being on time, but it didn't make any difference.

By the time Rachel got to school, first circle had already begun, so Rachel had to walk in late. She felt awkward because all the children turned and looked at her. Then they shifted around, making a spot for her to sit. This disrupted the presentation on zoology that the teacher was making to the children.

The next day, when she was late again, Rachel clung to her dad, crying. She felt embarrassed and did not want to enter the classroom. One of the teachers left first circle to come to his aid, which caused further disruption to the children already in class and more embarrassment for Rachel.

The next day the exasperated father tried to explain to his daughter again the importance of being on time, but to no avail. Rachel continued to dawdle, only this time it was even worse—she recalled her feelings when she was late and wanted to avoid them, so rather than speeding up, the opposite happened—she procrastinated. This time when she arrived at school, first circle was already over, so she had missed some social time (sharing books), the date and the next lesson in zoology, as well as an art lesson.

Rachel's tardiness affected others as well. Her friend, Becca, was upset that Rachel wasn't there and had a hard time getting started with work that morning. When Rachel finally arrived sobbing and screaming, the teacher had to leave another child right in the middle of a botany lesson to help Rachel come in. The teacher was concerned that it was unfair to interrupt a child who always arrived on time to tend to a child who was not on time. Unfortunately, Rachel was learning how to be inconsiderate of others.

After more failed attempts to get Rachel to school on time, John finally gave up, and she was late every day. Therefore, Rachel missed important presentations in the Practical Life and Sensorial areas. Later on in the year she completely missed sequential information in unit studies, which created gaps in her knowledge. When John went to conferences, he was disappointed to hear that Rachel had missed so many lessons due to her tardiness.

John's problem with Rachel is not unusual; in fact, it is very common to have difficulty getting a young child somewhere on time. Here are some suggestions for what to do:

The night before:

- Have the child prepare his snack/lunch for school
- Have the child set out the clothes he is going to wear the next day.

In the morning:

- Provide time for the child to get ready by getting up early enough.
- Have a set routine: The child should get dressed, eat, brush his teeth and then get his coat on.
- No TV watching or computer games.
- Set a timer and tell the child what you expect to be done by the time the bell goes off. Then have a consequence ready if it isn't done.
- Tell the child that if he isn't dressed by the time it is time to leave, you will take him to school in his pajamas. Then be prepared to

actually do it. Tip the teacher off beforehand so she can back you up. (Note: This is ineffective for two-year-olds.)

- Tell the child that you will count to ten, and if his coat isn't on by then, you will put him in the car without it. (Then once in the car, don't turn the heat on.) Counting is very effective in getting children to move, because even though they can't tell how long it takes to get to school, they quickly learn how long it takes to get to ten.
- If arriving at school late, explain to the child that to be considerate of others, he must wait quietly in the hall until first circle is over before entering the classroom.

As frustrating as it is, children are not being naughty when they dawdle; they simply do not understand the concept of time. It is our job as adults to help them by providing consequences for tardiness so that they can learn to be punctual. Self-discipline and social courtesies are learned early in life.

Computers

When Maria Montessori was alive, electronic devices were not present in learning environments as they are today. Therefore, these sections about computers and television are conclusions I have drawn based on my experience and my understanding of Montessori principles.

Jenny, age five, was a bright child and a good student. She loved school and was a good worker, but she was hesitant about challenges. For over a year she had been working on subtraction and was still having difficulty. She would read a problem, look at me and say, "What do I do? I don't remember."

"What does it say?" I said.

"Thirteen take away seven. I don't know what to do."

"Take thirteen counters," I reminded her.

She counted out thirteen and then asked, "Now what do I do?"

"What does it say?" I asked again.

"Take away seven. Can you count it for me?"

"You can do it."

"This is very hard." She took away seven counters. "Now what do I do?"

"How many do you have left?"

"I don't know. Six?"

"Count them and see."

She counted them and said, "Now what do I do?"

"Think about it. What do you do once you know your answer?"

Jenny wrote the answer down. And then…"Now what do I do?"

And so it went. She asked the same questions for the next problem, and the next and the next until she was finished. It took her all morning to do ten problems. Why was this so hard? It isn't like this was her first time. When she was finally finished, she said, "I do subtraction on my iPad. I do it every day so that I can get smart." My heart sank. No wonder this was hard for her.

It isn't that there is anything wrong with computers per se—quite the opposite. Computers are fantastic machines and it is phenomenal how much easier life has become because of them. When used, they do an enormous amount of work easily and swiftly, and have become so integrated into our lives that it is hard to imagine life without them. However, the use of computers to impart knowledge to a young child conflicts with the Montessori Method.

Knowledge does not come from looking at a screen and moving a mouse around. As Montessori noted, "The senses being explorers of the world, open the way to knowledge."[7] The child still needs to be gathering information with his hands by touching objects in the real world and making distinctions between them—this is the beginning of the development of intelligence. Presenting him with stimulation, such as images that appear and disappear on a computer screen that he cannot verify with his senses, results in mental chaos.

The Montessori classroom is based on reality, but computers are too removed from real things. Pictures of objects are not the same as the actual objects; the child does not yet have enough conceptual knowledge about these images to benefit from them. He sees a tree on the screen, but can't feel the trunk or leaves. He can't stand under it or walk around it. He can't throw a pinecone at it to hear what that would sound like. He can't stand in its shadow and feel a temperature change. He can't climb it to feel how big it is, or pull on one of the branches and feel the resistance. Adults have already integrated all this information; they did it when they were children. They can tell, for example, just by looking

_____

7 Maria Montessori, *The Absorbent Mind*, (New York: Dell Publishing Co., 1967), p. 183.

at a tree, the texture of the bark. The child cannot because he has to touch it. Marilyn George, former owner and directress of Blue Gables Montessori in Kirkland, Washington and former instructor at Seattle University, states it perfectly: "Any visual image is an abstraction and leaves out vast quantities of data. To teach using images leaves the child sensorially impoverished."

Therefore, children do not fully understand what the computer is trying to teach, but we are fooled into thinking that children do understand, since they appear to respond so well. Computer programs that beep when the user selects the right answer are like the conditioned response training of Pavlov's dogs, and keep children at an animal level of functioning. A parrot can repeat words—it can imitate speech—but that doesn't mean it can understand; it is merely imitating what it has heard. Children taught this way do the same thing—they repeat back what they've heard, often to please the adult. That doesn't mean they understand the concepts for the sounds they spout. One could liken these children to circus animals that do amazing things for the rewards and attention they receive.

Young children who have been taught with a computer have a harder time in the classroom. Jenny had not spent enough time using real objects to do subtraction so she was just memorizing information that she did not understand, and therefore could not remember what she was supposed to do. "I don't remember" is a common response from these children, as if the answer should have sprung out of midair rather than have been grasped by interaction with the real world. The child, frustrated when the answer is not immediately apparent, begins to guess, hoping to hit upon the right answer rather than trying to figure it out. One teacher reported that a child said, "There are no beeps to tell me if I am right or wrong."[8]

The optimum time to set the foundation for putting the mind in order is prior to age seven. Computer usage interferes with this because when the child is put in a situation where he understands very little about the information he is receiving, he feels overwhelmed. This makes it harder for the child to develop the ability to concentrate on one thing at a time. The child passively experiences sound, movement and imag-

---

8 Other common responses are: staring into space, crying, refusal to try, and putting work away before finished. For a more complete list of the negative results of computer usage, see appendix.

ery rather than distinguishing, sorting and integrating them himself. This over-stimulation can cause the child either to tune out or to be easily distracted. As Healy stated, "A young child's attention naturally jumps from one thing to another, and some forms of electronic media may prolong this immaturity. Distracting graphics and special effects, coupled with the temptation to click impulsively, encourage stimulus-bound behavior which, in turn, contributes to attention problems."[9] In addition, the computer performs actions for the child that he should be learning to do for himself. One example is that a child must learn how to form his own goals and formulate by himself the steps needed to reach those goals—but the computer does both for him. There is concern that the pre-frontal cortex, which regulates emotion, complex thought and problem solving, can become lazy or undeveloped. We must remember that the young child is developing his neurological system and that this is serious business.

Jane Healy voiced her major concern about children and electronic learning:

> Computers must never be allowed to supplant supportive human environments. And we must remember that children need practice integrating the senses through many different kinds of play experiences, managing their own minds—not having their minds distracted or programmed from outside. Symbols must be internalised through concrete experiences before they can be understood in the abstract, such as on a computer screen. Children need to hold the counting bears and place them in a pile of three to relate that concept to the number "three." When computers make up the images, children's minds don't have to work to create them. In addition, electronic media can cause over stimulation and prevent children from focusing on the task at hand.[10]

She fears that when children use computers instead of interacting with their physical environment, the time lost in the development of the active sensory and mental processing needed in order to reason and think accurately may be irreplaceable. These children may never reach their full potential; it takes tremendous mental effort for an older child or adult to

---

9 Jane Healy, "ECT Interview: Computers and Young Children," *Early Childhood Today*, (http://www.scholastic.com/teachers/article/ect-interview-computers-and-young-children.)

10 Jane Healy, "ECT Interview: Computers and Young Children," *Early Childhood Today*, (http://www.scholastic.com/teachers/article/ect-interview-computers-and-young-children.)

change his engrained thinking methods. I can't stress enough the immense difficulty involved and the precious time that has been lost.

Don't forget, the child has not had enough experience yet to know that reality remains constant. Jenny needs to see for herself that a quantity of thirteen minus seven is six no matter what position those objects are in, and the only way she can determine that is by moving real objects. When children are introduced to the computer before they are developmentally ready, it has detrimental effects on their ability to learn. Instead of using a screen, they should be gathering and integrating sensory information.

Television

Johnny's parents are worried about him. He just can't sit still and has a hard time learning in school. His teachers say he lacks self-direction, he can't ever find anything constructive to do and has trouble completing his work. He has very little (if any) self-control and gets into trouble with his classmates. They report that he has to be told every little step in a process because he can't figure things out for himself. Often, he has trouble learning new words, numbers and letters and one time when asked to identify a letter, he answered with the name of a TV show. In short, he can't concentrate and because he can't concentrate, his world is falling apart.

Over the years we've seen lots of children like Johnny. There are many reasons: perhaps he is immature or bored, or his parents do not discipline him properly. Perhaps he has an unidentified health problem, such as allergies, a vision or hearing difficulty, sleep deprivation or poor nutrition. However, Johnny's parents are consistent and fair in their discipline of him, and he has been examined by a physician, who found no health problems.

The parents did notice that there is one activity Johnny *can* stick to for a long period of time. While engaged in this activity he sits immobile for hours, with his eyes wide open, absorbed. A bomb could drop and Johnny would go on as if nothing had happened, still focused on the object at hand—television.

Johnny's parents decided that their son really didn't have a problem after all. He did have the ability to concentrate, which he demonstrated every day at home. This, on the surface, seems to be a logical conclusion, but something is wrong with this picture.

Parents erroneously conclude that because their child can watch television for hours, he can concentrate enough to learn. However, learning has two components: receiving information and processing it. When a child watches TV, he is only receiving visual and auditory input, which gives him very little, if any, knowledge because, as I have explained, the young child also needs to use his sense of touch in order to learn. But this isn't the only problem with television.

Often, children's television programs are geared toward a split-second attention span and do absolutely nothing to foster concentration. Imagine what watching the show *Sesame Street* is like for a young child as images whip past on the screen, cut off before his brain has time to process the stories or concepts which they portray. Since that is frustrating to the adult brain, I shudder to think how Johnny is reacting. It is not relaxing, nor is it educational.[11]

Johnny is so used to stimulation coming into his brain from watching television that his mind becomes an inactive receptacle which produces no output. He is so used to being entertained that he can't find his own things to do. He can't imagine. He can't think. He has no interest in learning, because it requires effort. He has become lazy and he says school is boring. No wonder he is having trouble in school.

But not all children are like Johnny. Is television bad for all children? The same problems that resulted in mental passivity for Johnny are problematic for every child. In Jane Healy's, *Different Learners*,[12] she explains that while the safe amount of viewing can vary from child to child, studies have linked television exposure to attention and learning difficulties, and more recent research indicates problems for pre-school children. Even a television that is on in the background is harmful. A child may not be watching it constantly, but periodically he turns to look at it and his attention is taken away from his activity. His thought process is interrupted along with the related circuits in the brain that control self-monitoring, language and problem solving. This is a major problem for young children who need to learn how to sustain their attention. Healy

11 For more information on the harmful effects of excessive television watching, I highly recommend Jane Healy's book *Endangered Minds: Why Children Don't Think and What We Can Do About It*, (New York: Simon and Schuster, 1990).

12 Jane Healy, *Different Learners* (New York: Simon and Schuster Paperbacks, 2010), p. 299–300.

wrote, "Periodic interruptions of play may seem unimportant, but they can have big long-term effects."[13]

Television watching for children ages 0–6 needs to be highly limited and some experts recommend it be eliminated altogether.[14] Should you decide to let your child watch television, pay close attention to not only the frequency of the viewing but the duration. If a child watches a movie, say one-and-a-half to two hours long, I recommend waiting a full week or more before letting him watch anything again.

If television is watched, it should be used in small (I emphasize *small*) doses for relaxation with the family and to promote a joyful sense of life through good movies, but parents must be very careful in selecting shows for their children to watch. (For recommendations please see appendix.) Some families enjoy documentaries which may be of some benefit depending on the child and his understanding of what he is watching.

While television is a wonderful invention that brings us information and stories quickly and efficiently, its main usage is not for education. The development of television was a logical progression from stage plays, movies and radio. It brings us dramatic performances right into our home, but performances are about entertainment, not about acquiring knowledge. Television is not a child friendly machine. Children need to be spending most of their time developing their minds through exploration of their environments with their hands. Decisions about watching television must be taken with care and thought. Johnny will not be missing much if he does not watch television during his early childhood. He has his whole life to explore the world of movies and documentaries, but he has only six precious years to experience the most crucial sensitive periods for his development. And once these sensitive periods are gone, they are gone forever.

---

13 Jane Healy, *Different Learners* (New York: Simon and Schuster Paperbacks, 2010), p. 300.

14 Jane Healy, *Endangered Minds: Why Children Don't Think and What We Can Do About It*, (New York: Simon and Schuster, 1990), p. 198.

Chapter Seven
Self-Esteem

One of the most remarkable characteristics of a "normal" child is his self-confidence and sureness in action. [1]

MARIA MONTESSORI

What is Self-Esteem?

Traditionally, at our spring program the children sing Whitney Houston's song, "The Greatest Love," which has the message that loving oneself is the greatest love of all. One of the parents in our school convinced us that the children should sing it every year because, she said, "This is what the school is all about."

I was thrilled to hear her say this. She understood that the Montessori Method fosters the development of genuine self-esteem in children and supported our efforts in the classroom. I have found that while loving parents want their children to have self-esteem, most don't necessarily know how Montessori helps them achieve it, let alone how parents should help them achieve it. And in order to help children achieve self-esteem, one must first understand what it is and how it is attained.

Most people think that self-esteem comes from others and therefore, if we love and praise children enough, they'll feel good about themselves. Yet many people struggle with self-confidence problems even though they were cared for deeply as children; so love, while important, is not the total answer.

If one's self-worth comes from being praised by others, then one is in the position of always having to please others in order to be accepted

---

1 Maria Montessori, *The Secret of Childhood*, (New York: Ballantine Books, 1966), p. 170.

(e.g. the person who buys new items not because he really enjoys them, but because he wants the admiration of others; or the teenager who takes drugs so he can belong). Are "others" always correct? Should the Jewish people of Nazi Germany have concluded that they were bad because that's what the majority of their countrymen thought? Should the overweight child who is brutally teased by his classmates automatically conclude that he is worthless?

Contrary to what we've been told all our lives, self-esteem is not automatic, inborn, nor does it come from others. Each individual must earn it on his own. As Dr. Montessori said, "[P]erfection and confidence must develop in the child from inner sources with which the teacher has nothing to do." [2] Self-esteem entails two interrelated aspects: that one is worthy of living and that one is competent to live. It is the knowledge that one's mind can grasp the facts of reality, that one can understand the world and then live rationally and morally. Only then can a person feel a constant inner peace deep down, secure in the knowledge that he is a good person, and glad that he is who he is. He is confident and he values competence. When he meets someone new, his first thought is not, "What does he think of me?" but rather, "What do I think of him?" Genuine self-esteem entails that one is honest with oneself and therefore can be honest with others.

A person with a low opinion of himself thinks, "If you really knew me, you wouldn't like me." He sees himself as a loser, and uses solutions that don't work and that set himself up to lose. This kind of thinking eventually leads to promiscuity, drugs, alcohol, lying and so on. Poor self-esteem can also lead to power-seeking. The power-seeker privately believes he is powerless and therefore strives to attain power over others (e.g. bullies). He thinks, "If I can't control myself, maybe I can control someone else; and if I can do that, I must be really something." Another type is the gossip, who tries to build himself up by tearing others down.

The person with a shaky self-image says to himself, "I'm not so sure I'm okay." He may drive himself hard to get stars (e.g. braggart), or he may put himself down, secretly hoping that others will disagree and build him back up. Then there is the pseudo-intellectual, always trying to impress others with how much he knows. Often, these people are hiding their true selves, and they can become so obsessed with what others believe to be true that they eventually lose all self-identity. Dictators love these

---

2 Maria Montessori, *The Absorbent Mind*, (New York: Henry Holt and Co., 1995), p.274.

types of people because they are so easily influenced and controlled and can be led like sheep.

Parents and teachers are vital to creating an environment that fosters genuine self-esteem in a child; but just as someone cannot teach French without himself knowing French, an adult cannot foster self-esteem without having his own sense of self-worth. A very young child gets his initial influence from his parents—the way they feel about themselves and him. (This is a strong influence, but not a determining factor.)

Adults often, unknowingly, sabotage the child's development of self-esteem. Montessori observed:

> A child…has yet to develop his habits of acting, but he is never allowed to lay out a continuous course of action. If a child is playing, an adult interrupts him, thinking that it is time for a walk. The child is dressed and taken out. Or a child may be working at a task such as filling a pail with stones when a friend of his mother calls. The child is then interrupted in his work and shown to the visitor. An adult is constantly interrupting the child and breaking into his environment. This powerful being directs the child's life without ever consulting the child himself. And this lack of consideration makes the child think that his own activities are of no value. On the other hand, when an adult addresses another adult in a child's presence …, he does not interrupt him without saying, "If you please," or "if you can." A child consequently feels that he is different from the rest of mankind, that he is inferior, subject to all.[3]

Maria Montessori was way ahead of her time in recognizing that genuine self-confidence was internally generated through one's work. She did not, therefore, advocate the use of praise, stars, or other external methods for rewarding children. Through his work, the child concludes that he is competent at living, and through proper behavior the child learns that he is worthy of living. Allowing the child to be independent fosters genuine self-esteem. Since Montessori education is individualized, no child has to compare himself to anyone else ("There must be something wrong with me because I can't read as well as the group"); and each child grows to accept himself as his own person, with his own individual traits and differences, and realizes that is okay.

---

3 Maria Montessori, *The Secret of Childhood*, (New York: Ballantine Books, 1966), p. 168–169.

Self-esteem builds when a child feels pride over his accomplishments.

There is no question more important to a human being than what he thinks of himself. We all live with that question every waking moment. Most of the problems we see in the world—the insecurities, the power seeking, the evil—get back to this personal, individual, all-important question of what one thinks of oneself. To be at peace inside is one's most crucial need. Early influences matter. If we give a child the opportunity to develop genuine self-esteem, we've given him the key to a happy life. One year, while at the post office, I encountered a parent whose son had been one of my kindergarten graduates. The mother said to me, "Our teenage son has never forgotten the song, 'The Greatest Love.' To this day, when he hears the song, he drops what he is doing to listen, and insists that everyone around him do the same."

Praise

Ronin, age four, was working intently on the metal inset pencil work, his head down and his eyes never wavering from the paper. He did this for some time, then looked up with a mile wide smile and said, "I'm good! I'm good!" I said, "How do you know?" He held up his paper and said, "Lookit! I stayed within the lines!"

When I hear children speak like this, like I do so often in the classroom, I know that they evaluate their own work. Sarah Cole Zimmerman, a child psychologist, noted this when her four-year-old daughter, Shandy, came home and announced, "My teacher doesn't know what 'good' means." The mother was surprised. "What do you mean?" "Well," said Shandy, "I showed her some work and she said it was good." Shandy went on to tell her mother in detail all the mistakes she had made while doing the work.[4]

Children are capable of thinking about and appraising themselves, yet, many people think that children need approval from others in order to develop self-confidence and we therefore get questions from visitors to our classrooms asking why we do not praise the children very much. I answer that this is because we want the children to evaluate themselves and not rely on *our* appraisal. Dr. Montessori said, "To tell a person he is clever or clumsy, bright, stupid, good or bad, is a form of betrayal. The

---

4 Sarah Cole Zimmerman, paper on self-esteem presented at workshop, Berkeley, California; Feb. 20, 1983.

child must see for himself what he can do, and it is important to give him not only the means of education but also to supply him with indicators which tell him his mistakes."[5] She also stated, "But, unless I can correct myself, I shall have to seek the help of someone else, who may not know any better than I do...This begets a discouraging sense of inferiority and a lack of confidence in one's self."[6]

I frequently observe parents praise their child for every little thing they do. Out in public I often hear, "Good job! Good job!" If we over-praise children, they can become dependent on us because they want to please us. They want to grow up and become adults themselves (they are incensed at being called "little": "No, I'm big. I'm five."). If they are working only for the sake of praise, however, they will be shattered by correction or criticism. And in trying to bolster a child's confidence by praise alone, we present him with an unrealistic view of reality: no one in the adult world is praised for every little thing he does.

Research at Columbia University by Carol Dweck from 1997 to 2007 strongly indicates that telling children they are smart actually causes underperformance.[7] Children given this type of praise think that their intelligence is innate and fixed. In essence they think, "I am smart, therefore I don't have to put forth effort." Then, when they encounter something that is difficult, they conclude right away that they can't do it. This causes insecurity and an obsession with their self-image, and they often react by tearing down other children. Children who are told that they work really hard, rather than that they are smart, conclude that their intelligence is something that can be developed—that they are in control of it—and have excellent persistence and performance. In some cases, these children ended up doing better than children with higher intelligence scores. (I highly recommend reading the entire article about this study, "How Not to Talk to Your Kids."[8])

The child can feel fragile as he builds his self-esteem. Perhaps this is why there is a tendency to over-praise, especially if we think the child has a poor self-image. A friend of mine couldn't understand why his son was

---

5 Maria Montessori, *The Absorbent Mind,* (New York: Dell Publishing Co., 1967) .p.250.

6 Maria Montessori, *The Absorbent Mind,* (New York: Dell Publishing Co., 1967), p. 248.

7 Po Bronson, "How Not to Talk to Your Kids," http://nymag.com/news/features/27840/, New York Magazine, August 3, 2007.

8 Po Bronson, "How Not to Talk to Your Kids," http://nymag.com/news/features/27840/, New York Magazine, August 3, 2007.

in trouble: "But we gave him plenty of praise!" People think that if you praise a naughty child, you will spare the child looking at his negative characteristics. If he isn't aware of them, he will feel good about himself. But faking reality does the child no favors. How will he know to correct himself when he hasn't been told what he needs to correct? Praise needs to be based on the facts of reality and feedback to the child needs to help him, not hinder him—and meaningless messages do not give anyone concrete proof that they are okay.

How, then, do we avoid over-praising the child, and instead encourage him to evaluate himself? We must be careful not to praise a child when he is in the process stage. In this circumstance, it is best to say, "You're learning how to make letters," rather than, "That's a good letter." We must also be aware of the child who works only to please adults and constantly seeks our approval. When this child asks, "Is my picture pretty?" we should respond with, "What do you think?" We can also try to reflect what the child might be feeling about his picture, such as, "I can see you enjoyed working on that," or "I bet you feel proud of all that work you did."

To be effective, verbal praise needs to be specific feedback, so that the child knows where to focus his attention the next time he does the activity. "I like the way you folded your legs, put your hands in your lap and sat silently, waiting for first circle to start." In the Montessori classroom, we have a distinct advantage: the child is largely freed from the teachers and able to evaluate himself, as the control of error is for the most part in the materials.

Under-praising is harmful also. A child who works and works and works to achieve a certain goal will want recognition for it. Dr. Montessori stated, "This, however, is the moment in which the child has the greatest need of [the teacher's] authority. When a child has accomplished something…he runs to the teacher and asks her to say if it is all right….After he has done the work, he wants his teachers' approval….The teacher must respond with a word of approval, encouraging him with a smile…." [9] If the adult is not sensitive to the child's need for recognition, the child will be disappointed. He'll feel that the adult didn't understand him or doesn't care. Children look to us for guidance and need to feel secure. When a child accomplishes something and is happy, the adult needs to show his happiness also.

---

9 Maria Montessori, *The Absorbent Mind*, (New York: Dell Publishing, 1967), p. 274.

When you are upset with the child's performance, however, ridicule is not a good means of feedback. Ridicule is not the same as constructive criticism, but rather is destructive attention. The child feels crushed when ridiculed. A message, direct or indirect, should never sound like this: "What's the matter with you? Can't you ever do anything right?" Remember, tone of voice and facial expression can convey ridicule just as much as words can. When angry, tell the child you are angry and state the reasons, but don't ridicule him. Montessori said, "To tell a child he is naughty or stupid just humiliates him; it offends and insults, but does not improve him." [10]

All children need praise and hugs and lots of love, but be careful not to over-praise. Don't use praise as a means to boost your child's self-esteem, use it as a means to help the child assess himself. If the child learns to rely on his own thinking in his self-appraisal, he gains independence and self-reliance.

---

10 Maria Montessori, *The Absorbent Mind*, (New York: Dell Publishing, 1967), p. 245.

Chapter Eight
Discipline

A teacher of experience never has grave disorder in her class because, before she draws aside to leave the children free, she watches and directs them for some time, preparing them in a negative sense, that is to say, by eliminating their uncontrolled movements. [1]

MARIA MONTESSORI

Consequences

Visitors to Montessori classrooms are often impressed with the benevolence and good behavior of the children. Most children go about their work, often without being told, and, while the classrooms are active, they are at the same time peaceful. There are many reasons why this happens, and one of the most important is discipline.

Discipline is not punishment, but rather training which corrects and strengthens behavior. What is unique about the Montessori Method is that the child learns how to discipline himself. Rather than the adult trying to control the child through external rewards and punishments, the child acquires internal control through his work. His achievements give him a sense of self-mastery and self-control, especially since the concrete materials allow him to make corrections and discoveries on his own. Montessori observed that even unruly children were transformed by their work. Once an engaging activity grabbed a child's attention, he learned to concentrate and the true child began to emerge. Until this happens, however, until the child achieves internal discipline, he requires external discipline from adults.

---

1 Maria Montessori, *The Absorbent Mind*, (New York: Dell Publishing, 1967), p. 268–269.

In our Montessori teacher training class, discipline was likened to a kite. Think of the kite as the child and the string as the gentle guiding hand of the adult. When the child exhibits maturity and responsibility the adult lets the string to the kite out, but when the child misbehaves the adult pulls the string in. While the child is growing up, the adult is constantly adjusting the length of the string, pulling it in and letting it out, depending on the behavior of the child.

The most effective type of discipline is the use of consequences. There are two types: natural (child runs into street without looking and gets hit by a car) and logical (child runs into street without looking and parent won't allow him to go outside to play). When the natural consequence is too dangerous, or if it doesn't work, the adult should set up logical consequences.

Logical consequences need to be tailored to each individual child according to his unique personality and set of circumstances. Any consequence given will depend on the age of the child, why he's doing what he is doing, household or classroom rules, number of times he's broken the rule, type of rule broken (for example a safety issue needs to be dealt with quickly), and so on. You have to find what works for *your* child. But whatever you do, always be prepared to follow through with the consequences that you have set up because if you don't, the child will cease listening to you. For that reason, consistency is *vital* to good discipline. Also, thinking of effective consequences and successful discipline is something you can learn, and it gets easier with practice.

Consequences should be given without long dissertations. Once you have determined what the circumstance is, declare and institute the consequence quickly and without further discussion. When the consequence is over, it is usually a good idea to ask the child to explain what he did wrong and have a discussion at that time. But if a parent lectures and lectures, before, during or after the consequence, the child will misbehave again because of the attention he received.

Parents often ask us for ideas for consequences when their child refuses to cooperate. An example is the child who won't get dressed for school in the morning. Usually these parents are at their wits' end by the time they come to talk to us about it. When we ask them what they've done, they tell us they've tried punishments, rewards, logic, yelling, threatening and spanking, and the child still is not responding. If the child is more than two years old, I often suggest that the parent give him two choices: either he gets himself dressed, or he goes to school in his pajamas. A few parents have responded, "Oh, but that would humiliate him. I could never do that."

Because of this fear, adults can be reluctant to do what needs to be done to get a child to behave. Usually when we think of humiliation, we think of a child wearing a dunce's hat, sitting on a chair in front of the class while his peers laugh at him. Humiliation is degrading someone else with the purpose of bringing him down and shaming him. A person could be humiliated for that over which he has no control and which has no moral element (e.g. a facial feature); or he could be humiliated for something that he does have control over and that does have a moral element (e.g. robbing a bank).

The purpose of discipline is not to bring the child down, but rather to help him develop control over his own actions and learn the difference between right and wrong. The child needs this help because he can't think long range and can't foresee consequences; but many adults don't realize this. They think the child can reason like an adult; they assume he understands and therefore expect him to cooperate when they talk to him about his behavior.

But the child does not understand. When we try to explain to him that he needs to hurry or he'll be late, he doesn't get it because he has no concept of time. When we try to explain that a car could hurt him if he runs out into the street, he doesn't understand how serious this is because he has no concept of death or serious injury. When we try to explain that he needs to eat now or he'll be hungry later, he still doesn't eat because he isn't hungry now and can't project into the future. When we explain that he shouldn't take his toy into the store because he might lose it, he does it anyway because he doesn't know what it would be like to lose something.

The child is perceptual. He lives in the here and now. So how do we get him to realize that there are consequences for his actions? How do we get him to think beyond what he knows only in this moment?

Spankings, long lectures and yelling don't work. Most of the time, the child cannot see how they relate because they don't relate to his actions, so he reacts to them without understanding what he has done wrong, and thus has no reason to change his behavior. Choices and consequences, however, appeal to the child's conceptual mind. When he has to endure the consequence of a choice he has made, he is compelled to think about his behavior.

Would we refuse to send the bank robber to jail because we were afraid he would feel humiliated? Of course not. He made a choice to steal from other people, knowing full well that he was harming them, and jail is one of the consequences. The child, who chooses not to get dressed, has also made a choice. Though he, unlike the robber, does not understand the full ramifications of his choice, he can begin to learn them by feeling the natural embarrassment that will ensue when he arrives at school in his pajamas. Will he think about the choice he made? You bet.

Something many adults miss about children is that children have the ability to assess adults and behave accordingly. When I was a child, about five years old, my mother's cousin would often come to baby-sit. I loved it when he baby-sat. Once in bed, I could think of a million excuses to delay going to sleep, and he always fell for them. If I claimed I was dying of thirst, he would bring me a drink. If I heard a terrifying noise outside my window, he would come and look for it. If I groaned in pain with a fake tummy ache, he would come take my temperature. I thought this was great fun and would laugh and giggle with glee. I always had him on the run and it was fun to think of new and unique reasons to call him to my bedroom once again to do my bidding. I thought it was a delightful game. He, however, didn't find this at all amusing and felt extremely frustrated, yet every time I called him, he came.

Children are testers—they are testers of reality and they will test to see what will happen or how much they can get away with. When the adult does not take charge, the child will manipulate him. Often the adult has no idea what is going on and unknowingly keeps catering to the child. If the child learns that he can get away with stalling, he will. If he doesn't have to get dressed in the morning, he won't. If he fakes being sick so that he can be home with Mom and it works, he'll try it again. One time I asked a three-year-old why he misbehaved with his mother. "Because I get what I want," he replied.

Once the adult recognizes and fully understands that the child thinks and acts differently, he will have the strength to let the child feel the natural consequences of his behavior. This is not the same thing as humiliating him. If an adult forced a child to stay in his pajamas and then forced him to go out in public, that would be humiliation. But no force is involved when the child is given choices and is told in advance what will happen with the choices he makes. Then it is up to the adult to carry through and make sure that the child experiences the outcome.

We cannot and should not protect a child from the consequences of his actions (provided they are not physically harmful). To do so is to hold him back from learning what the real world is all about. In the real world, if you don't get dressed, you don't go to work. If you don't go to work, you lose your job. If you lose your job, you won't have any money. Without money, you don't eat. A child cannot understand such abstract reasoning; but he can begin to take the steps needed towards self-responsibility by making choices and then reaping the consequences of those choices, good or bad.

I would much prefer that a child make mistakes and feel the effects when he is young, than wait until he reaches an age at which he could be making life and death choices—e.g. Do I get in that car with a drunk driver? If a child has had experience with making choices and has learned how to anticipate consequences, chances are he won't get into that car. But if he has been protected from making mistakes, and protected from the effects of his misbehavior, chances are he will get into that car. Which way would you rather have it—your four-year-old child feels embarrassed because he came to school in his pajamas, or your teenager dies in a car accident because he never learned what happened when he didn't think ahead?

The choice is yours.

Time-Outs

Edward, age 3½, has had a pretty good day at Montessori. For the first time, he attempted some brand new work on his own, work that prior to this day he had been afraid to try. He is gradually gaining confidence in himself and feels fabulous when he walks out of the classroom at dismissal time. He sees his mother and walks over to her elated. "Were you in the time-out chair today?" his mother asks. Edward's happiness immediately dissipates.

Parents are understandably concerned about their child's behavior. Nobody wants to raise a child who grows up to be defiant and unhappy, especially when he is deeply loved and cherished. But Edward did not have any major issues that the teacher was concerned about. Yes, he was in the chair every day, often more than once a day, but this is often normal when children are learning how to control themselves. However, when parents ask for a daily report about sitting in time-out, the child can conclude that something is wrong...and that "something" is him.

In addition, some parents worry when their child says, "I didn't get in trouble today." They think this indicates their child is obsessed with being in trouble, but it is a normal childhood expression. This is one way that the child expresses pride in the fact that he behaved well. Another example is the child who says, "I didn't spill at dinnertime." Translation: "I sat up straight, ate over my plate and didn't wiggle around. I'm getting control over myself." It doesn't mean that the child is traumatized by spilling.

In the Montessori classroom discipline is handled on an individual basis and consequences for misbehavior can include a verbal correction, a stern look, a presentation on how something should be done, natural consequences, redirection, and so on. In addition, Maria Montessori advocated another consequence that was very effective:

> As far as punishments are concerned, we frequently found ourselves confronted with children who disturbed others, but who would not listen to our entreaties. We immediately had them examined by a physician, but very often they turned out to be normal. We then placed a little table in a corner of the room and, there isolating the child, we made him sit in an armchair where he could be seen by his companions and gave him all the objects he desires. This isolation always succeeded in calming the child. From his position he could see all of his companions, and their way of acting was an object lesson in behavior more effective than words of his teacher could have been. Little by little he came to realize the advantages of being with the others and to desire to act as they did. In this way we imparted discipline to all the children who at first had seemed to us to be rebels...I do not know what happened within the souls of the isolated children, but certainly their conversions were always true and lasting. They became proud of their work and behavior, and they generally retained a tender affection for their teacher and for me. [2]

2 Maria Montessori, *The Discovery of the Child*, (India: Kalakshetra Publications, 1966), p. 86.

Time-outs give the child the concreteness that he needs in order to correct himself. He needs to feel and see that his misbehavior will not be tolerated. Time-outs appeal to the child's mind. By sitting in one spot, he can calm down and *think* about his actions while observing the proper behavior of the other children.

Time-outs were used in Montessori's original schools with success. E.M. Standing, author of *Maria Montessori: Her Life and Work*, recalls:

> I once sent a questionnaire round to a number of long-established Montessori schools, and one of the questions in it was this: What use do you make of punishments? One directress wrote: "Work is its own reward. Punishments are rare; a troublesome child might be removed from her companions until she is ready to behave properly." Another said: "With younger children the greatest reward is to be able to pass on to a new stage in each subject. It is a punishment to a child not to be able to use the apparatus, but to sit still and do nothing." Another teacher (with twenty years of experience behind her) said: "If a warning does not suffice, the offender is separated from other children and made to sit beside the directress. The lessons given by the directress to other children generally arouse interest and the child settles down to work. Either this or she becomes bored and returns to her place. This 'punishment' proves quite sufficient." [3]

Critics worry that time-outs can create social problems for the offending child. Several years ago another Montessori teacher came to observe my classroom. At the end of the observation time I asked her if she had any questions and her response was immediate, "Your children are so… they're so…well, they're so…calm!" She went on to tell me that she had a group of children who misbehaved every day. They were a disruption to the entire class. They terrorized everyone by kicking, hitting and running. They abused the materials by swinging the bead chains around. She was never able to make any presentations without constant interruptions and said she really needed help in the area of discipline. I said, "Have you ever tried putting those children in a time-out chair?" "Oh no!" she stated emphatically. "Then everyone would know they were naughty."

I couldn't believe this. Did she really think that none of the children knew who was being naughty? Her motive was to shelter the misbehav-

---

3 E.M. Standing, *Maria Montessori: Her Life and Work,* (New York: New American Library, 1957), p. 44.

ing children by trying to hide the fact that they were misbehaving, rather than correct their inappropriate actions and protect the well-behaved children. She was more worried about social problems than moral development and safety. If something isn't done to stop misbehavior, the entire class is disrupted and the children feel violated. They can't work. They are afraid. But when the offenders are removed they feel safe. The class can carry on—they are free to learn again, now that the disruption has been stopped. And one more thing: they no longer feel threatened by the wrongdoers, so they can still be friends with them.

Some people think that if a child is continuously disciplined, no one will like him, as if it were the discipline that was affecting the children's affections for each other, rather than the child's own behavior. But it is correction which helps children socially.

Some people fear that time-outs increase the child's separation anxiety. They think it gives the child the message that only his good side is acceptable and that he is being sent away because the adult can't deal with his bad side. They think the child feels shunned, so they use "time-ins" instead. With a "time-in," the adult stays with the child during his tantrum. Depending on the age of the child and the reason that he is upset, this can be the right thing to do. In most cases, however, this is not a good idea, because it rewards the child for his misbehavior by giving him more attention. In fact, the message that only his good behavior is acceptable is exactly what he needs to learn, and alone-time gives him the chance to think about his misbehavior without distraction. The purpose is not to make a child feel that you don't love him, but that you love him enough to take the actions required for him to learn the difference between right and wrong.

Another criticism is that the child won't learn anything if he is in the chair too much. Yet, what is the child learning when he is cruising around the room, disrupting the work of others? What is he learning when the only time he settles down and does any work is when an adult is sitting right there by his side? A child has to learn *self*-control. He has to learn how to sit still and pay attention on his own before he can learn anything else. When a child sits in time-out, he has no choice but to sit still and observe.

Montessori's method was revolutionary in the area of discipline because, instead of giving the child more work to punish misbehavior, she advocated withdrawing him from work and putting him in a position where he could observe work all around him and so see what he was missing. (In the Montessori classroom, work is rewarding.) Children like to be active and on the go, so this is very effective. Once the child finds engaging work, he is transformed and his behavior changes. Then he feels great, not in anticipation of external rewards, but because of the inner satisfaction from being able to control himself.

We must learn to be realistic when raising children and we must be careful in the messages we give to them. Needing correction is normal in childhood and we don't want to give children the impression that it is abnormal by drawing constant attention to it. Rewards such as treats draw the child's thoughts away from his misbehavior, and denying reality serves only to make the problem worse. The only solution is for the adults in the child's life to find out what it takes to get him to behave… and then have the courage do it.

"Saying No Will Hurt Their Self-Esteem"

I have known people who think it is a good idea to spare children direct correction and avoid using the word "no," for fear of making them sad and hence hurting their self-esteem. Saying no, in this view, should be reserved for emergency situations when a child could get hurt, such as crossing a busy street. There are two underlying premises here. One is that self-esteem comes from others, and therefore one should always present a positive view to a child about himself so that he can have high self-esteem. The second is that that temporary sadness or negative emotions hurt self-esteem and that this is what causes a child to behave poorly. Both views are false.

Self-esteem, as I discussed earlier, does not come from the approval of others. Children initially develop their self-evaluation from the conclusions that they draw about the world through their experiences. If they think reality is understandable and that they are capable of understanding it, they will have a positive view of themselves; but if they think reality is chaos, that they can't comprehend it, and that anything goes, they will have a negative view of themselves.

Think a minute about the idea that saying "no" will hurt a child's self-esteem. This idea presupposes that a child already has self-esteem but, as we have seen, self-esteem must be earned and takes time to develop. If a child is misbehaving by hitting, shoving, pushing, kicking, name-calling and disrespecting others, I don't see how he can possibly feel good about what he is doing. (If he does feel good about it, that is a serious psychological problem, which is outside the range of this discussion.) The more he is allowed to do these things, the worse he feels about himself, and if this goes on long enough, he won't have much (or any) self-esteem. Self-esteem is not a starting point. If we want him to have high self-esteem it is his behavior that needs to change, and the purpose of discipline is to persuade him to change it.

The idea also assumes that correction hurts a child's self-esteem because it makes him sad. It is important to understand, however, that emotions cannot affect self-image—they are not responsible for creating self-esteem, improving it, or damaging it. Emotions are a result of value judgments that a person has made; and if a child judges that he has behaved poorly, he *should* feel bad about it. How else can a child learn the difference between right and wrong unless he feels uncomfortable when he does something wrong? To deny a child that is to deny him the development of a conscience; and if he doesn't develop a conscience, there is no self-esteem to be had.

Some argue that the child be given choices instead of being told "no." It is true that choice-making is essential to independence, and is very effective in developing self-control; but there are times when we can't give the child a choice. It is fine to say, "Would you like to climb into the car seat yourself or should I put you in it?", but what happens when he refuses both choices and runs away—then what do you do? Some children refuse to cooperate no matter what choices are given, and you can't allow a child to choose what is not allowable. (Nor can you wait until an emergency before saying "no": if the child has never heard that word from you before, how will he know what it means?)

I have also heard people say that adults should give the child limits, but not impose any external consequences on him should he exceed those limits—that he should feel only the natural consequences of his actions. This is only half of the equation, though: other people do provide consequences to those who violate individual rights. A natural consequence of murder is that someone dies; an external, logical consequence is that the murderer loses the right to his own life and goes to jail. A natural consequence for a cheater is the inner knowledge that he didn't actually win; the logical, external consequence is that once people learn that he cheats, they won't invite him back for another game. The child needs to learn that what he does affects others, and if it affects others in a negative way, negative consequences will be imposed on him as a result. Sheltering a child from this fact is doing him no favors in preparing him for real life in the adult world.

When it comes to an issue of morality or safety, we must be unwavering in our approach with him. We have to set the boundaries by telling him, "No!" If he is defiant with us or continues to misbehave, we need to make him stop by giving him an immediate consequence such as removing him from the dangerous situation. Doing this is an important measure in helping a child learn correct behavior and gain control. Children are impulsive and on the move and when made to stop, the child can then see for himself that he is able to stop.

We had a student at school who was choking other children—a very serious problem. We isolated the child at his own table for three months. The mother was upset because she thought he would conclude he was naughty and it would damage his self-esteem. She thought the other kids wouldn't like him. At the end of the three months, however, when it was time to give him his freedom again, he told his mom he didn't want to leave his table because while working there he didn't hurt anybody. Telling him "no" gave him the boundaries he needed to start controlling himself. As I heard someone else say, "A child needs to hear the word 'no' said to him so that he can say it to himself later."

A child may protest at the moment when he is told no, but this doesn't mean that correcting him was the wrong thing to do. Of course, he doesn't want to stop, he wants his own way, but part of growing up is learning how to deal with the fact that you can't always do whatever you feel like doing. By not saying "no," adults send a child the message that everything in life will go as he wants no matter what he does. That isn't reality.

However, despite their objections, children actually appreciate correction. Firmness makes them feel secure. It is interesting to see that children who have been corrected and disciplined surround their teachers with love and affection. Montessori reported the same phenomenon. [4] Countless times I hear these same children brag to their parents about the fact that they have rules that they have to obey at school. When our oldest daughter was eight years old we had this conversation:

---

4 Maria Montessori, *The Discovery of the Child*, (India: Kalakshetra Publications, 1966), p.86.

"Mom, do you remember Amy, who used to baby-sit for us?"

"Yes."

"Does she still work there at Target?"

"I don't know."

"Well, when she baby-sat us we couldn't get away with a *thing*. She used to sit with her back to us doing her homework. We figured she wasn't paying any attention so we would jump on the bed. As soon as we started jumping, she'd turn around and tell us to stop. She was so stern, but she was only stern about the things we *couldn't* do. She was very stern. Mom I *really* liked her!"

If the child is always presented with a positive view of himself, even when he is doing negative things, he isn't helped: he is actually hindered. This is shielding him from reality. He has no way of distinguishing right from wrong and has no guidelines for changing. We shouldn't give him the view that everything he does is wonderful, and we are lying to him if we do. It is not wonderful when he misbehaves.

Saying "no" will not hurt a child's self-esteem. Let's not reverse cause and effect. To have a good self-image, the misbehaving child needs to change his behavior. If people are concerned about a child's self-esteem, they should learn what it is and how it is attained. Self-esteem is the result of a positive appraisal of oneself based on one's ability to understand and deal with the real world. We need to give the child a firm and loving guiding hand so that he can develop that ability. Nothing brings self-esteem to the soul of a child more than his own competent mind.

"The Strong Willed Child"

A four-year-old races madly around the classroom, throwing materials and hitting children. Then he begins to walk on the shelves. The teacher takes no action because the child is "expressing himself" and she doesn't want to "stifle his creativity." A five-year-old refuses to sit quietly at dismissal time and makes defiant faces at his teacher. The parent says the child is expressing his supposedly "strong will." When these same adults observe the calmness and self-control which children exhibit in a Montessori classroom, I have heard them conclude that those children have been stifled and regimented. But which children have really been stifled?

Up until this time, the child's every move and thought had a purpose: to develop his own being. He grew from a helpless newborn into a walking, speaking person in only three years. His nature was not to be violent and disorderly, but to learn. Now, suddenly, it is believed that a child would rather play than work, would rather be disobedient than self-disciplined, would rather break things than build them.

Montessori stated: "... confusion springs from the belief that children's natural actions are bound to be disorderly and even violent. Usually this belief is based on the fact that people, seeing a child act in a disorderly way, always assume that these actions proceed from his will. But this is far from the truth." [5] (Montessori defined the will as "the intelligent direction of movements." [6]) Montessori thought that the rebellious child is not being disobedient because of the presence of a strong will, but because of its *absence.* This child is not directing his movements by making intelligent choices: he lacks self-control, so he is acting from a state of weakness.

Before the child becomes a conceptual being, he only reacts to events. He starts to make choices as he builds up his conceptual framework, as he acquires knowledge and understanding. It is knowledge that makes good choice-making possible. With limited knowledge, a child can only make limited choices, and children misbehave when they do not understand enough to make good choices. For example, they know that stealing is wrong, but because they do not have the conceptual framework of an adult, they do not know all the reasons why it is wrong. Therefore, most children steal at some time in their childhood, whereas most adults do not steal. Children also misbehave when they receive conflicting information, e.g. from the parent who says "no" to a child, but then backs down or does nothing when the child disobeys. This confusion hinders a child's choice-making ability. The child needs to be able to develop his mind logically so he can make choices based on rational thought. The greater his understanding of logic which he learns through his work, the surer he can be of making the right choices. Then he can be strong, because he can act with confidence.

Montessori thought that a pattern of disorderly and violent behavior in a child were "signs of emotional disturbance and suffering." [7] I couldn't agree more. A child who "acts out" is not a self-assured, happy child and

---

5 Maria Montessori, *The Absorbent Mind*, (New York: Dell Publishing, 1967), p.253.

6 Maria Montessori, *Spontaneous Activity in Education,* (on line book: http://www.read-central.com/chapters/Maria-Montessori/Spontaneous-Activity-in-Education/008), chapter 7.

7 Maria Montessori, *The Absorbent Mind*, (New York: Dell Publishing, 1967), p.253.

he needs a caring, loving adult who has the courage to give him the help that he needs—discipline. The child has to learn the difference between good and evil, what is safe and what is dangerous, and so on. A child learns that adults know more than he knows. He also learns that the world has dangers and that he can get hurt. He *needs* adults to correct him, to protect him, to keep him safe. If this isn't done, the child feels insecure and frightened of his own power. He knows he shouldn't have that kind of power. He is not the big one, the knowledgeable one. When you're scared of yourself, how can you build self-confidence? Note how often these children are also angry. They have every right to be—they have been abandoned.

Montessori was very clear in her view of the adult's role in correcting the child. She stated:

> When the teachers were weary of my observations, they began to allow the children to do whatever they pleased. I saw children with their feet on the tables, or fingers in their noses, and no intervention was made to correct them. I saw others push their companions, and I saw on the faces of these an expression of violence, and not the slightest attention on the part of the teacher. Then I had to intervene to show with what absolute rigor it is necessary to hinder, and little by little suppress, all those things which we must not do so that the child may come to discern clearly between good and evil. [8]
>
> ...
>
> If at this stage there is some child who persistently annoys the others, the most practical thing to do is interrupt him. It is true that we have said and repeated often enough, that when a child is absorbed in his work, one must refrain from interfering, so as not to interrupt his cycle of activity or prevent its free expansion; nevertheless, the right technique now is just the opposite; it is to break the flow of the disturbing activity... [9]
>
> ...
>
> A vigorous and firm call is the only true act of kindness toward these little minds. [10]

---

8 Rita Kramer, *Maria Montessori,* New York: Capricorn Books, 1976) p. 118.

9 Paula Polk Lillard, *Montessori: A Modern Approach*, (New York: Schocken Books, 1972), p. 88.

10 Maria Montessori, *The Absorbent Mind*, (New York: Dell Publishing, 1967), p.268.

A child is not "expressing himself" when he is walking on shelves. Since the child is still in the process of developing himself, he hasn't yet much of a self to express. He *is* expressing frustration and anger, and is acting in a reckless manner which, if allowed to continue, could land him in the hospital. Correcting misbehavior is not "stifling creativity." What has a child created by hitting and throwing objects? Destruction is not creative. Adults who allow this misbehavior are doing the child no favors. He will learn soon enough that the real world doesn't operate this way and, not knowing correct behavior, will feel like a misfit.

The child has one very important job—to grow up. He will make choices from what he learns, whether or not he is allowed to run wild or is disciplined. Parents and teachers have a job as well—to help him grow up. In order to do that, they have to make a choice. They have to choose either to recognize the true nature of the child and provide him with the greatest opportunity for success, or to ignore what is required for his proper development and stifle his human spirit.

Rewards

Years ago, I had a student who was hitting others and was in constant trouble in school. When disciplined for it, he didn't seem to care. Finally one day, when put in a chair for hitting again, he sat and cried with his head in his hands. "Hurray!" I thought to myself, "We finally made a breakthrough!" But I was sorely disappointed when he choked out these words in between his sobs: "Now that I've had to sit in the chair, I won't get to see a movie when I go home." Unfortunately this is what happens when a child is offered a reward for good behavior—he focuses on the reward rather than his actions.

It is understandable that parents offer children rewards. Parents are often frustrated when their child misbehaves or does not cooperate despite repeated efforts to get him to do so. They also may feel guilty, thinking they must have done something wrong to cause the misbehavior. But parents need to understand that the child is an individual with a free will. Children draw their own conclusions independently of us and they can form misconceptions about some things without our knowledge. For instance, a child may observe that his older sibling is more competent, but not understand why this is, and therefore conclude that he is inferior. He may lack self-confidence, and therefore choose not to venture out and try new things. He may notice that adults are not afraid of dogs, while he is, so feels unsure of himself. He may have speech difficulties and not know how to express his frustration, and so just lashes out when angry. And so on.

Because the child is his own person, he must learn to bear the consequences of his own actions. The child needs to be held responsible for his behavior and parents must let that happen. But when parents offer rewards, they take over the responsibility. The parent is now in the driver's seat, deciding when the child's behavior is good enough, instead of letting the child judge for himself. The parent has the power and grants the child a prize if he cooperates.

The child's focus shifts to the envisioned prize. He thinks, in essence, "What will I get?" rather than, "How should I behave?" Because he is so focused on the reward, whether or not he behaves becomes a matter of chance rather than conscious effort on his part. On a particular day when he does happen to behave, he gets a reward; but even though he is told why, he may not be able to figure out how to get himself to do it again—he wasn't paying attention to his *actions*—so now he feels helpless and at the mercy of others.

It isn't surprising that the child now feels helpless. He was treated like an animal. Animals are trained to behave with the use of treats. This type of learning is called conditioning, more specifically Pavlovian conditioning, which is not contingent upon the willful actions of the subject, but rather quick, non-thinking responses. But the child is not an animal, the child is a human being and that is how he needs to be treated. Any consequence needs to help the child learn how to think, not respond like a rat running around in a maze. Discipline needs to help the child learn to think about the proper connection between what he did and the consequences.

Sometimes the teacher, also anxious for the child to be successful, will sit the child next to her all day, giving him work, watching his every move and preventing every infraction of the rules. Then at the end of the day, when he tells his parents that he didn't get into trouble, he receives the reward. But who should really get the reward? Who was really in charge? And we all know the teacher cannot do this every day. She has other children to think about.

Children growing up have a lot to learn and figure out. So if you throw in one more thing—if you tell a child that he will get a star or a piece of candy for not hitting—he will not think about *why* he was hitting. If there was a conflict, he will not think about how to resolve it. If he was angry, he won't face it. Rewarding him for walking away from his anger serves only to make him repress it. He needs to learn how to express emotions properly. Often, just stating his feelings will help him to feel better—more in control—and, therefore, allow the thinking process to be easier. Once he knows that he is angry and why, he is empowered to think of how he will deal with it and learn how to resolve it; but external rewards prevent the child from doing this because they don't help him form principles for handling disputes.

One of the worst messages that a child can take away from this type of discipline is the expectation that he will get something from others in return for acceptable behavior: "What are you going to give me?" This thought process can turn the child into a manipulator as he gets older: "I won't behave unless I get something." If the child likes external rewards, then he may continue to hit once in a while so that adults will give him a reward when he doesn't hit. He may feel that the world revolves around him, and that what happened to the other child doesn't matter.

Behavior improves gradually as a child figures out the ways of the world and how they relate to him. It is not an overnight change—it takes time and conscious effort. Another problem with rewards is that they demand an immediate transformation, and even when the child is improving, he may get the message that he isn't good enough because he didn't get a reward. So he may feel like a failure even though he is making progress.

If you think that your child needs a concrete way to see his development so that he can evaluate his progress for himself, setting up a chart to record his behavior may be acceptable in some cases. However, the adult should not place any stars on the chart—the child should do that; he should be evaluating his own behavior and deciding if he should give himself the star. At the same time, the parent should monitor this process and not allow the child to lie or fake reality by letting him have a star if he hasn't really earned it. If the child reaches his goal of a certain number of stars, the parent can say, "Doesn't it feel good? Would you like to celebrate in some way? What would you like to do?" This puts the ball in the child's court and gives him a sense of control over his life.

One of the most important things that we want a child to develop at this age is a sense of ethics. We want him to start discerning the difference between right and wrong. If he feels bad when he does something wrong, it gives him an incentive to change his behavior. Then when he does change, he can feel internal gratification and pride, knowing that he is learning how to control himself.

Rewards have their place, but shouldn't be used as a form of discipline. Rewards, used as a way to change unacceptable behavior are bribes, not actual rewards. Real rewards are used to celebrate accomplishments and are secondary to the inner satisfaction one feels from those accomplishments. Furthermore, rewards are not given for every little triumph, but rather are used for long range achievements. When a child is given rewards for his every success, he becomes used to being the center of attention and continues to expect it from others as he grows up. And he has been denied the pride that he could have felt had he focused on his accomplishments, rather than the rewards.

Giving a child external rewards for good behavior may seem good as a short-term solution, but it does not work in the long run. The child needs to observe what happens when he behaves or misbehaves and to feel the natural consequences, good or bad. And he has to feel those consequences inside himself, without expecting anything else beyond that. Kids want to please their teachers and parents. Once a child can do that, once a child can behave using his own free will, his parents have reason to celebrate one of the greatest rewards of parenthood—a child with a conscience.

Patience

Early on in my career as a Montessori educator, I was having a conference with some parents about their child, who had some behavior issues. When I asked them what they did at home when he misbehaved, they replied, "We tried sending him to his room for a week, but that didn't work, so we stopped doing it." I found this puzzling, but I encouraged them to continue to send him to his room and not give up. Over the following years, I often encountered similar attitudes about discipline. Occasionally parents, knowing that their child is in trouble a lot at school, will worry and fret and ask at the end of every day, "How did he do? Did he sit in the timeout chair today?" Or, "Has he stopped hitting the other children yet?" Teachers also have these kinds of attitudes, coming to me with, "I have been putting him in timeout and it isn't working," or "We have separated him from so and so and it isn't working." Some adults can become discouraged if a child's behavior doesn't change quickly, and some become so discouraged that they give up.

I think there are two reasons that this happens. First, some people subscribe to the theory of determinism. They think that the child's personality and behavior is already set—that nothing can change it—and they easily give up, believing there is nothing they can do. However, a child is not determined by forces outside his control. While he obviously has no choice as to who his parents are, how he is disciplined, what school he attends and so on, he does have a choice in how he responds to the environments he is given. All humans have free will and the child is in the process of shaping his own life by the decisions he makes.

Secondly, many people have an unrealistic expectation of how quickly a child can change his behavior; if he doesn't alter it immediately, adults can view this as a failure, but children can take a long time to change (depending on the type of behavior). There are several explanations for this: they are in the process of learning that reality is constant and doesn't change; their concepts are very limited; they can't transfer information from one context to another; they don't understand cause and effect; and they can't think long range yet. Because of the nature of the child it can take months, years or even his entire childhood for change to take place. That is why adults need to persevere and must not give up.

When our oldest daughter was four or five years of age she used to love to run out to the mail box each day to get the mail. The problem was, she was repeatedly running out into the street without looking. We tried banning her for short periods of time. We started with one day, that didn't work, so we went to one week. That didn't work. Then one month. No dice. She was still running out into the street when she went to get the mail ... so I banned her for a year. And you know what? It worked. After the end of that year, she never ran out into the street again. It's a good thing we didn't give up—but wow, did I ever get flack for this. One whole year! The poor thing—didn't that damage her self-esteem?

I did start to wonder, as she got older, what her perspective was on how this had been handled. So one day, after we'd come home from school and she'd retrieved the mail as usual (she was seven years old by then), I asked, "Do you remember when I wouldn't let you go get the mail?"

"Oh, yes!"

"Why was that?"

"Because I kept running out in the street and you were worried I might get hit by a car."

"Do you remember how long I wouldn't let you get the mail for?"

"Oh, yes! It was a LONG time!"

"How long was it?"

"A week."

In her mind it took her only a week to change, but in reality it took one year (and no, her self-esteem wasn't damaged). Change takes time with children, and adults have to learn to wait it out.

Waiting is hard, however, because it can be embarrassing when our children don't behave. It is frustrating enough when they don't behave at home, but when they go out in public we can feel particularly down-hearted, especially when their behavior disrupts other people.

Rest assured that in Montessori we recognize these facts about children—that their behavior is their own and not their parents'—so you don't need to worry, if your child has to sit in the timeout chair, that we are blaming you. We may give you suggestions to help him, just as you may have suggestions for us, but we know that it takes time for any change to become visible. In Montessori we don't view the child as a static entity; we know that he is evolving into the adult that he will become.

You can be the best parents in the world and be doing all the right things, but your child will still challenge you at times, or maybe even all of the time. Parenthood is not easy. The key is to understand that your child is his own person. He is completely separate from you, with his own thoughts and his own conclusions. He is responsible for the choices he makes, and the responsibility begins, not at age ten, or sixteen, or twenty-one, but *now*. This needs to be recognized and he needs to be held responsible when he misbehaves.

As parents, we all worry about our children. We have a huge emotional investment in them. Their future happiness is very important to us and we are anxious to have them learn the difference between right and wrong so that they can be successful in life. While some of our worries as they grow up are warranted, some are not. If we want to enjoy their childhood, we need to stand back and look at what is going on objectively, so that we can let go of the worries that have no merit. We can't spend time worrying that he is a "bad boy" or that he will never change. We have to learn to be patient.

Chapter Nine
Social Development

The only social life that children get in the ordinary schools is during playtime or on excursions. Ours live always in an active community. [1]

MARIA MONTESSORI

Social Interaction in a Montessori School

Guests to Montessori classrooms cannot help but notice the perpetual interaction of the children as they work. There is a constant buzzing of conversation as children hover over each other, watching each other work. "No, John, you shake the bottle first, *then* you put the polish in the dish." In another corner, a couple of four-year-olds work on the geometric solids, placing the shapes in different parts of the room and then walking around to find them again, discussing the difference between an ovoid and an ellipsoid as they do so. A three-year-old needs her shoe tied, but the teacher is busy, so a six-year-old comes over and ties it for her. A new student is feeling sad and bursts into tears, so a child leaves his work and puts his arms around her, saying, "Don't worry, Mommy will come back." Suddenly, a two-year-old spills his work on the tile floor and several children rush over to help. One time, a visitor who had been observing my class said, "I was told that children don't socialize in Montessori classrooms. Nothing could be further from the truth!" I replied, "Yes. And not only do the children socialize, they do it well."

Montessori children are impressive in their concentration, independence, thinking skills and initiative, but they are also remarkable in the manner in which they socialize. They respect each other and accept each

---

1 Maria Montessori, *The Absorbent Mind*, (New York: Dell Publishing, 1967), p. 225.

other as individuals. Every year I accompany the older elementary children on a three-day camping trip. Even though their personalities could not be more diverse, I never cease to be moved at the regard that they have for each other. They range from the child who is so shy he can barely be heard when he speaks, to the chatterbox who cannot refrain from letting his every thought be known to every person within hearing range. There are the quiet children who love to take some time to be by themselves, and the boisterous children who are constantly whooping with laughter. Some prefer to read, others want to play ball. There are differences among them, yet they all get along. Not that all children are best friends or that no one squabbles, but they all treat each other with consideration and they all have a good time. Another thing I noticed—there is no "in-crowd." It was very different for me when I was growing up and had a fear of "not fitting in" with the group.

There are many reasons that the children socialize so well, but the most important one is the most surprising. It is that the primary attention in the classroom is on the child's individual *cognitive* development, not his social development. Montessori children focus on developing their own minds through their work. As the child does his work, he is developing his inner self, building up his confidence in himself as he acquires knowledge. The confident child has a better chance of socializing successfully, because when a child values his own life, he understands the value of someone else's and can treat others respectfully. Only when a child develops in this manner is he ready for social relationships.

The Montessori child progresses academically at his own pace; he does not have to advance as part of a group. No child is required to "keep up" with others or to "slow down" so that others can catch up. This way, no child feels he must be the same as everyone else. He can be his own person, and he accepts others as being their own persons too. Since everyone is allowed to be different, everyone is respected, even if they aren't necessarily liked. Every child in Montessori is regarded as an individual, as unique, with his own distinctive thoughts and interests.

If a child does not focus on developing his own self first, his knowledge about reality is not first-hand, so he cannot know anything for sure and will feel confused and scared inside. He may look to others to take care of him. Friendships are painful, because he is insecure in who he is and constantly worries whether his friends like him or not. This may drive him to try to control them, or he may avoid friendships altogether. The self-confident child, however, views friends as a positive value, someone he can share his thoughts with and whose company he can enjoy. As Michael Berliner explained[2], this independent child "respects the rights of other children and deals with them as equals." Good socialization is a by-product of children's focusing on inner development.

In Montessori's early schools, there was much skepticism about the ability of the children to develop benevolence towards each other due to this stress on the individual.

> Many people asked Montessori, "And how will the social senti-ment be developed if each child works independently?", but Montessori wondered that these same people could imagine that the traditional school setting, which regiments the children's ac-tions and prevents them from helping one another in their work or even from freely communicating with each other, could possibly be considered as fostering social concern.

> (Montessori answered) "We must therefore conclude that this (traditional) system of regimentation in which the children do everything at the same moment, even to visiting the lavatory, is supposed to develop the social sentiment. The society of the child is therefore the antithesis of adult society, where sociability implies a free and well-bred interchange of courtesies and mutual aid, although each individual attends to his own business."[3]

Montessori's solution was to give the children freedom throughout the day to interact with their classmates and the natural interest and concern for each other developed spontaneously.

This is not to say that Montessori children do not go through all the normal stages of social development. Two- and three-year-olds are not very interested in socializing yet, because their primary goal is to figure out the world. They often work alone or prefer to observe the older children. When they get a little older and become interested in having friends, they don't understand that you can be friends with more than one person at a time, so when a friend wants to work with someone else, they feel hurt. Not yet understanding cause and effect, they will then try to manage one another through physical control (hitting, pushing, etc.) or verbal

---

2 "Montessori and Social Development," *Educational Forum*, Vol. 38, no. 3.

3 Paula Polk Lillard, *Montessori: A Modern Approach*, (New York: Schocken Books, 1972), p. 74.

control ("You can't come to my birthday unless you..."). Then, when they reach the age for the elementary class, there can be lots of drama regarding friendships; one day they are best friends with someone and the next they are enemies forever, only to change their minds an hour later.

While this is all a part of growing up and learning through experience, the Montessori Method eases the growing pains in learning how to deal with social difficulties. Montessori limited the actions of children when they interfered with the rights of others. "We must ... check in the child whatever offends or annoys others, or whatever tends towards indecorous or impolite acts," said Montessori. [4] Therefore, the classrooms have clear, objective rules that are consistently followed. The most fundamental of these concerns property rights: every child has his own space to work in and is not to be interrupted. If a child invites a friend to work with him, that is permissible; but if that friend starts disrupting him and is asked to leave, the friend must leave. If a child takes out a piece of work, it is his and he is in charge of it until he puts it away. This system solves most social difficulties before they can even begin. When a conflict does arise over who may do an activity, the teacher has only to ask, "Who took it out?" to end the problem then and there, because the children know that whoever took it out has the final say on who does it. The children learn not to interfere with each other's work. This includes not giving away the answers to someone who is struggling; instead, they learn how to give cues to help each other think and solve problems. When children respect each other's work, they respect each other. Not to respect someone's property is not to respect that person; but because property rights *are* respected in the Montessori classroom, fighting is kept to a minimum.

When the rights of others are disrespected, it is not tolerated. A child who has perpetrated an infraction in the classroom may be given a time-out as a consequence which limits his activity so that he can watch learning without disrupting it. The well-behaved children can continue to work, safe from further interference, and because of this may still feel like giving the offending child another chance, often offering to work with him at a later time.

The Montessori environment is carefully thought out so that good social behavior can develop successfully. Children learn patience because (for the most part) there is only one of each material and they have to

---

4 Maria Montessori, *The Montessori Method*, (New York: Frederick A. Stokes Company, 1912), p. 87.

A child cries and out of nowhere another child appears with a tissue to dry his tears. Compassion for one's classmates is common in the Montessori classroom.

Children often gather around in order to watch a child doing work and offer to help if necessary. (In addition, they also discuss the work. These children are trying to figure out which objects will sink and which ones will float.)

wait their turn before they can do an activity. In addition, Dr. Montessori created lessons that help the children learn how to work out their problems and how to relate to each other. They are given a demonstration, for example, on what to do when they are upset with someone. They are shown how to approach that person and what to say to him and then they are given time to practice.

Work is not segregated according to gender: the boys get to do what would typically count as "women's work" and the girls get to do work that commonly interests boys. One year, my class was studying dinosaurs, and another teacher gave them a big plastic dinosaur to scrub that she had found at a garage sale. Both of us supposed the boys would think this was great work. Well, weren't we surprised to see that it wasn't the boys, but rather the girls, who found the work exciting! So I asked some boys who were intensely concentrating on another activity, "Hey, I thought you boys would love this dinosaur-scrubbing work. How come you're not doing it?" "'Cause we'd rather do this," they replied with their heads down, sewing a button onto a piece of fabric. Children have the opportunity to experience a wide variety of activities, not just what is expected of them because of their gender. This creates an atmosphere of acceptance and respect for the interests of others.

Montessori classrooms are not segregated by age. This is a huge advantage in creating a positive social atmosphere. Maria Montessori explained it best:

> The charm of social life is in the number of different types that one meets. Nothing is duller than a Home for the Aged. To segregate by age is one of the cruelest and most inhuman things one can do, and this is equally true for children.
>
> ...
>
> There are many things which no teacher can convey to a child of three, but a child of five can do it with the utmost ease. There is between them a natural mental 'osmosis.' Again, a child of three will take an interest in what a five year old is doing, since it is not far removed from his own powers. All the older ones become heroes and teachers, and the tinies are their admirers. These look to the former for inspiration, then go on with their work. In the other kind of school, where children in the same class are all of the same age, the more intelligent could easily teach the others, but this is hardly ever allowed. The only thing they may do is to

answer the teacher's questions when the less intelligent cannot. The result is that their cleverness often provokes envy. Envy is unknown to little children. They are not abashed by an older child knowing more than they do, for they sense that when they are bigger their turn will come. There is love and admiration on both sides; a true brotherhood. [5]

The social interaction that takes place between the different age groups is remarkable. The younger children look up to and admire the older children and learn from observing them do the advanced work. They like children who are in the know, and express it: "Wow, that's great James!" "Look at what Emily did!" As Montessori said, "Something else very uncommon can be seen in our schools: it is admiration for the best. Not only are these children free from envy, but anything well done arouses their enthusiastic praise." [6] Competence and accomplishment is their own goal, so they admire others who have achieved it; and someone else's achievement gives them the fuel to continue their own work.

The older children remember what it was like to be two years old and to feel helpless when unable to perform a task, so they readily give assistance to the younger ones. (Interestingly enough, the younger children will also help the older ones, usually when their sense of order is upset.) The older children also enjoy giving lessons to the younger children, however, this practice has sometimes been criticized as being detrimental for the older child. Montessori answers:

> People sometimes fear that if a child of five gives lessons, this will hold him back in his own progress. But, in the first place, he does not teach all the time and his freedom is respected. Secondly, teaching helps him to understand what he knows even better than before. He has to analyze and rearrange his little store of knowledge before he can pass it on. [7]

There is even interaction between the youngest and the oldest children in different classrooms within the school. Young adolescents can be seen helping the toddlers in the hallway, sitting and reading to them or even playing with them at school events.

---

5 Maria Montessori, *The Absorbent Mind*, (New York: Dell Publishing Co., 1967), p. 226–227.

6 Maria Montessori, *The Absorbent Mind*, (New York: Dell Publishing Co., 1967), p. 231.

7 Maria Montessori, *The Absorbent Mind*, (New York: Dell Publishing Co., 1967), p. 227.

When I went to school, I didn't experience the benevolence towards others that I observe in our school. It is because I went to a government school where social interaction was the main focus instead of the development of the conceptual faculty. This is completely backwards. How can you interact with others if you have no self? And how can you have a self without having a mind?

Education that focuses on socialization (as I explained in Chapter One, "The Individual Montessori Child") produces children who are focused on others rather than on the facts of reality. Without knowledge, they don't know how to think or reason. They are insecure, so they seek safety in groups. It is interesting that in Montessori schools, which emphasize individuality, you won't see gangs or cliques. The children feel no need to form or join groups of this nature to gain acceptance because they already accept themselves. Instead, these self-confident children seek out other individuals who value learning as they do. When children have work to do that they work hard on and enjoy, and when their friends share this same joy, they feel a bond with their classmates. And that is how it should be.

Sharing

Shortly after I began my career as a Montessori teacher, someone from the news media came to observe my classroom for a story about Montessori schools. Afterwards, she was very open about her impressions: "The children are so calm and well behaved! And the fighting…Why, there is none! You should see the other daycares I visited, where the children were constantly hitting and yelling. And your children share so nicely. Why is that?"

I replied, "Well, there are lots of reasons that Montessori children get along so well, but the main reason is that we recognize that children have rights and treat them accordingly. Children have the right to work undisturbed so that their concentration can develop. [8] And the reason our children share is that we do not force them to do so."

I went on to explain that forcing young children to share does nothing but create a climate of fear—children in such an environment never know when something will be taken away from them—and when their

---

8 Maria Montessori, *The Absorbent Mind*, (New York: Dell Publishing Co., 1967), p. 279–280.

classmates do grab their property, they feel angry. This does not exactly make for a good social atmosphere. Montessori children are given the choice as to whether or not they want to share or interact with others. "They are not forced, subtly or otherwise, to join in any group activities or to share themselves with others when they are not ready or interested." [9] When a child prepares his own food, he may either eat it himself or serve it around to his classmates. If a child chooses to work alone, he is allowed to do so. The result is a feeling of safety and trust, and once the children decide that they want to work or play with a friend, they share willingly and enthusiastically.

Forcing young children to share is a common practice in our culture. Even when children are not outwardly pressured to share, there is usually the expectation that they do so. This attitude stems from the moral code of altruism, the idea that man has no right to exist for his own sake and that he must give up his values for somebody else. Yet, if we want our children to be happy, they should not give up their values. Instead, they should be pursuing them. In addition, sharing should not be a sacrifice—it is something we do with people we esteem. But the child has to reach a certain level of maturity before he understands that friendships are a value and discover the joy of sharing.

The two-year-old is not yet at that stage. He is not ready to share because he is still trying to figure out the nature of reality and it is physical objects that provide him with the information that he is seeking. Montessori noted: "In the normalized child, his freedom to take an interest in all kinds of things, leads to his interest in focusing not on the things themselves, but on the knowledge that he receives from them." [10] He is also not ready to socialize because he is trying to figure out the nature of people and thinks that other children are similar to these objects he is curious about, rather than beings with thoughts and feelings like his. So he doesn't really have any friends yet and without friends, there is no reason to share. Additionally, he has to understand the concept of property. In order to learn the real meaning of possession, the child has to possess his own things. He has to understand: What is mine? What is yours? What is ours? What is okay to give away? What must I keep? What happens when I share? What possessions are precious to me? What

9 Paula Polk Lillard, *Montessori: A Modern Approach*, (New York: Schocken Books, 1972), p. 55.

10 Maria Montessori, *The Absorbent Mind*, (New York: Dell Publishing Co., 1967), p. 219.

does "expensive" mean? Also, all through toddler hood, the child has heard, "No—give it back!" and, "Don't touch, that's mine," and at two he begins to practice what he has heard. He feels the need to really have things of his own and it is vital that he not be *forced* to share them. If forced to share, he may feel threatened by other children, and will often end up hitting and fighting with them.

Several years ago, I was reading a magazine while waiting for an appointment with my doctor. The silence in the waiting area was broken by the screams of two toddlers nearby. I looked up. Daniel had taken from his mother's bag a book that had sparked his interest, and was looking through it when another small child, Alex, tried to grab it.

Daniel's mom, instead of sticking up for her son, reprimanded him: "Daniel, give him your book."

The commotion continued. Alex, insistent and screaming, pushed Daniel over, hoping to win; but Daniel, tears streaming down his angry face, clung to the book. His mother commanded his obedience: "Daniel, let it go! Give it to him. You need to share!" Alex's mother said nothing.

Daniel continued to refuse to cooperate, so his mother yanked the book out of his hands and gave it Alex. She turned to Alex's mother. "I'm sorry. My son is so selfish."

Alex learned that any time he wants something, all he has to do is demand it—and if he doesn't get it, he can throw a tantrum and behave inappropriately, no matter whom it hurts. He received a lesson in how to be a bully. Daniel learned that his personal feelings are not important—that he should sacrifice himself to someone else, that it is okay for another child to hurt him, that he can't rely on his mother to bring him justice, and that he is a bad person because he wanted something for himself.

Forced sharing gives children two messages. To the child who is in possession of the object, the message is, "Your desires are unimportant"; and to the child who is not in possession of the object, the message is, "It's fine to take something away from someone else, even when he doesn't want you to." (Even in a situation where the child is not forced to share, the unspoken expectation is, you don't have to give it to him, but you should.)

One time a parent came to me all upset because of what had happened after her younger daughter had gone into her sister's room and taken one of the dolls. The parent said, "My older daughter had a fit! And I don't understand why—after all, she hadn't played with that doll in six months!"

I thought to myself, okay…I have a snow blower that I haven't used in six months. How would I feel if my next door neighbor just walked off with it without asking me if he could use it? And how would I feel if I then called the police and was told that I shouldn't be upset, that I should learn to share? Would I be resentful? You bet! I would resent the person in authority (the policeman) and the person who had taken my property (my neighbor). Force does not create a feeling of benevolence and trust between people.

When a child is made to share against his will, he is put in an awkward position. He feels resentment toward the child who stole from him, yet he is required to be nice to the thief. When a child is not pressured to share, he is left free to be truthful, develop honest relationships and the result is spontaneous generosity. I have observed time and time again children in the classroom who take great delight in making or preparing something to give to their friends. I had a father argue with me once about our policy on sharing. He told me that if I didn't force his son to share, that he would grow up to be uncaring and inconsiderate towards others. This father had bought into the common belief that children are mean, but children are *not* mean by nature—they are basically good.

The notion of eliminating forced sharing will, of course, create problems for you, the parent, because most people in our culture expect children to share, even when they don't want to. You, however, can be a very good example to your child (and to other parents) and can teach sharing without forcing. Montessori did not address what should be done outside of school, but here are some ideas.[11] Try having a few toys that belong to you and not to your child. When visiting children are present, share your own toys—your two-year-old will be impressed. Another tip: when you want all your children to be able to use a toy (e.g. swing set), don't give them community ownership. When this sort of item comes into the family, make it clear to all the children that it belongs to the parents, but is for the children to use. That way, when fighting occurs over the use of the item, the parents have the final say as to what is to be done, because *they* own it, not the children.

At three years of age, a child is usually able to share *some* of his things *some* of the time, with *some* children whom he trusts. Plan to invite a friend over. Put up those things your child doesn't want to share and let

11 Marilyn George, "Two and Three Year Olds" and "Four, Five and Six Year Olds," Blue Gables Montessori School, Kirkland, Washington.

him select a few things he will let his friend play with. And keep *your* box of toys handy. Try not to push this issue. Companionship is a value and sharing is fun, and if all goes well, your child will become a typically over-generous five-year-old, wanting to give gifts and, perhaps, even his own possessions.

True sharing comes from within rather than from orders and tears. Let your child learn naturally from doing—from normal interaction with other children. The end result will be a pleasant, generous child rather than a resentful one.

The Excluded Child

I'm sure most everyone has had the experience of being excluded. It isn't fun, but everyone needs to learn how to deal with it. You can't be invited to every party. Besides, being the outsider isn't always a bad thing; it depends on what you were excluded from and why you were excluded. Maybe it was because you were an independent thinker. When I was a child, I didn't go to a Montessori school. I went to schools where there were always "in" crowds. I wanted them to accept me, but I was rejected— not just once, but over and over again. Now, as an adult looking back, I am glad that it happened, because I think I am stronger for it. It wasn't the end of the world to be excluded.

Yet, parents are usually disturbed when their child is excluded. Maybe their child comes home and says that the other children won't play with him. Or perhaps the parent, when observing in class, notices that her son works alone and concludes that it is because the other children are excluding him. The parent then worries that their child is lonely and upset about it, but I have found in my experience that there is often more going on with the excluded child than meets the eye:

- The "excluded child" is new to the school. The other children need some time to get to know him and make friends. In the Montessori environment, children are typically welcoming to new children, but it still may take some time to form friend-ships.
- The "excluded child" enters the room and the rest of the children are already engaged in an activity. A newcomer can be an inter-ruption. It is nothing personal. Usually it is best for the newcomer to just stand nearby, watch, and not interrupt.

- **The "excluded child" is too young for friendships.** Two- and three-year-olds typically prefer to work alone or sit on the sidelines and watch others work. They are typically not too interested in social relationships.
- **The "excluded child" is not ready for friendships.** This child has not matured enough yet to have friends.
- **The "excluded child" wants to be alone.** In this case he is not being excluded; he just loves being by himself and working alone.
- **The "excluded child" has poor behavior.** Children don't want to be friends with him because he interrupts them, tries to control them, or hurts them with his words or actions.

If a child is upset that he is being excluded, it is best to ask him questions to see if he knows why he is not included. Find out if he asked the other children why he wasn't allowed to play with them. Most of the time, he hasn't asked them, so he has no idea why he was not invited to play. Tell him he needs to find out, because if he did something to upset his friends, he needs that information so that he can change his behavior. Often, the rejection has nothing to do with the child who was excluded. When I have asked children why someone can't play, I hear, "I just want to be alone," or "I want to be with another friend," or "I'm having a bad day." It was nothing personal against the child who was excluded.

It is detrimental for children to automatically draw the conclusion that the reason they were not included is that they aren't liked. They may grow up and assume every time they aren't invited to a party, that it is their fault. Or every time the boss doesn't give them a raise, it is because the boss doesn't like them. Or every time someone doesn't say "Hi," it's because he is angry. Making these kinds of assumptions causes unnecessary distress. Not everyone gets invited to special events; people can only invite so many. Maybe the boss can't afford to give anybody a raise. Perhaps the person who didn't say "Hi" was absorbed in his own thoughts about a problem. Things are not always what they seem, and it is best to look at things objectively. Now is the time to help the child begin to understand this.

But maybe the reason the child was excluded is that he did something that caused the children to reject him. Maybe he interferes with their work, tries to control the direction of their activity too much, or abuses them physically (hits, pushes, spits, trips, etc.) or verbally (name-calls, uses inappropriate language, bosses them around, etc.). If this is the case, the parents need to make it very clear to their child that he is the cause of the rejection and he is the one who needs to change his behavior. It does no good to blame the other children, who were just sticking up for themselves.

What about the child who has done nothing wrong and is still being excluded? While I have found that this type of situation isn't very common among Montessori children, there are still times when individual, insecure children try to control relationships through exclusion. The parent of the excluded child should explain that children who do this don't know how to make and keep friends and encourage him to find new friends. If this doesn't work and the child feels especially miserable, a talk with your child's teacher is advisable.

Parents are sometimes at a loss as to what to do when a child complains to them that he was rejected. It is easy for them to take their child's word for what happened because parents and children are so emotionally attached. Parents can then worry and overreact. If the parent becomes obsessed with the child's problem, it will become bigger in the child's mind than it really is. Then the child will start to fret about it. Instead, here are some suggestions for how to handle it:

- Determine if the action is justified. Does the child with the toy want to be alone? Or perhaps the child just wants to work with certain children? Does the outsider have a reputation for bothering others?
- Reflect feelings to the excluders. "Gee, John would really like to work with you. Are you sure you don't want him to join in?" Sometimes, when children realize how upset the outsider is, they change their minds.
- Explain: "Katrina still likes you, she just wants to be alone right now."
- Distract: "John, you can come do something with me."
- Be supportive, yet firm: "I know it hurts when you are not included, but I didn't send you to school to have friends. I sent you to school to learn."

At any rate, it is hard to accept the fact that we can't control our children's lives. We can't control their social relationships. We can discipline them for inappropriate behavior, meanness and rudeness, but we can't control whom they choose to like. We can teach them social graces, but it is up to them to use them. We can encourage friendships, but we can't force them to be friends. Forcing relationships always backfires, causing full-fledged resentment; it doesn't do anybody any good and is counterproductive.

Most of us were raised in schools that emphasized "getting along with others" and we grew up thinking that there was something wrong with children who weren't accepted by their peers in school. What were the standards for acceptance, and what had to be done to meet them? No answer; yet those who were rejected by the group were made to feel like a scar on the face of humanity. However, social relationships are not the primary need of the child. Once a child develops himself, he will have values, and thus a reason to want friends—the sharing of those values. Friendships like this mean more than having a friend for friendship's sake, or for the sake of feeling accepted.

When a child is consumed with the desire to have friends, rather than the desire to learn, the stage is set for dependency later on. Children like this grow up worrying about what other people think rather than evaluating reality firsthand. It is better to know what you think and expect others to live up to your standards than to agonize about acceptance all the time. If you have an excluded child, give him support and love, acknowledge that it is hard to be excluded, and reassure him that he will find friends when he is ready. Help him to focus on what is truly important now—the development of his own independence.

Humor in the Montessori Classroom [12]

Laughter in the classroom was such a rare occurrence when I went to school that, when it happened, I felt as if I wanted to engulf it with my entire being so it wouldn't go away. Someone would say something funny, we would laugh for a few moments with wide smiles on our faces, our eyes sparkling, and then the teacher would say, "Back to work," and the gloomy, boring mood would return, like a dark shadow descending upon us. It was as if humor and learning were not possible together.

---

12 While humor is not a major educational component in Montessori, it was still considered important enough to be one of the topics covered at the annual AMI conference in 1976.

The Montessori classroom is completely different. Occasional laughter or a stream of giggles can often be heard amongst the constant chatter during work time. This happens because work is not viewed as a negative. There is no expectation, as I experienced in class, that most of the time we must work but now and again we can have fun. There is no conflict between work and fun in Montessori because work *is* fun. Laughter also happens because the children are able to interact socially in a benevolent, happy and safe atmosphere.

In addition, the Montessori Method actually prepares the child for humor. To understand how, it is important to realize that a child must go through two stages in order to develop a sense of humor: first, he must acquire knowledge; second, he must become secure in that knowledge. In other words, he must get to feel comfortable with reality. When a child knows reality, contradictions are humorous. For example, when a child has learned colors and is secure in his knowledge of color names, he laughs when the teacher points to red and says "blue"; but without that security he would be confused and uncertain. Similarly, once he is sure of the facts, he enjoys what is called "topsy-turvy" humor (e.g. "The dog meows" or "Trees are purple").

According to Bobbi Atahy of the former Blue Gables Montessori School in Kirkland, Washington, the Montessori child develops a sophisticated sense of humor at an earlier age, and more strongly, than other children, because the Montessori Method is based on reality. The children are so aware of what is real and what is not real that when an absurdity is presented, they see it immediately. Because in the sensorial area materials are graded and contrasted, children come to understand the meaning of both total opposites and subtle differences. Marilyn George, former owner and directress of Blue Gables, points out that joking with Montessori children encourages in those children a healthy assertiveness. For example, when a youngster takes out work and the teacher smiles and says, "Oh, you're not ready for that yet" (both teacher and child know that the child is ready), the child says delightedly, "Oh yes, I am!"

We can see, then, that environment has an impact on the child's development of humor; but it is equally important that the adult who is relating to the child be tuned into the fact that there are sensitive periods for humor, just as there are sensitive periods for all other areas. When young children enter school, we take time to discover if they have yet taken those first two steps necessary for the development of humor. Each is observed individually; and, as for other areas of development, each indirectly prepares himself by watching the older children as they respond to humor. It is important that the adult judge carefully as to when a child is ready for humor. This readiness develops just like readiness for the cubed tower, the first reading lesson, and so on. As an interesting side note, I have observed that readiness for humor in a very young child can be a sign of intelligence.

There are countless examples of humor in our classroom. The children think it is hilarious, for example, when they put one of us in "the chair" for being "naughty," or when we threaten to go home because "we don't like being teachers." The common response is, "Yes, you do like being teachers! You love us!" They have a clear grasp of reality. They know the facts (that we love them) and are secure in that knowledge. Hence, they tease and can be teased.

Strengthening this security and basis for humor is the fact that the children understand very early in their Montessori experience that deliberate destruction is not tolerated. Just as no one is allowed to purposely knock over the tower, so also is no one allowed to deliberately hurt feelings. A joke, then, is fairly obvious.

Some people have asked, "But when you're joking with an older child, is the younger child frightened?" Not any more than when an older child is disciplined. The young child looks to the older as the example. He sees how the other responds to getting into trouble, and how he responds to joking. Laughter and hugs are preferable to sitting in the chair. Remember, each child is treated as an *individual,* and sensitive periods for humor are as respected as sensitive periods for anything else.

A critical aspect of humor is confidence. Once confidence is achieved, jokes are fun. People who are comfortable within themselves because of a secure self-esteem often have a good sense of humor. We see this in our classroom too. We can enjoy humor because we are at ease with ourselves and others, understand reality, and are having a good time.

Anger

Steven was bothering Evan all morning. He kept poking him and talking to him, trying various things to get his attention. Finally, he grabbed

Evan's pencil and ran away with it. Evan, feeling angry, ran after him and socked him right in the eye. Steven ran to the teacher sobbing, pointing his finger at Evan.

The teacher called Evan over. "What happened?"

Evan shrugged his shoulders.

"Why did you hit him?" she persisted.

Evan shrugged his shoulders again. "Were you angry?"

Evan finally spoke: "NO! NO! I wasn't angry!"

"It's okay to be angry," the teacher explained.

"Well, Steven kept touching my work and poking me. And then…" Evan went on to describe in detail all the events that led up to the hitting incident. He was willing to explain the episode then because he knew the teacher wouldn't be upset with him for being angry.

This is a pretty typical exchange at school. Many children have already received the message at this young age that anger is wrong, and therefore do not want to admit to it; but once they know their emotion is acceptable they come forth with the truth.

Anger is a commonly misunderstood emotion. People think if you *feel* angry you will *do* something horrible. So when their child says, "I hate my sister," parents say, "No, you don't, you love her," thinking that if they squelch the emotion, no one will get hurt and love will conquer all. But that is not at all what happens. The child will conclude from this that anger is wrong and will seek to suppress it by not talking about it or the incidents which caused it.

It is important to understand that just because you feel a certain emotion, that doesn't mean you have to act on it. When a child feels angry, it is important to let him know that it's okay to feel angry, but it is not okay to hit, name-call, or threaten. If your child says, "I hate my sister," respond by saying, "You sound really angry with her right now. What happened? Want to talk about it?" You can even practice "I" statements with your child: "I feel angry," "I'm mad at you right now," "I feel furious when _____."

Often, all a child wants is understanding —someone to listen to him. Imagine how you would feel if you expressed fear or anger to another adult and heard, "That's nothing to cry about." Would you choose to tell this person about your feelings again? Wouldn't you rather hear, "You seem very upset. What's wrong?" Which response would make *you* feel safe, unthreatened, and understood?

Maria Montessori understood the importance of anger in the child's development:

> ...It often happens that children do not react violently. It might be better if they did, because the child who gets angry has discovered how to defend himself, and may then develop normally. But when he replies by a change of character, or by taking refuge in abnormality, his whole life has been damaged. Adults are unaware of this, and think there is nothing to worry about unless the child gets angry. [13]

When a child expresses fear or anger, we must never discount his emotions. If children think certain emotions are bad, it can become almost impossible to get to the bottom of their feelings and resolve them. Help your child identify his emotions and see that his feelings are normal. He will feel understood and will be more likely to tell you what is on his mind.

Apologizing

It is a very common practice in our culture for adults to insist that children apologize when they have done something wrong. In fact, the adult usually hovers nearby, prompting the child by saying, "What do you have to say to Jimmy?" or, worse yet, "Tell him you're sorry." While this practice was not addressed by Montessori, I think it is an important topic because I have observed that forcing a child to apologize is not only unproductive, it is likely to be harmful.

A typical pattern is for adults to prompt children to apologize immediately following the misbehavior. For example, you, the teacher, just saw Katy hit Jimmy, and you want to step in and insist that Katy apologize. At that moment, Katy is still very angry, which is why she hit in the first place. Forcing her to say she is sorry will teach her two things. One, it will teach her to repress her anger, because it gives the message that anger is not okay. Two, it will teach her to lie since, at that moment, she is *not* sorry for what she did. So what should you do in this situation?

---

13 Maria Montessori, *The Absorbent Mind*, (New York: Dell Publishing Co., 1967), p. 132.

It is important to identify, or help Katy to identify, exactly what her feelings are. You can do this by asking questions such as, "Did Jimmy call you a name? Is that why you hit him?" Validate her feelings by confirming that name-calling would make you angry too. Then go on to suggest that there may be better ways to resolve the difficulty—"Can you think of any, Katy?"—and help her to find some, such as saying to Jimmy, "That hurt my feelings, Jimmy. Don't call me stupid."

When the child has calmed down and can see that the anger is understood and accepted, then suggest making amends with words such as, "Is there anything you'd like to say to Jimmy?" Give Katy an opening through which she can apologize. She may or may not respond in a positive way, but you've provided the opportunity for her to talk. That's all some children need to be able to honestly say, "I'm sorry."

Another common pattern that occurs when children are forced to apologize is misbehavior immediately followed by the child's insisting, "I'm sorry! I'm sorry!", thereby, in his mind, making everything okay. In such a short interval, however, he can neither have admitted his anger nor experienced remorse. What he is hoping is that his "apology" will keep him out of trouble. When the adult expresses displeasure he pleads, "But I said I was sorry!!!"

Like Katy and Jimmy in the example above, this child needs help in understanding that anger is okay, but expressing it inappropriately and then offering a meaningless apology is not okay. In fact, the apology constitutes a lie. The child needs first to feel the remorse and understand the need to change his behavior. Only then will "I'm sorry" be valid.

At times it is apparent that the child is genuinely sorry for what he has just done. In this case too, validation is important. "I can see that you feel bad about what you did." Then go on to explain, "When we've done something wrong we can go to the person we hurt and say we're sorry. Sorry means you feel bad about what you did and that you're going to try and make things better." Then leave it up to the child to decide what to do. Being forced to speak at that moment could provide an extremely humiliating experience for him. If it appears that he does want to apologize at once, he may need you along for moral support; but it is more likely that he will wait until the adults are absent. Apologizing is a private, personal matter. The wise adult will allow the child to learn that through experience.

"Tattle-tales"

Every adult has experienced the "tattle-tale." This is the child who approaches the teacher every other moment and reports every teeny tiny infraction of every single rule that he observes or hears about in the classroom. He is sure to include every minute detail and stands waiting for a reply with a sense of urgency. This often irritates adults. Why do children do this?

In reality, the child is beginning to establish his own moral code. He is making judgments and wants to know just how wrong an act is for someone else.[14] This helps him to evaluate how bad the act is for him. In effect, the child patrols everyone else's acts and verbalizes what he perceives as wrongdoing to the adult in authority. How the adult acts then verifies or nullifies his judgments.

The adult must try to be sensitive to this stage. In most cases, she should encourage the child to handle the problem on his own: "Tell Johnny that is against the rules." In other instances, the child will need her support: "That must have hurt your feelings," or "That was not a nice thing to do." In circumstances where a serious violation has taken place, the adult should act promptly to correct the situation herself, and then thank the child for telling her about it.

The adult should never call the child names like "tattle-tale." He will learn not only that it is okay to call people names but also, very early in life, that he should not speak his own conscience. As an adult himself, he may witness a serious crime but be reluctant to tell the proper authorities because that would be "tattling" (I've known people like this!).

Instead, we must try to help the child to judge for himself which wrongdoings need to be handled by him, which reported, and which just ignored. Because this child is beginning to make moral judgments, and so is very socially conscious, discussions regarding rules and their reasons are important. The child is interested at this age and therefore very receptive to these discussions and your ideas.

Uniforms

From time to time, questions come up about school uniforms. Shouldn't

---

14 Chulanganee Fernando, who had been trained by Maria Montessori and was an AMI trainer at the Montessori Training Center, St. Paul, Minnesota, confirmed this in a conversation with me in 1991 or thereabouts.

they be required? Aren't they beneficial to the child's development? Wouldn't it be easier socially if everyone looked the same? No, no, and no! Although Maria Montessori did not address this issue, in my view, school uniforms are actually detrimental to the development of the child's individuality and, hence, contradictory to the Montessori philosophy.

School uniforms are viewed positively by some parents. They like the thought that they do not have to fight with their children over what to buy or what to wear. They think that children won't have to worry about "fitting in" at school by wearing certain styles, because no one will be wearing those styles, and that children who don't have fabulous wardrobes won't need to feel inadequate or inferior. These parents think that since children won't have to compete to look the best, or wear designer labels, they will behave better. The premise is: if everyone looks the same, it will level the playing field and everyone will be equal. Therefore, they will all get along. Materialism is divisive, so let's get rid of it.

Uniforms are intended to convey that materialism isn't important, and that having name brand clothing doesn't make someone a better person— that you can't judge a person by what he wears. While children do tend at first to judge people by appearances, they learn through experience that there's more to it than that—that you have to base your judgment of a person on his behavior, that one person may be dressed to the hilt but lack enthusiasm for life, while another may look slovenly but be highly intelligent and fun. However, the child does not get this experience with his peers when they all wear uniforms and look the same: he can't directly learn the lesson that you shouldn't judge a book by its cover.

In fact, uniforms don't remove materialism—they accentuate it. The message is: "We think clothing is so important that we are going to make everyone look identical. Name brand jeans are so significant that we are going to take them away." Once, people were concerned that children all wanted to look alike by wearing expensive jeans; now, they help them to all look alike by requiring uniforms. The first thing you see when you see a bunch of children standing outside their school in uniforms is not individuals, but a mass of clothing. What is accomplished when children look identical to one another? Do they learn that it's okay to be different —or that it's important to conform?

Uniforms will not eliminate the problem of "fitting in." This psychology has more to do with the system of education that the child has experienced than with what he wears. If the child's education is based on individual development and respect for his individuality, "fitting in" will be less of an issue. But the child educated under a system in which he can progress only as part of a group will strive to conform to the standards of that group; and, not valuing himself as an individual, he will be insecure. The insecure child often wants to feel superior to others and if he can't do it with his clothes, he'll find another way such as sports, jewelry, shoes, hair, possessions, accomplishments, etc. A child who wants to fit in by wearing name brand clothing is no different from the adult who wants to keep up with the Joneses. He is consumed with what others think of him, rather than what he thinks of himself. He is relying on what he wears to give him a sense of self-worth rather than regarding his clothing as an expression of himself.

Children need to learn what they like, regardless of what their friends like or wear. They need to learn their own values. They should wear something because *they* like it, not because of peer pressure. Wanting something because everybody else has it is not independence; wanting something because *you* value it, is. If children think they need name brand clothing to fit in with their friends, they need to learn that that is not friendship. It is best to understand these things before reaching adulthood, and children won't learn them from wearing uniforms.

Parents like the idea of uniforms, thinking they would spend less money on clothes if uniforms were required. True, children can put pressure on their parents to buy expensive name brand clothing. But here is a good learning opportunity: teach your child self-control and the value of money by letting him earn the money himself to buy the clothes he wants. Another suggestion is to give the child a clothing allowance. Let him learn how much things cost, and how to save up for them; let him find out what he has to do without so that he can get what he wants most; let him discover that, for the price of one name brand item, he could buy three others just as good.

Education should be holistic, but by making a child look like a clone, parents are taking away part of his learning experience. Children want to express themselves and need an outlet to do so. They need to learn what is appropriate, what isn't, and why.

I do agree that clothing can affect behavior. Some children try to draw attention to themselves by wearing inappropriate clothing. This can be very disruptive to the learning process as it distracts children from what they should be doing. This is where a dress code comes in. Give the child some rules and guidelines and let him choose and learn on his own what is acceptable. In addition, the teacher's guidance and comments to the child about his inappropriate dress often have a far larger impact than do the parents' comments.

It is important that children be allowed to dress as individuals. As children approach the teen years, girls need time to discover their femininity and explore it through dress. They need time to discover what looks good on them and why. They need time to create their own uniqueness, their own style. In addition, you can't make everyone look the same by making them wear uniforms, because everyone's physical makeup is different. If a child is differentiated by physical traits only, he can't work with them and make the best of what he has. For example, the child with a weight problem can't minimize it by choosing a more flattering style.

Most school uniforms look dowdy. If a child looks dowdy, he may feel dowdy. Adults don't want to go around looking like everyone else, and neither do children. When I asked some elementary children what it would be like to wear uniforms to school, they said, "It would be dull and boring."

Montessori said, "The school must permit the *free, natural manifestations* of the *child* if in the school scientific pedagogy is to be born. This is the essential reform." [15] If children think wearing uniforms would be "dull and boring," and then they are made to wear uniforms, the freedom for them to develop a normal, personal aspect of their individuality is being impeded. This violates Montessori's principle for educational reform.

Our 2003 Minnesota Renaissance School Yearbook had a page where the children were asked, "What do you like about our school?" One middle school child answered, "We don't have to wear uniforms." I found this very interesting. Even though the child most likely did not realize the significance of this statement, on some level he was aware that he was allowed to be an individual, and he liked it.

---

15 Maria Montessori, *The Montessori Method*, (New York: Frederick A. Stokes Company, 1912), p.14.

Chapter Ten
Parental Concerns

Although our natural inclinations are all toward helping him in his endeavors, this philosophy teaches us never to give more help than is absolutely necessary. The child who wants to walk by himself, must be allowed to try, because what strengthens any developing power is practice, and practice is still needed after the basic power has been attained. [1]

MARIA MONTESSORI

"Thirty Children! Isn't That Too Many?"

The most common question we get from parents interested in our school is about the teacher-student ratio. People typically think that if there are lots of adults in a pre-elementary classroom and a low number of students, the children will learn much more. This view is false.

The fallacy stems from the belief that a child learns more when a teacher is teaching him. In reality, children do not learn from being pumped with information by an adult. You can tell a child that 1+1 = 2, and he can repeat it back to you, but he is only parroting. It isn't until he understands the process of addition by taking objects, putting them together, and counting them that he can truly understand what addition means. Similarly, an Olympic athlete can learn only so much from his coach; he learns much more by practicing his skills tirelessly, day after day and year after year, as he prepares for the upcoming Games.

Children learn from observation and hands-on experience with objects in the real world, and by thinking and understanding that experience. I can remember as a child being told that diamonds are hard enough to cut glass, but I didn't believe it until I took my mom's wedding ring,

---

1 Maria Montessori, *The Absorbent Mind*, (New York: Dell Publishing, 1967), p. 155.

ran it along the window in my room, and saw for myself the result. My father used to tell me the value of hard work and how good one feels from accomplishment, but I never understood what he meant until I had experienced it for myself many times. My mother used to tell me that it didn't matter what some of my peers at school said about me, but I didn't accept that until I had developed self-confidence and then thought through all the reasons that people gossip about others. All this I figured out on my own—with adult guidance, yes, but under my own control.

Having too many adults in the classroom is actually detrimental to learning. Children require an environment that allows them to learn by figuring things out on their own, *without interference from adults.* This is crucial: adult interference usually slows the child down. If a child notices that an adult is watching him, he may feel self-conscious, wondering if he is doing his work wrong; or he may get distracted because he likes the attention. This breaks his concentration, disrupting his thought process, after which it may be difficult for him to start again. Children who are constantly interrupted by adults hovering, correcting, directing, prompting, lecturing, explaining and informing become dependent on adults rather than doing their own thinking.

Dependent children, children whose mode of learning is through being given information, just accept others' judgments and become guessers. Guessers think they should automatically know facts. When they encounter a new problem, they stop. They think, "I don't know," rather than, "How can I solve this?" Guessers are used to being told the answers, so they are dependent on the minds of others.

In Montessori education the child is taught how to think for himself. He uses concrete objects to experiment with and confirm reality. The Montessori child develops an independent mind because we do not tell him what to think. We allow him to learn independently—on his own—without flooding the room with adults. We also let him learn by interacting with lots of other children.

Lots of children are a necessary component of the Montessori classroom. The more children there are in a classroom, the more independent activities go on, and the more there is for children to observe and learn. It is not uncommon for Montessori children to know how to do math processes long before they are officially presented with them in class, because they have been watching their older friends do them for years. Lots of children mean lots of individual interests, which makes the classroom exciting and fun. John likes geography, Anna loves grammar, Lucas enjoys doing algebra, Susan likes to cut apples, Dean is thrilled with his first reading lesson, and so on. Lots of children also mean lots of social interaction, which enables children to develop friendships, help each other, understand the differences between them, and learn how to resolve conflicts. From my personal experience I have found that a class with a low teacher to student ratio is good with twenty children, but better with twenty-five, and terrific with thirty.

Parents worry that with thirty children in a classroom there isn't as much one-on-one time. I don't know of any other system of education that systematically provides children with more one-on-one time than Montessori. Because Montessori is an individualized system, children get individualized attention. Do children receive individual lessons every day? No! Nor should they, as they need time to learn from practicing the lessons that have been presented to them. Do children receive individual monitoring and direction every day? Yes! This is provided by the head teacher and her assistants.

Contrast this to traditional forms of education, where the goal is dependence. Children are trained to obey rather than think, to memorize rather than understand. Lessons are given as a lecture to the class as a whole, and all the children are expected to learn and progress at the same time, regardless of ability. One-on-one time happens only after the lesson has been given, and even then only if the teacher is not busy. Children are not accepted as individuals—they are expected to learn at the same rate as the group.

Maria Montessori said that a Montessori teacher can easily handle 35 children with one assistant. This is because of the nature of our method. We have a prepared environment that meets children's sensitive periods for learning and fosters independent mastery. In traditional schools, every child works on the same activity at the same time. The teacher simply can't get around to help everyone who needs help, and the children can't help each other because they are all doing the same thing. In Montessori, however, the teacher isn't swamped with requests for help all at once, because the majority of children are practicing lessons they have already been shown. When a teacher is busy giving an individual lesson and can't immediately offer assistance to those who need it, there is still no problem. Since the children are recognized and treated as individuals, they develop an understanding of the needs of others, and just spontaneously step up to help and teach each other. This unprompted consideration for each other simply does not happen when there are too many teachers, because then the children rely on adults to take care of things.

The system that promotes independence gives children as much one-on-one attention as they need, while the system that promotes dependence does not give the children enough one-on-one time. It is, therefore, frustrating to me that traditional education sets the standard for the teacher-student ratio, a criterion that cannot be applied to us. The reason the Montessori Method works and is so successful is that it does not conform to the standards of methods that do not work. We Montessorians have our own standards, and they are higher.

However, one-on-one time isn't what Montessori is all about. The teacher isn't what it is all about. Creating geniuses isn't what it is about. Montessori is about fostering the independent thinking and learning of the individual child. In a word, Montessori is all about independence.

Frequently Asked Questions:

"How can a teacher keep track of the progress of 30 children?" It really isn't that hard. Because we work with the children individually, with sequenced materials, we know exactly where they are and what they are ready for. Teachers write down their observations of the children and enter them into a record keeping program that regularly documents the child's progress.

"Since the assistants haven't been formally trained in the Montessori Method, are they qualified to make presentations?" Each head teacher trains her own assistants, supervising and guiding them in the classroom. At some schools, assistants observe the children and confer with the head teacher, help with record keeping, conferences and discipline, make presentations, and help prepare materials and the environment. For more information, please read *Montessori: A Modern Approach* by Paula Polk Lillard.

"I have heard that the reason some children are really excelling is that the teachers work with them most of the time. Is this true?" Children who really excel have learned how to be independent and pursue knowledge on their own. We typically have to make a presentation only once; they understand and repeat it without our asking them to do so, then go on to pursue something else or even come up with new ideas to challenge themselves. Often, these children learn from each other, receiving presentations from their friends. Children who have achieved competency in their work are often eager to show other children who are ready. Most of the time they have been in Montessori for three years and already have a solid intellectual foundation.

"My child practices the same thing in school every day. Isn't it true that if there were more teachers, he could learn more new concepts?" No. We *want* him to practice his work over and over. A person learning how to play a musical instrument cannot become competent by playing it only once—he practices repeatedly for days, weeks, even months. Then, once he has attained perfection, he plays for sheer enjoyment. A child goes through the same process when he is learning. He must understand and feel proficient at what he has learned before moving on to the next concept, otherwise he will become confused as the concepts become harder and more complicated.

"What did you do at school today?"
"Oh, nothing."

Are you one of those frustrated parents whose child will never tell you what he does at school? Join the club. If you are unhappy because your child doesn't share his day with you, don't despair. This is a very common phenomenon with this age group and almost every parent who comes to conferences bemoans this fact. There are several reasons why your child won't tell you what he did at school.

First of all, young children literally cannot recall information if they can't see it in their minds. This is due to the fact that they are in the process of learning how to visualize, and since they can't 'see' the materials they have been working with in the classroom, they will respond, "Nothing." There is a game that we play in the classroom where we line up some objects, have the children close their eyes, take one object away, then let the children open their eyes and try to figure out what's gone. This game is great fun. They also like the activity where they feel the object with their eyes closed as they try to name it. It is the youngest children who typically have the most trouble with these games. (Parents often comment that their child has such a good memory that he can recall events that happened years ago. This is because the child has a very vivid mental picture of those particular experiences. Conversely, we as adults cannot recall most of our early childhood because we have very few visualizations from that period of our lives.)

Secondly, even if a child is able to visualize what he has done in school, he may not know the official name of the exercise. For example, he might have worked on the abstraction game with the geometric solids and doesn't know how to communicate that.

Some children feel that school is their own very special place and don't appreciate being asked about what they do. As adults, how would we feel if at the end of every day our spouse asked, "What did you do at work today?" I don't know about you, but I would get tired of it. In addition, knowing that no one else was asked this question as much as I was, I would wonder if something was wrong with me. Children aren't stupid and they notice that adults don't pester each other about what they do each and every day.

If you want to know about your child's day, I recommend that you learn all you can about the Montessori Method and the materials we have in the classroom, and attend conferences, so that you can ask him more specific questions when you see an opportunity. For example, when he rolls up your rugs at home, you could ask him if he has been working on that at school. Or when he walks around the house uttering, "Buh, buh, uh, guh," you would know that he had been working on the pre-reading sound games and could offer to play them with him. When your child mentions a rectangular prism or a square-based pyramid, you can ask him how he likes learning the shapes and what games he plays with them. Often parents at conferences, upon learning what their child does at school, will say, "Oh, now I understand why he has been doing that at home."

Lorraine was intensely interested in the growth and development of her son and daily asked her six-year-old what he did at Montessori school that day. "Oh, nothing," he answered consistently. Weeks went by and Lorraine was starting to worry, but she decided to wait and see what the teacher had to say. At conference time, the teacher had so much to tell her about the work her son had done, she almost ran out of time. When

Lorraine went home that night she confronted her son with what she thought was a blatant lie. "Every day," she told him, "when I ask you what you are doing at school, you tell me 'nothing.' Yet, the teacher told me about all kinds of work that you have done." "Well," replied her son, "the teacher didn't tell us that we had to do the work and we were having fun, so I figured we weren't doing anything."

So relax. This phenomenon is completely normal. And remember, Montessori parents can look forward to conferences, when they are told as much as possible about what their child does in school. But if you are one of those rare parents who is concerned that your child talks too much, I only have one thing to say to you…Congratulations!

What follows is my adaptation of a poem that is used for pre-school and early elementary teachers to share with parents. The original author is unknown.

> When children come home at the end of the day,
> The question they're asked as they scurry to play
> Is, "Tell me what you did today!"
> The answer they give makes you sigh with dismay:
> "Nothing, I did nothing today!"
> Perhaps "nothing" means that I folded socks
> Or learned the igneous kind of rocks.
> Maybe I counted the short bead stair,
> Put on my shoes and combed my hair.
> Maybe we played the silence game,
> Blew out the candle when I heard my name.
> Maybe today was the very first time
> That my scissors followed a very straight line.
> Guess what? I no longer take a nap,
> Hooray! I'm ready for a map!
> Perhaps I learned to work alone
> To do the work I call my own.
> And hey! I did it by myself,
> That work you see there on the shelf.
> Today I felt so good inside
> I worked so hard, I felt such pride.
> I concentrate, a worthy goal,
> Which forms the basis of my soul.
> With Montessori my mind has wings,
> So "Nothing" means a great many things.

"I'm Bored"

Parents understandably get upset if their child says he is bored at school. They usually call the teacher with visions of their child sitting around doing nothing or simply repeating easy activities while they pay money for it. How could the teacher let this happen?

In most cases, this is an example of the adult not understanding how a child thinks. To illustrate this, a few years ago I took a survey of my students. I called each one over independently and asked him the same questions:

1. How old are you?
2. Have you ever said, "I'm bored?"
3. What does "bored" mean?

Out of twenty children (one was a four-year-old, the rest were five- and six-year-olds), only three knew what "bored" meant. Here are some of the definitions they gave:

"That you did everything and you don't want to do anything else."

"If you don't want to do something but you have to, it makes you tired."

"I wanna play around and do stuff like that."

"It means that you are tired."

Just because a child uses a word, does not mean he understands it; but if it gets a big emotional response out of the adult, he will continue to use it. What reactions he gets from words! Words have such power!

If your child uses a word that alarms you, instead of jumping to conclusions, ask him what the word means. I have done this countless times over the years in the classroom and in most cases children have told me they don't know, or have attempted a definition that may be way off or close but is not correct; rarely have they known the exact meaning. They hear us say something and they repeat it. Do not assume they completely understand the words they use.

Some parents worry, nonetheless, that there isn't enough for their child to do at school. However, the Montessori classroom provides literally hundreds of activities. Even before he is ready to do an activity himself, the child observes others doing it and his mind is engaged. He mentally progresses, whether or not we can see it. It is not unusual for a child to work exclusively in one area of the classroom, yet still progress in another. The teacher is often surprised to see how far he has advanced when she reminds him to take out something he hasn't worked on for a long time.

Parents in a Montessori school can easily believe their child when he says he's bored, because Montessori children often bring home the same work day after day. The parent assumes the child isn't learning anything new; she thinks, "I would be bored if I did the same thing over and over, day in and day out, so I know it must bore my child." But a motivated child doesn't freely choose activities that bore him.

In the event that your child is saying he is bored at school and is using the word correctly, there could be several reasons. Maybe he is missing his mother and has a hard time finding something to do without her. Perhaps he is on the verge of moving on and needs some new work. Usually this is not a problem: he moves on anyway, since he absorbs facts from the classroom environment and learns from the work of others who are ahead of him in the sequence of materials. But if it is a problem, speak to the teacher about it or encourage your child to ask for new work.

Some children want to do work that someone else is doing even though they are not ready for it, so they use the word "bored" as an excuse not to find their own work. Usually, however, the child who says this is used to being entertained by someone (an adult or another child) or something (TV, computer, or video games) and therefore doesn't know how to find something to do at school. In this case, the primary problem isn't boredom, it is lack of independence, and *this is* serious; it means that he doesn't know how to take the initiative and use his mind.

If this is the case, the child needs to learn to occupy himself at home. He needs lots of books to look through and contemplate. He should be given some tools for inventiveness such as dress-up clothes or construction activities. TV and electronic games must be turned off. He should go outside to play. He needs to spend time by himself so that he feels comfortable being alone. The parent must let the child know that it is his own responsibility to find something to do. When children are independent at home, they do not wander aimlessly around the classroom waiting to be told what to do.

The three children, who gave me the correct definition of the word "bored," interestingly enough, were self-starters who took the initiative in learning and were very independent. I then asked them another question, "When you are bored, who should find you something to do?" All three responded, "Me."

"My Child Says He Has Done Everything in the Classroom."

Occasionally children will go home and announce with great pride, "I have done everything in the classroom!" Then the parents ask, "Is this true?"

No. It isn't even possible.

Learning does not stop on a dime because a child masters one lesson on a material; many other lessons can be given with the same material. Many materials first encountered in the pre-elementary classroom, such as the bead cabinet, geometric solids, binomial and trinomial cubes, fraction insets, grammar activities and so on, are also used in the elementary classrooms, some even in the upper elementary classrooms. This is because more advanced lessons are given with those materials as the child masters the basic concepts and moves onto higher-level concepts.

In addition, we have materials in each classroom that go beyond each age group. Most children in the class do not work on those materials, but Montessori is an individualized approach and we want to have the advanced materials available for the few children who are ready for them.

Some children set their sights on an activity they have seen the older children do; then, when they are ready to do that activity, they think they must also have done all the others. This is why a child may go home and announce that he has done everything in the room. One child told me he thought he had done everything because he had done the bank game. Another child told me she thought she had done everything in the room because she was finally ready for all the beads in the bead cabinet.

What if a child in the upper elementary classrooms has worked with and understands all the materials? Then does the learning stop? No. The whole idea is for the child to eventually leave the materials behind as he forms abstractions in his mind. The Montessori teacher's job is to continue to challenge the child at his individual level.

When you look at a Montessori classroom, there is much more to it than meets the eye. Suffice it to say, I have never had a child who has "done everything in the room."

"My Child Doesn't Have Any Friends"

Almost every year, a parent comes to me with a heavy heart: "My child says he doesn't have any friends." When we hear this we instantly feel sympathy, because it brings back memories of our own social struggles when we were children. We recall the times when we were rejected or teased and the agony we felt. But it is important that we avoid projecting our own experiences and feelings onto our children.

When children aged two to six say they don't have any friends, the meaning behind their words can be completely different from what we suppose. This is the age when children are figuring out the meaning of the concept "friend" (See "How The Young Child Communicates" in Chapter 4) and commonly think that you can have only one friend. Children can think that if you are working with one child, you can't be friends with anyone else, because only that one person is your friend.

Young children are not very social. Two- and three-year-olds are not too interested in their peers; they are more interested in learning. When reality becomes more stable and clear in his mind, then the child becomes more interested in other people. Once he is secure within himself, he is ready for social relationships. The more secure the child, the better relationships he can make.

Children also don't know how to handle social situations yet, so they will say they don't want to be someone's friend because they want to work alone, or they are angry with the other child, or they want to work with someone else, or they are shy or scared (I heard a four-year-old give this as a reason to another child). We must not rush to conclusions when a child comes to us upset about someone who says he doesn't want to be his friend. Instead, ask the child questions. "Was he mad at you? Did you do something to make him angry? Did he just want to work alone? Was he feeling shy? Did you ask him why he didn't want to be friends? Well, I think you should ask some of those questions."

Maybe your child really doesn't have any friends, because he behaves badly or he is shy. If it is because of misbehavior, you will need to remind him why he doesn't have any friends. If he is shy, the best thing to do is to accept the way your child is and not force friendships upon him. You might try encouraging some relationships by making suggestions (e.g. "Would you like to invite Annie over for a play date?"), but in most cases it is best to just wait and let friendships develop naturally and in their own time. Since the Montessori Method is based on individualism, the children learn to accept each other as individuals and a shy child doesn't strike them as odd or abnormal.

In the meantime, don't worry about it. The primary reason he is in school is to acquire knowledge, not friends. When he matures, social relationships will have more meaning for him and there will be a better chance for success. When the time is right, friendships can develop, so don't push it faster than this natural process allows. The relationship issue is something that will take time and social skills are learned, just like everything else in life.

Chapter Eleven
How Long Should My Child Stay in Montessori?

*Intelligence is the ability to deal with a broad range of abstractions. What-
ever a child's natural endowment, the use of intelligence is an acquired
skill. It has to be acquired by a child's own effort and automatized by his
own mind, but adults can help or hinder him in this crucial process.* [1]

AYN RAND

Kindergarten and Elementary School

As your child's progress in school continues, you may be thinking about
his transition to the next level of his education. Should he continue in
Montessori or transfer to a public or neighborhood school? Or perhaps
you are trying to decide if your child should enter a Montessori school for
the first time. Many parents have been in your shoes, and they have some
reservations about continuing or starting their child in a non-traditional
school setting and how it will affect their child. Here are some concerns
or questions that parents typically have in making their school decision,
with my responses.

"Should I send my child to Montessori for his Kindergarten year?"
The last year in the Children's House (pre-elementary level), which public
schools and some Montessori schools refer to as "Kindergarten," is the
time during which the child completes the journey of his first stage of
development. Regrettably, some parents decide to enroll their child in
a government school instead of letting him continue in the Children's
House, not realizing that they are preventing their child from attain-

---

1 Ayn Rand, "The Comprachicos" in *The New Left: The Anti-Industrial Revolution*, (New
York: New American Library, 1971). p.160.

ing his full potential and the self-confidence that results from that. It is important to understand that the Montessori learning experience is cumulative. What a child learns during the first two years in the Children's House prepares him for his Kindergarten year, when he moves from the concrete materials to abstract thinking. If this transition takes place in the Montessori classroom, the child still has access to the Montessori materials to complete the process. It is not uncommon to see children in the Montessori Kindergarten blossom into joyful readers and enthusiastic mathematicians, begin to think about the world in terms of integrated facts, and start to socialize with their peers in a meaningful way. The learning from the child's previous years is fully deployed and he is much more likely to achieve inner satisfaction and happiness. Montessori Kindergarten is a critical year in the child's education. (There are a large number of activities that children who have attended Montessori for three years accomplish before going on to the elementary level. See appendix for details.)

"I want my child to have friends in the neighborhood." This is like saying that if you choose private education, your child won't have any friends in the neighborhood, but this isn't a choice of one or the other, education or friends. Your child can still have friends in the neighborhood even if he doesn't go to school with them. When I was a child, I played with the kids who went to private schools in my neighborhood just as much as the ones who went to public school like me (and they weren't necessarily in the same class as me anyway). However, when I got older (junior high and high school age), I spent time only with friends who lived far away—just like children who go to private schools.

Now that I am grown and have my own children, who have gone to private Montessori school, I realize that I like the fact that they chose to socialize more with the children at school. I liked the fact that their social skills were developed in a safe, loving close-knit environment, rather than on the street. They were in a comprehensive social system where they had the opportunity to learn to socialize properly. They didn't have to sit and be still and quiet all day long. They were able to move around and talk to each other about what they were learning and thinking during class time rather than waiting until class was over.

You can't choose who lives in your neighborhood, but because I knew the families of my children's friends from meeting them at school, I had confidence in allowing my children to be with them outside of school.

The only disadvantage was that we had to drive them to their friend's homes, but the safety factor and appropriate influences that they were getting made it worth it.

When our oldest daughter left our Montessori school and went into tenth grade, she had many comments to make from her observations about the social life in her new school away from us. But the most revealing comment was this, "You never realize how good you had it until you don't have it anymore."

"My child wants to go to the same school as his friends in the neighborhood." When a child says he doesn't want to leave his friends, he is saying he is apprehensive about going someplace new. When parents cave into that, the message they give their child is that he has good reason to be scared—that he can't possibly make it on his own—so he doesn't learn to venture out, make new friends, and get over his fear. He ends up passing up opportunities that could improve his life because he has become dependent on his friends. But children need to learn that friends don't always have to be there in order to experience what life has to offer. Fear of change and new situations is normal, but when a child steps out and overcomes his fear, he increases his self-confidence.

But let's presume this is not the case. Let's say that the child is mature, has good friends in his neighborhood and he genuinely wants to go to school with them. Yes, it would be very nice if they could all go to the same school together, but if it comes to a choice between that and a good education, pick the good education. Parents are often concerned about the bonds that their children form during childhood, but a great social life does not stem from friends in the neighborhood—it stems from having a good, self-confident mind. Neighborhood friends are not more important than a strong education. Your friends are your friends when you are growing up, but you have your mind for life.

"I want my child to fit in." Fit into *what*? The group, the crowd, the gang? Relationships are with individuals, not with unknown collectives. When someone wants to fit in with the unnamed "others," he puts himself at the mercy of what others think of him. Instead, he should be defining what his standards are for relationships, decide which individuals are worthwhile, and choose his friends accordingly.

Are you saying that your child is having social problems and at a different school he would have new children to choose from to find friends? You need to determine if your child's social struggles are normal. Children's relationships as they grow up can be very unstable. One day the world has come to an end because the friendship is forever ruined, the next day they are best buddies again. Some parents have become so upset by these social conflicts that they have enrolled their child in a different school, thinking that surely he can find children with whom he can get along. But this doesn't solve the problem. Instead of the child learning how to deal with other people, he just runs away from them, never staying with one relationship long enough to resolve things. What should he do if he encounters the same problems at his new school? Run away again? And when he grows up, there will most likely be people in the work place who annoy him. What should he do then? Change jobs? The child needs to face the social problems, unpleasant though they may be.

Some parents seem to think that private schools should be immune from children with social, behavioral or learning problems. This is wishful thinking. Children are children and they present challenges that can be found anywhere. The difference that you will find from school to school, however, is how the administration and teaching staff deal with those difficulties. The private school setting has the ability to provide more support for children by providing consequences for inappropriate behavior.

Or are you saying that you want your child to go to a school where he will be popular? It is the quality of relationships that matter, not the quantity. The desire for your child to be popular stems from the misconception that you get your self-esteem from what others think of you—if lots of people like you, then you must really be a great person. But as I pointed out earlier, self-esteem doesn't come from others. Being well-liked has no relation to whether or not a person has a good self-image. There are countless examples of people who have been popular but have poor self-esteem (Britney Spears, for one).

"My child has decided that he wants to go to a school that has more sports." Sports is a big topic, involving many fundamental issues which I cannot go into here, but let me just say this. Sports focus mostly on the development of body muscles; yet it is the development of the mind that is needed for one's survival. Yes, children who play sports learn about sportsmanship, following rules, and persistence, and these are all valuable skills. And yes, sports can give some children a sense of confidence if they do poorly at academic subjects. Nonetheless, sports do not provide a child with a comprehensive way of dealing with his life.

If your child loves sports, get him involved in activities in the community, but keep him at his Montessori school. Don't let your child make a decision that he isn't ready to make. He does not have the full range of knowledge or life experience to make decisions that will affect him for the rest of his life.

I think that traditional school was boring for most people and the only way they coped was through extracurricular activities like sports or relationships with their friends, so they think these are likewise important for their own children. But these are temporary, short range solutions. When a child goes out into the world he will need to feel ready to deal with it in a successful way, so making the right decision for a child's education matters.

"Anything else?" As you consider your options, keep this in mind: education is more than just learning how to add and read. Education is preparing the child for adulthood. When he grows up, he will need to know how to listen and remember what he hears, read and assimilate information, follow a train of logic, and make decisions. He will need to apply his math skills in order to figure out if he can afford to buy that new car. He will need a strong sense of self and the ability to introspect about his values and emotions for all the important life changing steps he will take, such as whom or whether he should marry. He will need to use his best judgment when deciding whether or not he should send his child to a Montessori school. He will need to know how to consider alternatives, how to evaluate which are the best ones, and how to set priorities in order to have a stable, happy life. All this will greatly depend on the thinking ability that he develops during childhood.

You also need to be aware of this: not all Montessori schools are the same. Some Montessori educators think it is a great system, but do not understand the Montessori philosophy. They do not understand how it teaches a child to think or even the importance of the reasoning process in the development of the mind. Some educators, not understanding Montessori's concept of freedom, will even allow children too much leeway. If a child doesn't feel like learning his multiplication tables, for example, they think he shouldn't have to learn them. In addition, any school can call itself a Montessori school. So do your homework. Visit potential schools, read their literature, observe classes in action and ask lots of questions. Then choose carefully.

Middle School

(Maria Montessori did not create a middle school learning environment, but stated her views about adolescents in lectures and papers. Therefore, Montessori schools must develop their own programs based on her principles and the nature of adolescence.)

You started your child in Montessori at a young age. Maybe it was the Children's House or first grade. Your child has done very well. He loves to learn, he's doing well academically and socially. You are happy and he is happy. Now your child is twelve years old and it is time to decide if he should continue in the Montessori Middle School until he is fourteen or go to a larger public school.

Perhaps you think that your child should go to a bigger school, somewhere sports are offered, more after-school events, more activities. Certainly being around more kids would be good—he'd have more friends. And anyway, he's going to have to make the change eventually, so he might as well do it now. Is this a good idea?

Here is some background on changes going on in adolescence:

The beginning of adolescence is a critical time in your child's life. It is a time of consolidating personal identity while immense changes are going on. The child is going through massive biological growth, which hasn't happened since he was an infant. Puberty begins. His hands and feet grow, then the limbs, then the trunk. The facial structure matures. His body keeps changing and because of this he spends a great deal of time looking in the mirror. All these changes are frightening; he doesn't know when they will stop, and this makes him feel self-conscious and insecure.

The timing of this change can vary from child to child, but for most, a major transformation, almost like an explosion, begins to take place in the brain around age twelve. He is changing in his thinking from a dependency on concrete experiences to abstract ideas. As he starts to enter the adult world of abstract thought, he moves away from his reliance on concrete objects. This means he begins what is called 'possibility thinking,' where he thinks in essence, "If this, then that." He starts making logical connections from one thought to the next. This allows him to engage in systematic inquiries and, much to the consternation of his parents, he begins to engage in complex arguments with them. He wants to try out new things. He tests things to the limits. Emotionally, it seems as though he is two years old again.

With these drastic physical changes going on, he begins to define who he is as an individual. He wants to feel that he has control over his life and show the world that he is responsible and intelligent. He wants to make his own decisions. He wants to make contributions to the adult world. He starts to change socially. He begins to develop friendships based on common values, goals and interests as opposed to proximity. He learns how to assert himself with others, negotiate, listen and get feedback. Elizabeth Johnston Coe, author of "Montessori and the Middle School Years," calls this developmental period the 'Age of the Mouth,' "because young people are either eating to keep up with their physical growth, arguing to test their new cognitive skills, or talking—the number one activity of adolescents." [2] But the scariest part of being an adolescent is this: he senses that soon he will be going out into the world. Can he take care of himself on his own? That's why I prefer to call adolescence the Age of Worry.

In 1985, School of the Woods, a Montessori school in Houston, Texas, added a middle school (which has since then become a model for other Montessori middle school programs [3]). At the end of the school year the administration conducted an extensive evaluation of their program by using tests, questionnaires, classroom records, observations and the Piers Harris self-esteem inventory. The results were interesting.

> The Pier Harris self-esteem inventory indicated that the students had a very high self-concept score… According to the test, all students gained in self-concept. These are remarkable results, because literature reveals that young people aged twelve to fourteen have the lowest self-concept of any age group (Simmons, Rosenberg, & Rosenberg, 1973). [4]

Based on their responses 100 percent of the students thought of themselves as smart, trustworthy, good and happy. They thought of themselves as different and lucky. They all thought when they grew up they would be an important person. They liked school and thought they were good

---

2 Elizabeth Johnston Coe, "Montessori and the Middle School Years," *Montessori and Contemporary Social Problems*, p.244.

3 Elizabeth Johnston Coe, "Montessori and the Middle School Years," *Montessori and Contemporary Social Problems*, p. 259.

4 Elizabeth Johnston Coe, "Montessori and the Middle School Years," *Montessori and Contemporary Social Problems*, p.257.

at their school work and were important members of their class. The bottom line is that they liked who they were.

At the same time ninety percent of those same students answered in a way to cause concern: I worry a lot (yes), I cry easily (yes) and I have a good figure (no). This confirms the theory that worry can be normal for adolescents even though they have a good self-concept. This is most likely because of the drastic physical transformations that are taking place.

All these changes can be a difficult time for everyone, because adolescents move through the physical, emotional, intellectual and social stages at different, irregular rates. For example, there can be a difference of six to eight years in physical growth in an average group of thirteen year olds. It is imperative that adults in the child's family and school are aware of these changes and create developmentally responsive programs.

So we return to our original question, is now a good time to move your child to a bigger school?

Since there are so many dramatic changes happening to your child at this time, a new school environment can be overwhelming to the twelve year old. If he is beginning to worry about himself, he is likely to have more worries if he moves to a new school now.

At traditional schools, the child is herded around from place to place every 45 minutes. In every class there are different teachers and different kids. He is no longer with the small, intimate group of children he knew in his old school. Your child is used to the Montessori Method, which accepts everyone as an individual. Now he is thrown into a group where everyone is expected to be the same. Will he feel comfortable voicing his new, abstract thoughts with people he can't trust? If he says something unpopular, will he be treated with respect? What if those new thoughts are wrong? What happens to a young mind in a setting like that?

The task of developing autonomy and identity at this age can best be done in small, secure peer groups. The large junior high school does not provide a place where close, trusting relationships with peers can be established. With the smaller group, the adolescent feels more comfortable communicating his ideas and develops the skills of relationship building.

In Montessori, your child has also been taught to be independent with a sequential learning approach. Now he is in a system that tells him what to do, how to do it and when to do it. He is not given the opportunity to learn a skill or concept well before moving onto the next one. At the crucial time of searching for an identity and self-confidence, he is thrust into a frustrating system that gives him little control over his life.

Adolescents need time to relax and reflect, kick back and think. Maybe they need help with some homework and want to ask a friend or teacher about it. They also benefit from periodic snacks to meet the needs of their growing bodies. If the students do not change classes every hour, they can spend time in relaxing breaks instead of rushing from place to place. But this isn't done at traditional middle schools.

Children at this age need to form a close relationship with a significant adult at school whom they know well and who knows them well. Adolescents want input from these adults and it is important that the teacher is willing to listen actively and to guide them in their own problem solving rather than spoon-feeding them facts and information. Learners need to participate actively, make choices and take responsibility for their learning, and the teacher's role is to facilitate this process rather than viewing the student as a sponge waiting to soak up knowledge.

Since this is the Age of Worry, the adolescent needs to feel as safe and secure as possible in his school environment. He will also need to be closely watched as he tests out his new thoughts, misbehaves and experiments.

Making the decision:

Having laid out the predicaments of adolescence and the potential problems of changing schools, you will, nonetheless, still need to evaluate your individual child. Some children are not bothered by a larger environment, and some children are not plagued with self-worry. Your personal circumstances (financial, location of school, etc.) will also enter into your decision. You will need to keep all that in mind as you consider your options. Here is a list of questions for you to think about as you make your decision:

- Will your child have the benefit of developing a relationship with one significant adult whom he trusts and with whom he can feel safe and secure?

- Will he be in an environment where he will feel accepted when his voice suddenly changes, or his face breaks out, or his body goes through some other change?
- Will he feel secure enough to tell his peers what he *really* thinks?
- Will the new school system foster independence?
- Will he be closely watched and will you be communicated with if he misbehaves?
- Does the new school understand the major change taking place in his brain, as his process of thinking shifts from a dependence on concrete objects to thinking more in the abstract, contemplating possibilities?
- Will he feel safe and secure at a time when he is beginning to worry about himself?

Children will never be able to live these years again, never be able to develop with a good school opportunity again so choose wisely. In reflecting on my own childhood, it would have been much easier to develop my mind as I was growing up, rather than struggle with insecurities into adulthood. The California State Department of Education sums it up perfectly. "Intellectually, early adolescents are at risk because they face decisions that have the potential to affect major academic values with life-long consequences."[5] So, my advice is: If you have found a good Montessori school, keep your child there for as long as you can.

---

5 California State Department of Education, *Caught in the middle: Educational reform for young adolescents in California public school,* 1987, p. 144.

Chapter Twelve
Beyond School

A child develops through personal effort and engagement…It is of utmost importance that a child be able to recall the impressions he has received and be able to keep them clear and distinct, since the ego builds up its intelligence through the strength of the sense impressions which it has received. It is through this hidden inner labor that a child's reason is developed. And reason in the final analysis is what distinguishes a man from irrational beings. A man is one who can make a reasoned judgment and then, through an act of the will, decide his own course of action. [1]

MARIA MONTESSORI

Summer

As the end of the school year rolls around, some parents express concern about the upcoming summer break. Will their child forget much of what he has learned over the long vacation? Will he lose the progress that he has made? How will their child stay occupied for such a long time? Should he go to summer school?

There is no need to worry about the child losing too much ground during the summer. Elementary aged children can forget some of the facts or procedures that they have learned, but the Montessori child gets back into the swing of things fairly quickly when he returns to school in the fall. Unlike children in traditional schools, most Montessori children go back to the same classroom with the same teacher. The teacher already knows where each child is in his work, and can have him return to it right away so she can see what he remembers and decide if he should

---

1 Maria Montessori, *The Secret of Childhood*, (New York: Ballantine Books, 1966), p. 96–97.

move on. If he has forgotten some information, the concrete materials are available for him to review and practice. With this system the teacher can guide her students more quickly than a teacher who is just getting to know them for the first time. Plus, even for children going onto the next level, the teachers know where they have come from academically because of the logical structure of the Montessori curriculum. More importantly, Montessori children become excited about learning and this excitement doesn't stop because school stops. (As a matter of fact, it is not unusual for children to be so enthusiastic that they don't want the school year to end.) If your child is learning how to take the initiative in learning, there is no reason why he can't continue to find things that interest him during the summer.

The long summer break can provide the child with opportunities that he wouldn't otherwise have if he went to school all twelve months of the year. He can be enrolled in summer programs where he can explore some subjects in more depth. Some summer schools offer drama classes where the children perform various plays throughout the summer; some offer art classes where children learn about customs in countries from all over the world and do art projects related to those customs. Children can also learn how to run a simple business where they sell something they make, like lemonade or cookies. Summer is the best time for families to take car trips to another area of the country to see the sights. Some children visit their relatives who live too far away to visit during the school year and can then spend some quality time with them. Others go to camp and learn how to canoe or ride horses. Summer is a time to relax, read and to try new experiences.

If you cannot afford to enroll your child in a summer program, sign him up for camp, or take a car trip, there is still a lot for your child to discover and create on his own. When I was a child I spent my summer vacations at a lake in northern Minnesota. We spent hours and hours exploring the woods, fishing, catching creatures in the water, hiking, swimming, playing cards, playing board games, creating plays, playing dress up, going boating, investigating "haunted houses," hiking, going berry picking, building structures, playing kick the can, going to the dump to see wild animals, collecting rocks or pine cones, socializing with friends, and countless other fun activities. Since our lake place didn't have any electricity, we never watched TV. As a matter of fact, when electricity finally came through the area and my parents purchased a television we grumbled about it and it was rarely, if ever, turned on. We were too busy occupying ourselves with our own self-initiated activities.

Summer is a time of growth and the outdoor air is good for a child's health. People who live in the colder areas of the country are often cooped up inside during the winter, so summer gives children the best opportunity to be outdoors and run and play. Spending time outside can also help children who have trouble finding things to do and have trouble concentrating. While outside, and if alone, the child has no choice but to find things to do which occupy his mind and summer vacation offers a long span of time for him to do this.

I am not an environmentalist nor do I advocate environmentalism, but summer is a good time for the child to connect with the earth. When he is outside, he is not surrounded by the comforts that are inside his house. The rocks are hard beneath his bare feet, not soft like the floors of his home. Lying on the ground naming cloud shapes is quite different from lying on his bed. The contrast between the two environments can be stunning. While outdoors, his access to technology is limited and his activities of necessity revolve around outdoor elements (like wood, stone, water) in order to have fun. When a child tries to create something using the things he finds outside, the end result could teach him a very important lesson about man's struggle with nature.

I remember once a group of us decided to build a wooden raft to swim on. It took us many hours and many weeks. We would think we finally had it, put the inner tubes underneath and take it for a test run. Nope—too many boards sticking out on one side. So we'd take it ashore and work on it some more. After a few more weeks, we knew we had it this time—but once in the water, it sank too much. So, back to the shore with hammer and nails again. This went on for most of that summer, and we never did figure it out, but it is one of my best summertime memories. Most importantly, the experience gave me an appreciation for the amount of work it must take in order to achieve technological progress.

Summer can provide a long stretch of time for the child to initiate and create long range projects, pursue his interests, and learn new skills. The value of summer and what children can learn during that time, if only to initiate their own activities outside, is overlooked. No matter whether your child goes to summer school, stays home or goes to the cabin, he still has opportunities to learn and develop independence.

Montessori in Action

Every summer our family goes to Canada to visit my brother at a lake in the middle of the wilderness. His beautiful log cabin is located on an island with magnificent white pines and a variety of wildlife all around. From every window we can hear the sound of loons and see a different view of the lake. He likes to take us on great adventures, where we explore haunted houses, abandoned gold mines, old trapper's shacks, bear traps, and various other escapades. I always feel like a child again, anticipating every visit with great excitement. One summer we had an adventure with our children that can only be described as 'Montessori in action.'

It was a beautiful, sunny day. The water was calm and it was a perfect day for a picnic. So what else was there to do but go on a picnic? We packed the coolers and set out on the pontoon boat, straw hats on our heads, pop in our hands, and our bare feet up on the seat cushions. Life was good.

We weren't on the lake very long when we noticed smoke coming up over some trees on the mainland, in the general direction we were headed. We went as close as we could to the smoke, found a place to stop near a secluded cabin, and got off the boat to investigate. We walked behind the cabin and then climbed up a hill that was thick with brush. We had to keep looking up to figure out where the smoke was coming from. My husband led the way. Next came our daughters, Cassie (age 16) and Samantha (age 13), and their cousin, also named Samantha (age 13), and then me. As we got closer to the source of the smoke, Dan and the girls discovered a fallen, burning tree and I looked up and saw the top of a Northern pine on fire. Dan said, "We'd better get out of here!" and we all turned around and went tearing out.

By now it was past lunch time, and because my brother is a diabetic, he needed to eat immediately, but we also needed to do something—and quick. There was another cabin around the bend and the occupants were there, so we quickly got back onto the boat, sped over, alerted them to the problem and told them to contact the Canadian Ministry of Government Services with a short wave radio. (Getting help in the wilderness is not as simple as dialing 911.)

As we set off again we could see that the fire was gathering momentum, so we decided to scrap the whole picnic idea and do what we could to contain the fire until the Ministry arrived. We went back to the island and quickly gathered hoses, a pump, buckets, and a sandwich for my brother; then we got on the boat and raced back to the fire.

On the way we discovered that the fire hose had been eaten through by mice, so we were going to have to rely on the garden hoses, which weren't going to get us very far.

When we arrived back at the fire, everyone jumped off the pontoon boat and the children immediately sprang into action. Cassie grabbed some buckets and hoses and went up the hill with her father. Samantha, my niece, went to the nearby cabin to look for extra hoses. While this was going on, my brother taught me how to operate the pump so that we could get water into the hoses and up the hill, and then left with the boat to go find more people and hoses. Then our daughter, Samantha, went back and forth between her father and me, telling me when to turn the pump on and when to turn it off. When the other Samantha couldn't find any extra hoses, she returned and helped our Samantha. The Two Sams, as we call them, started looking and listening for the helicopter and, when they heard it coming, waved life jackets in the air to bring attention to our location.

To make a long story short, I was never so happy to see a helicopter in my life. The Ministry finally arrived and put out the fire, which had started from lightening that had struck two days prior.

I was extremely proud of the children. No one told Cassie to grab some buckets and hoses and head up the hill. No one told Samantha, our niece, to run to the nearby cabin to look for more hoses. No one told our daughter, Samantha, to be a messenger so that I would know when to turn the pump on and off. No one told the Two Sams to look for the helicopter and to wave their orange life jackets in the air when they saw it. The children didn't wait to be told what to do, they just figured out what needed to be done and did it. This incident was a remarkable example of the principle of independence, which is the essence of the Montessori Method.

If you want to know why a good education pays off, and why teaching children how to think is important, this incident clearly illustrates it. In a crisis situation, adults don't have time to keep track of everything the kids are doing, so the ability of the children to reason and do the right thing while staying safe is vital. The children used their minds and acted with competence. It was what I like to call Montessori in Action.

This doesn't guarantee that if you send your child to a Montessori school, that he will choose to think. This also isn't to say that no child will learn how to think unless he goes to a Montessori school. But this is an example of the kind of thinking that a good Montessori school, a school that adheres to the fundamental principles of the Montessori Method, is trying to produce in its students.

The ability to think is essential for man's survival and happiness. I don't know of any other educational system other than the Montessori Method that uses a highly specialized, integrated methodology for the specific purpose of teaching a child how to use his mind. Maria Montessori discovered what children are and how they really learn. And she recognized that in order to reason, it takes much more than just an accumulation of facts. The Montessori Method is a realistic approach to learning based on the true nature of the child. And it works.

Quick Referrals

How Can I Help My Child at Home?

Parents don't need to be Montessori teachers at home in order to help their child be successful. The best strategy is to apply the *principles* of the Montessori Method as much as possible. Here are some suggestions:

1. Have clear rules in your home. Disrespect for people or property should not be tolerated.
2. Discipline needs to be consistent. Consistent discipline makes children feel secure because they know that you care enough about them to make them behave. It also gives them a firm grasp of reality. The most important thing is not to present contradictory messages.
3. Routines need to be as consistent as possible. Order is very important to children at this age; change in routines can be upsetting.
4. Let your child take the lead in learning. Pressure to learn creates anxiety. Support his interests instead.
5. Read to your child every day. This is one of the best ways to prepare a child to learn how to read.
6. Teach letter sounds rather than the letter names. The sounds of the letters prepare the child for reading.
7. Limit, or better yet, eliminate TV, computer usage and video games. Your child still needs to be exploring his world with his hands and these mediums are too abstract. They also do not help the development of his initiative, imagination and concentration.
8. Make your child fulfill his commitments. If he decides to commit himself to something (providing it is reasonable and acceptable to you), he needs to follow through. If he tells someone he will help him pick up his toys, he needs to do it. If an older child asks to take music lessons, he needs to understand that he must continue

for a specified amount of time before he can stop. Then make sure he takes the lessons for that much time.

9. Encourage independence.
   - Allow time for your child to dress himself. When he can take care of himself he feels confident.
   - Encourage alone time. Children need to initiate their own activities so they can learn how to concentrate.
   - Encourage your child to go outside and play. Being outdoors gives him a good opportunity to come up with his own things to do.

10. Encourage thinking. Let your child figure things out for himself. You don't have to fill him full of answers that he could have discovered by his own efforts.

11. Limit praise. Allow the child to evaluate his own accomplishments.

12. Respect the child's rights. Do not force him to share or apologize.

13. Let the child participate in activities around the house. This helps him develop independence and self-confidence and also makes him feel a part of the family unit. Here are some ideas:
   - Folding the laundry
   - Arranging flowers
   - Taking care of plants
   - Shoveling snow
   - Planting seeds
   - Raking leaves
   - Climbing up and down a step ladder
   - Polishing
   - Cleaning
   - Helping take care of a pet
   - Carrying objects properly
   - Handling objects carefully such as turning pages of a book
   - Preparing food such as buttering toast, putting toothpicks in fruit, cracking nuts
   - Setting the table
   - Loading the dishwasher
   - Sewing a button
   - Using tools such as a hammer or screwdriver
   - Putting clothes into the washing machine or dryer
   - Washing a small corner of the car

Tips for the "Helping Too Much" Syndrome

When we explain that parents should be encouraging children to figure out their own solutions to problems instead of giving them the answers and refrain from giving children too much help, the age old question pops up, "Well, what *are* we supposed to do?" Here is a copy of information that we give to new assistants in the classroom who are not familiar with the Montessori Method. Perhaps this will help answer that question.

1. General Rule of Thumb: Never do for a child what he can do for himself.
2. "I can't" often means "I don't want to."
3. Take time during class time to sit by the head teacher and observe her presentations.
4. If the child is able to do it alone, leave.
5. If all the children are busy, do nothing. Don't be afraid to do nothing. Our goal is to get them to work without us.
6. You don't need to be everywhere at once, even though it feels that way.
7. When a child asks for help, and you are busy, don't be afraid to say no (provided his request doesn't involve a safety issue). Then observe what happens: a) an older child may step in to help, b) he may decide to do it himself, or c) he may change his mind and do something else.
8. If you are doing it all, it's too much. Then it's your product, not his.
9. Don't worry if the finished product isn't perfect. Remember the young child is in the process stage, therefore it shouldn't be perfect. He is learning how to do it and he'll eventually get there with practice.
10. When a child makes a mess or drops something on the floor, he needs to clean it up. You can say, "I see some crumbs on the floor" and show him where the broom is kept. Remember that young children will make a mess as they clean—relax, re-demo, let them do the best they can. We can always get it later.
11. If the child makes a mess that is too much for him to clean up himself, invite him to watch you do it. If appropriate, invite him to finish (i.e. hold dust pan or sweep it into the dust pan and put

it in the garbage which even a two-year-old can do).

12. If the child keeps saying, "You do it" he is used to adults doing it for him.

13. Utilize older children for helping younger ones who need help. Get into the habit of saying, "Is there anyone who could help Johnny?" Encourage children to ask other children for help.

14. Do not make decisions for children that they can make for themselves even if they ask.

15. Observe first before taking action. When in doubt, take cues from head teacher, observe or ask her what should be done. Don't be afraid to ask—she had to learn too and understands how you feel.

16. Step in immediately if there is danger to a child or equipment.

17. Helpful phrases:
    "Try a different one." "Try again a different way." (puzzles)
    "See how I hold it."
    "Watch me again."
    "Try again."
    "Think about it."
    "Count it and see."
    "Figure it out."
    "Go get the broom."

18. Get into the habit of asking children questions:
    "What do you need to do first?"
    "What do you need to get?"
    "What should you do now?"
    "How did I do it?"
    "What do you think?"

19. Relax and observe. You don't need to be busy every second. Much of our job is to observe the child.

20. Don't worry. The children will get it in time.

Fostering Self-Esteem in Children

Adults can provide an environment that either encourages the development of self-esteem or stifles it. Just like everything else the child learns, genuine self-worth has to be acquired *first hand*. We can foster it, but not give it. How do we create an environment in which the child can learn that he is worthy of life and competent to live?

In order for a child to feel competent to live, he must be confident that his mind can understand reality. He achieves this competence through his work. To foster this, parents and teachers should:

1. Encourage independence. The child should be able to separate from parents and see himself as a separate entity. Also, the child should constantly be taking steps toward taking care of himself (e.g. dressing himself, bathing himself).

2. Allow the child to make age-appropriate choices. "Do you want to wear this outfit or this one?" "Do you want to do your homework before or after dinner?"

3. Tell the child the truth, so as not to undermine his view of reality. When a parent lies to the child, his first conclusion is, "What's wrong with me?" It also makes him feel that he can't trust his parents.

4. Let the child *initiate* his own age-appropriate activities.

5. Let the child repeat his work as often as he finds necessary, so he can master it. The parent who says, "You did that booklet *again*? Don't you ever do anything else?" undermines the child's self-esteem.

6. Let the child learn at his own rate rather than pushing him or holding him back. Holding a child back creates an angry, frustrated child. Pushing creates a frightened child.

7. Encourage your child to think. Say, "What do you think? Why?" Give him cues and hints. Know that the child learns only from direct experience, so requiring memorization of unrelated facts is meaningless and a waste of time.

8. Encourage learning through natural consequences. Concrete lessons work better than a hundred sermons (e.g. the child sees his friend leave because he won't share his toys).

9. Encourage your child's values (providing his values are moral) *without spoiling him*. Teach him how to value and he will learn to value himself. If your child loves books, take him to the library. Let him wear that favorite outfit that you are so sick of seeing. Encouraging values fosters a love of life.

10. Help your child to learn to evaluate himself by setting the example. Within earshot of the child say things like, "I really did a good job today at work and I feel just great!" or, "I feel really bad that I botched that up, but I'll try to do better next time."
11. Parents and teachers should give reasons instead of orders.

In order to conclude that he is worthy of life, the child must feel confident that he is a good person. Secondarily, he needs to feel understood and valued. To foster this, teachers and parents should:

1. Accept the child's range of emotions. Say, "You sound angry right now. Do you want to talk about it?" rather than, "Don't you say you hate your sister. You love your sister."
2. Use "I" statements when communicating with the child: "I'm angry because…" "I don't like it when…"
3. Direct all corrections towards the child's actions, not his person. "I still see dirt on the floor," rather than, "What's wrong with you? How many times do I have to tell you to clean up that mess?"
4. Treat the child with dignity. Don't shame or humiliate him (e.g. don't force him to apologize).
5. Avoid over-correcting. The child will eventually figure it out on his own when he is perceptually and developmentally ready.
6. Avoid over-praising. Instead, be a mirror: "I bet you feel just great about that." Praise keeps a child dependent on what others think.
7. Respect the child's rights (e.g. don't force him to share).
8. Be consistent in disciplining the child so that he can learn to behave properly. He will feel more secure if he knows someone cares about what he does.

Most of us were raised with the view that self-esteem comes from others, so we are not used to the idea that self-worth is earned. With awareness and practice, however, we can make it easier for our own children.

Appendix

Ages and Stages

1. Sensations to Perceptions (Sensorimotor) Age 0–2

The child takes in reality by moving and touching, moving and feeling. This is the only way to get to the perceptual level. Eyes and ears come later, as they don't give the infant much information at first. This is the building of the perceptual stage and by the end of it the child is forming many first-level concepts.

2. Perceptual to Conceptual (Pre-Operational) Age 2–6

- The child gradually passes into thinking with concepts. However, he doesn't think by means of concepts alone — he has to be physically active if he is to figure things out and make connections. During this stage his mode of learning slowly changes from using real objects to using symbolic substitutes (i.e. language and mental images). The child is building up his own system of logic during this time and can't use language and mental images in place of sensory-motor activities. For example, adults can picture the tower with a cube missing without having to build it first, but the child can't. He can picture what *is*, but not what isn't.
- The child can't learn from logical explanations yet; he has to see for himself.
- The child can't necessarily transfer information from one context to another.
- Logic is not automatic.

3. Conceptual to Higher Level Conceptual (Concrete Operational) Age 6–12

- The child has a beginning grasp of logic and can be deductive (reach conclusions from generalizations); but the primary way that he learns, and will continue to learn throughout adulthood, is by induction (forming generalizations from observation and experience).
- Thoughts are freed from physical performance (i.e. now the child can imagine the cube missing from the tower).
- The child starts thinking in principles ("What's fair?" "Why are these answers the same?")
- The child doesn't accept answers on faith; he looks for reasons for what's going on.
- Because the child starts to think logically, he makes judgments (e.g. "That is good." "That is bad.")
- The child is starting to use language for problem solving.
- The child can visualize pictures in his mind.
- He takes in tons of data, which helps him move into the next stage.
- The parent will know that the child is getting ready to move into phase four when he asks questions such as, "Does space go on forever? If not, when it stops, what is beyond it?"

4. Abstract and Philosophical (Formal Operations) Age 12–18

During this phase the child gradually passes into thinking in adult terms. He begins to have really abstract thoughts and form his own principles. He is truly self-aware. "I'm the only one in the world like me." He is monitoring his own thoughts. He tries to understand abstractions. Many adults never get here.

If Your Child Can't Read, It Might Be His Hearing, Even if He Hears

A child's reading difficulties can usually be traced back to some problem. Perhaps it was a physical problem, such as poor vision or allergies. Or maybe the child spent too much time on the computer, or in front of the television, and never learned to concentrate properly. Teaching a child to read by memorization rather than phonics might have been the cause of the problem. Quite often, however, I have found that children with reading problems had frequent ear trouble as infants, toddlers or pre-elementary students. When I express my concern about this to parents, they often respond, "Well, we've had his hearing checked and he hears perfectly now." But the fact that he can hear *now* doesn't alleviate his reading difficulties. Here's why.

The infant is very sensitive to language, and he homes in on human words and sounds. He concentrates hard, and strengthens and coordinates the muscles in his mouth so that he can imitate the sounds that he hears. When he doesn't hear sounds accurately at this stage, he learns to make them incorrectly. Hearing the sounds properly later is often too late; he has passed the sensitive period for forming them. Notice how we, as adults, no matter how hard we try, cannot form certain sounds in foreign languages. We can hear the foreigner's speech clearly enough but we cannot say the same words without an accent.

However, we have already learned language as such by learning to speak in our native tongue; and we already know how to read. For the young child, this is not the case. Learning to make the sounds of his own language incorrectly when he was very young hindered his ability to learn how to read later on.

When a child has fluid on the ear drum, what he hears is similar to what we would hear if we were underwater. Instead of hearing the word "see," for example, he hears "thee." When he gets older and can hear "see" correctly, he is still saying "thee," because he never learned to make the sound of "s." Now imagine what happens when he tries to learn how to read. He sees the "s" and makes a "th" sound. But "thee" doesn't sound like the word he is now hearing, so he is confused. It is almost like trying to reconcile two different languages—the language he hears now, and the language he learned to speak. (Interestingly, vision problems can also cause speech problems, because if the infant cannot see a speaker's mouth clearly, he finds it difficult to reproduce speech sounds accurately.)

Children like this may also appear hyperactive and have difficulty concentrating. One can understand why. The child has had a hard time deciphering the sounds around him. When his hearing problems went away, maybe things sounded too loud and put him on edge. He probably couldn't hear directions and instructions when he was little and was punished for disobeying. The world probably seemed pretty hard to figure out. That would make me nervous too.

But the good news is that there is help. Often, the best solution is to see a reading specialist for an evaluation. She may recommend a speech teacher or tutor. Also make sure that your child is in a phonics-based reading program, where he can learn the relationships between sounds and their symbols. The child also needs to hear individual sounds put together to make words. Merely memorizing words will bog down his mind and frustrate him, and will not clear up the confusion. He needs practice, and lots of it. And keep reading to him.

But the best solution is prevention in the first place. Insist on medical help when you suspect your infant or toddler isn't hearing you. Pay close attention to your child's health: early problems will have consequences later on.

How to Encourage Your Child to Think

- Direct the child's attention to relationships in his daily life. "Look at the gerbils. Do they look different to you? How?" "Why do you think your sister is upset? Did you notice what happened at dinnertime?" "Why do you think the plant is drooping? What do you think we should do about it?"
- Do not give direct answers, but instead encourage the consideration of other options. For example, if your child says, "Can I eat at Jane's house?" reply, "We are having company. You choose." (This response is appropriate if both alternatives are acceptable to you.) Keep putting the decision-making in the child's court. Stop and think every time you are about to say "yes" to your child. Instead of saying yes, give an alternative. "You want to play with Jim. We can go to the park together or you can have Jim over." "You want a snack. You can have a cracker or a piece of toast." "You want to watch the TV special. If you do, you will need a nap tomorrow. If you don't, you may ride your bike all afternoon." This forces the child into decision-making and thinking. A simple "yes" gives the child permission not to think, or consider alternatives, or assert his personality.
- Give the child choices that are within his capabilities.

- Do not give the child a choice to be lazy. Do not say, "Do you want to put on your coat or shall I?" We must not give the child this choice in areas where he has already mastered the skill.
- Encourage thinking of alternatives. "That is one way to build a fort. Can you think of another way?"
- Foster persistence by letting the child complete an activity; and allow for a fair amount of frustration, as it takes frustration to learn and change. When you do have to help the child, let him put on the finishing touch, such as the last puzzle piece, so that he knows he has achieved some success. Guide the child with encouragement, not the answers.
- Give logical reasons for rules of conduct. Modify rules as the child gets older and develops better judgment and control.
- Assume intelligence. Encourage responses from an older child by giving him diminished cues. Say, "It's raining today," as you look at his feet, rather than, "Put on your boots."
- Adults do not have to be walking encyclopedias answering the child's every question. Let the child reflect on possible answers or do the research on his own.
- With some questions, it's okay to say, "You'll figure it out when you get older," and leave it at that.
- Try to distinguish between giving the child relevant *information* and giving him the *answers* to questions on conservation, classification, quantity, length, and how to solve problems. Let your child know that he can figure it out.
- Let your child experiment with cause and effect. Let him put some water in the freezer. Don't tell him it will turn to ice. Instead ask, "What do you think will happen?" Then let him peek and observe for himself.
- Try as much as possible to let the child search out answers on his own. Use the lines, "What do you think?" "Why?" and "Think about it."

Advantages of Books, Harmful Effects of Electronics

Advantages of Reading Books to a Child:
- The child can snuggle up to the person reading him the book.

- Indirect preparation for writing: as the child turns the pages, he uses the same fingers that he will one day use to hold a pencil.
- There is control of error when the child doesn't pay attention: if he wiggles, mom stops reading.
- The reader can tell when the child is losing interest in the story and regain his interest by hamming it up, reading faster, slowing down, etc.
- The child learns sequencing by verbalizing the events of the story in order.
- When the child verbalizes the story, he is being prepared for thinking skills.
- The child performs more and more abstraction, because the number of pictures decreases as he gets older.
- The child's vocabulary increases. He learns new words from the context of the events in the story and can ask the meanings of words. Stories also introduce him to words he wouldn't necessarily use every day.
- Books motivate the child to understand: he puts effort into comprehending what is being said.
- The child gets time to contemplate the story. He can stop and think about it as he turns the pages, or can pause before reading the next page.
- The child gets motivated to learn how to read. He admires the human who's doing it.
- The child can take the book anywhere—he can carry it around, it can be his best friend.
- The child can ask the reader questions about the book to get more information.
- When the child learns how to read, he can re-read his favorite parts for enjoyment.
- When the child learns how to read, he can go back and re-read parts that he doesn't understand.

Harmful Effects of the Computer:
- The child becomes confused about the permanence of objects, because objects appear, disappear and reappear before his eyes. He may even think that magic is possible.

- The child cannot develop good fine motor control, because fingers do not get strong by pressing on keys.
- The child cannot ask questions to get more information.
- The child thinks that answers come from a machine rather than from the real world. When the machine is gone, he has no idea how to arrive at those answers.
- The child does not develop a muscular memory for letters or numbers by moving a mouse around or by pushing a button. [1]
- The child gets used to quick and easy answers so gives up easily when the computer is gone.
- The child thinks that speed is important in learning because the answers come quickly.
- The child accepts information from a machine without questioning its validity.

Harmful Effects of Television:
- The child becomes passive. He becomes used to sounds and visual images coming in while he does nothing.
- There is no time to think about stories; they go too fast.
- Why read? The television tells the child the story.
- When the child does learn to read, he may be able to read the sentences, but won't understand the meanings because he can't picture the story in his head. He hasn't learned how to visualize—television has been doing it for him!
- The child does not develop good large motor control because TV discourages movement. He spends too much time sitting rather than running, jumping, walking and so on.
- The child's language development doesn't progress because the level of language on television stays the same. No one stops and repeats a word for the child to try and pronounce or slows down while talking to make sure he understands.
- The child needs to hear words pronounced slowly so that he can hear the individual sounds. This is important for proper speech development and learning to spell accurately later on. The speed of language on television is too fast.

1 Gulnaz Saiyed "Writing by Hand Better for Learning Study Shows," *Medill Reports*, January 27, 2011, http://news.medill.northwestern.edu/chicago/news.aspx?id=177291#. UokxnwTI0p4.facebook

- The child thinks that what is happening on the screen is actually happening. He will wonder if the people on television can see him, because he thinks that the television screen is a window.

Harmful Effects of Video Games:
- The child doesn't learn how to take the initiative in finding his own activities to do.
- The child becomes dependent on entertainment rather than knowledge.
- The child may become competitive before he is ready.
- Objects appearing and disappearing on the screen do not help the child with understanding reality.
- Too many video games do not encourage relaxation because most of them are paced too fast.

Standards for Television Viewing

When deciding if a show is appropriate for children, parents should evaluate the following:

- Humor. Is it really funny, or are good people being ridiculed?
- Sense of life. Is life portrayed as good and are problems solvable?
- Morality. Is there a clear distinction between good and evil? Are honesty, integrity, justice, independence, and so on presented as admirable traits?
- Characters. Are they heroic? (Children need people to admire as they grow up.)
- Music. Is it really music or just noise? (This is especially important if they are watching a musical.)
- Language. Are the words used appropriate? Does the show encourage proper language development, or does it use immature language (e.g. *Teletubbies*)?
- Conflict resolution. Are there violence or death scenes that will cause your child to have nightmares (e.g. *Jumanji, Titanic*)?
- Theme. Does it reflect your family's values? The movie might be good, but is the subject matter too mature for your child (e.g. *To*

Kill a Mockingbird)? Is there a hidden political agenda (e.g. Walt Disney's *Pocahontas*)?

- Format. Does the show encourage a long attention span, or a short one (e.g. *Sesame Street*)?

Unfortunately, movie ratings have become inadequate and inaccurate, so that trying to decide what movies are appropriate for children to see is frustrating. These web sites can take the guesswork out of determining movie content and can be very helpful in making wise choices: www. screenit.com, and www.moviemom.com.

I recommend musicals such as *The Sound of Music*. Not only do they present children with a sense of joy about living, but if you later play the soundtrack, children will also learn the music and replay (visualize) the story as they listen to it. This helps them learn to sequence events. However, children need to learn how to create their own visualizations when they read rather than just recall pictures that they have already seen, so don't overdo it.

I also highly recommend the old classics with icons such as Judy Garland, Shirley Temple, Gene Kelly and Fred Astaire. There is nothing inappropriate in these films and children love to watch all the dancing and singing. Most importantly, these movies portray a benevolent sense of life and they are enjoyable for the entire family.

Can You Tell the Difference?

At one of our parent/teacher meetings a parent asked, "Can you tell the difference at school when parents don't carry through with the Montessori Method at home?" Generally speaking yes, but bear in mind that when a child has a difficulty, it may have *absolutely nothing to do with the parent!* Other factors come into play such as the child's health, his own reactions to information he receives, his sensitivity, his own conclusions and so on. None-the-less, I have listed the most common results we see in school when the Montessori Method is not followed at home. A child may exhibit one, some or all of these characteristics.

Independence
Action: Too much is done for the child. He does not dress himself, does

not feed himself, is not allowed to make choices and is carried everywhere.
Result: The child may

- lack persistence.
- be fearful of new situations.
- be afraid to try new or challenging work.
- expect to be waited on.
- not figure out how to do things on his own.
- stand around looking puzzled about what to do.
- not finish work.
- be immature.
- have a hard time following directions.
- be lazy.

Action: The child is told the answers without being allowed to figure them out for himself. He isn't allowed to make any mistakes.
Result: The child may

- become fearful of trying.
- become dependent on others to do his thinking for him.

Discipline

Action: Consequences and follow-through for misbehavior are inconsistent.
Result: The child may

- be defiant and disruptive.
- not listen.
- think reality can be manipulated.
- be angry.
- think the world revolves around him.
- expect others to satisfy his desires.
- be immature.
- be unable to delay gratification.
- lack self-confidence.
- be fearful.
- have trouble concentrating and be easily distracted.
- feel that no one cares about him.
- be insecure.
- eventually view the disciplinarian as a wimp.
- manipulate others.

TV
Action: The child watches as much TV as he wants, often for hours a day.
Result: The child may
- have trouble concentrating.
- lack initiative.
- lack body control and be clumsy.
- lack social skills.
- imitate what he sees on TV (such as threatening other children or using inappropriate words).
- become sensory deprived.

Computer
Action: Working on the computer is allowed and even encouraged.
Result: The child may
- have trouble with processing.
- lack problem solving skills.
- expect quick answers.
- want to quit when work is too hard.
- become a guesser instead of a thinker.
- lack small motor control.
- have trouble with pencil work.
- lack social skills.
- be sensory deprived.

Forced Apologies
Action: The child is forced to apologize whenever he does something wrong.
Result: The child may
- learn to lie.
- learn that he can do something wrong as long as he apologizes afterwards, so he repeats his misbehavior. When adult reprimands him, he replies, "*But* I said I was sorry."
- feel humiliated in front of others when he apologizes.

Forced Sharing
Action: The child is forced to share his possessions with others.
Result: The child may
- feel threatened by and be afraid of other children.

- not socialize well.
- try to control others.
- not trust adults, perhaps be angry with them.
- retreat from socializing.

Action: The child is allowed to take a possession away from another child in the name of sharing.
Result: This child may
- not learn to respect others.
- tromp on the rights of others.
- be aggressive and controlling.
- not be liked by other children.

Praise
Action: The child is over-praised in order to build his self-esteem.
Result: The child may
- become dependent on what others think of him, rather than evaluating himself.
- feel insecure.
- seek approval and attention from others.

External Rewards (such as stars, movie time, candy, etc.)
Action: Correct behavior is rewarded.
Result: The child may
- perform for the reward, rather than inner satisfaction.
- feel that other people are in control, because they are giving him the rewards.
- not focus on his behavior.

Communication
Action: Believing everything the child says. A child may lie in order to change reality, express a desire, or avoid trouble, etc.
Result: The child may
- learn to manipulate adults.
- become afraid to tell his parent things.
- become embarrassed by the parent who overreacts to these "stories."
- become confused about reality.

Pushing
Action: The child is pushed to excel.
Result: The child may
- feel that he can never measure up, he's never good enough.
- withdraw and become depressed.
- have poor self-esteem.
- be scared to pursue learning and therefore doesn't enjoy it.
- become bossy with other children.

Tattle Tales
Action: The child is told not to tattle.
Result: The child may
- not learn what is important to tell an adult and what is not.
- become afraid to share his thoughts with adults.
- have trouble forming his own moral code.

Accomplishments of Montessori Kindergarten Children

There are a large number of activities that children who have attended Montessori for three years accomplish before going on to the elementary level. Because children are different and progress at their own individual rates, it is not guaranteed that each child will master or work on all these activities, but generally speaking this is what most achieve.

Practical Life
- Masters following a sequence of steps that prepares a child for mathematics and thinking logically: food preparation, polishing and washing dishes, etc.
- Perfects fine motor work that refines handwriting skills.

Sensorial
- Works on advanced sorting (necessary for children to be able to sort and think through abstract ideas later on).
- Works on advanced sensorial work (combining the concepts of size, height, width, etc. which leads to creativity and advanced math).
- Works on the decanomial square (preparation for squaring and cubing that leads to abstract algebra).

- Masters the binomial and trinomial cubes (preparation for the binomial and trinomial theorems that leads to algebra).
- Works on the cubing material (preparation for squaring and cubing numbers that leads to algebra).

Mathematics

- Consolidates the ability to identify geometric shapes (cube, sphere, cone, rectangular prism, triangular prism, square based pyramid, triangular based pyramid, cylinder, ovoid, ellipsoid. Through the use of the concrete geometry materials, the children will later discover the advanced algebraic formulae that will be required for high school mathematics).
- Accomplishes advanced work with bead cabinet (cubed chains, counting to one thousand, leads to skip counting, better math fact knowledge, the actual size of a number, patterns within numbers. This is part of their forthcoming algebra curriculum).
- Learns the processes of addition, subtraction, multiplication and division, then the child is prepared for memorization of the tables, and some children start to memorize them.
- Experiences the decimal system (exchanging ten of one power for one of the next power, e.g. ten tens make a hundred).
- Does advanced work with fractions (equivalencies and addition).
- Is introduced to algebra in some Montessori schools (learning that "x" stands for an unknown number, learning how to make rectangles and reading the sides).

Language

- Learns how to read or starts sounding out phonetic words.
- Works on a workbook or other advanced reading materials (a child's love of reading and concentration skills are solidified).
- Learns grammar (parts of speech such as verbs, nouns, prepositions are identified and symbolized).
- Does additional reading games (Ha Ha, Bring Me Game, etc.).
- Learns phonograms (reading and spelling all 42 booklets with words containing phonograms such as sh, th, silent e, kn, ph, or, ar, oe, eigh).
- Learns how to do simple research skills (airplanes, volcanoes, planets, animals, Presidents, etc.).

- Writes phrases, sentences, stories.
- Participates in unit studies (often children really catch on to these studies in their Kindergarten year and can recall lots of information with excitement and will raise their hands at circle time to answer questions about what we are studying).

Geography
- Makes maps of some or all of the continents and learns more about countries all over the world.

Music
- Masters rhythms with instruments.
- Displays confidence during performances.

Art
- Displays creativity using different mediums.

Social/Emotional
- Teaches other children, which is a real confidence builder.
- Is admired. (All the previous years that your child was in Montessori, he looked up to and admired the older children. They were "in the know." Now, *he* is an older child, now *he* "knows", now *he* is admired. This is also a real confidence builder—not because he is admired, but because his knowledge is firsthand and he knows that he deserves the admiration.)
- Becomes more solid in the foundation for his sense of independence and individuality.
- Is guided according to his individual needs, as opposed to being grouped and taught according to his age.

Bibliography

Berliner, Michael, "Reason, Creativity, and Freedom in Montessori," *The Educational Forum*, November 1975.

Berliner, Michael and Binswanger, Harry, "Answers to Common Questions about Montessori Education". *The Objectivist Forum*, Vol. 5, June & August 1984.

Bernstein, Andrew, "Why Students Can't Add or Subtract" http://www.aynrand.org/site/News2?page=NewsArticle&id=5320 *Miami Herald*, July 21, 2000; *Buffalo News*, August 13, 2000; *Charlotte Observer*, July 23, 2000; *San Jose Mercury News*; July 18, 2000; *Las Vegas Review-Journal*, July 24, 2000; *Spokesman-Review*, July 19, 2000.

Binswanger, Harry, "Logical Thinking" (paper presented at Objectivist conference, Williamsburg, Virginia), July 1–7, 1992.

Bradley, Michael, *Yes, Your Teen is Crazy,* Port Charlotte, Florida: Harbor Press, 2003.

Briggs, Dorthy, (paper on self-esteem presented at workshop, Tacoma, Washington), Spring 1982.

Bronson, Po, "How Not to Talk to Your Kids" http://nymag.com/news/features/27840/, New York News and Features, February 11, 2007.

California State Department of Education, "Caught in the middle: Educational reform for young adolescents in California public school," 1987.

Coe, Elizabeth Johnston, "Montessori and the Middle School Years," *Montessori and Contemporary Social Problems*.

Coloroso, Barbara, *Kids are Worth It: Giving Your Child the Gift of Inner Discipline*, New York, Harper Collins Publishers, 1994.

Cline, Foster and Fay, Jim, *Parenting with Love and Logic*, Colorado Springs, Colorado: Pinon Press, 1982.

Dewey, John, "The School and Social Progress," *The School and Society*, Chicago: University of Chicago Press, 1907.

Faber, Adele and Mazlish, Elaine, *How to Be the Parent You Always Wanted to Be*, (audio cassette), New York: Simon & Schuster, 1999.

Faber, Adele and Mazlish, Elaine, *How to Talk so Kids Will Listen and Listen so Kids Will Talk*, New York: Avon Publishers,1980.

Faber, Adele and Mazlish, Elaine, *Liberated Parents, Liberated Children*, New York: Avon Books, 1974.

Faber, Adele and Mazlish, Elaine, *Siblings without Rivalry*, New York: W. W. Norton and Company, 1987.

Faull, Jan, "Your Brilliant Baby in Week 25, Crawling and Judging Depth Perception" http://www.babyzone.com/baby/nurturing/baby_week_by_week/article/week-25-baby, Baby Zone, Week 25.

George Marilyn, "Two and Three Year Olds" and "Four, Five and Six Year Olds", Blue Gables Montessori School, Kirkland, Washington.

Ginott, Haim, *Between Parent and Child*, New York: MacMillan Company, 1965.

Glenn, Stephen and Nelson, Jane, Raising *Self-Reliant Children*, Rocklin, California: Prima Publishing, 1980.

Gordon, Thomas, *Parent Effectiveness Training*, New York: Peter H. Wyden Inc., 1970.

Healy, Jane, "ECT Interview: Computers and Young Children," *Early Childhood Today*, (http://www.scholastic.com/teachers/article/ect-interview-computers-and-young-children.)

Healy, Jane, *Different Learners: Identifying, Preventing, and Treating Your Child's Learning Problems*, New York: Simon and Schuster Paperbacks, 2010.

Healy, Jane, *Endangered Minds: Why Children Don't Think and What We Can Do About It*, New York: Simon and Schuster, 1990.

Healy, Jane, "An Interview with Jane Healy," *Wild Duck Review*, Vol. IV, No.2, 1998.

Healy, Jane, *Your Child's Growing Mind: A Guide to Learning and Brain Development from Birth to Adolescence*, New York: Broadway Books, 2004.

Hughes, Dr. Steve, "Good at Doing Things: Montessori Education and Higher Order Cognitive Functions," (paper presented at Bergamo Montessori School, Sacramento, California), http://www.goodatdoingthings.com/, September 1, 2012.

Jackson, Deborah, "We Don't Push Children Here," *Montessori International Magazine*, 18 Balderton Street, London, 2003.

Jacob, S. H., *Your Baby's Mind*, Halbrook, Massachusetts: Bob Adams Inc., 1991.

Kramer, Rita, *Maria Montessori, A Biography*, New York: Capricorn Books, 1977.

Lillard, Paula Polk, *Montessori: A Modern Approach*, New York: Schocken Books, 1972.

Maleskar, Kanchan, "Are You a 'helicopter' Parent?" *Rediff News*, India, February 22, 2007, http://www.rediff.com/getahead/2007/feb/23parent.htm

Montessori, Maria, *The Absorbent Mind*, New York: Dell Publishing, 1967.

Montessori, Maria, *The Advanced Montessori Method*, New York: Frederick A. Stokes Company, 1917.

Montessori, Maria, *The Discovery of the Child*, India:_Kalakshetra Publications, 1966.

Montessori, Maria, *The Montessori Method*, Fresno, California: Schocken Books, Inc., 1964.

Montessori, Maria, *The Montessori Method*, New York: Frederick A. Stokes Company, 1912.

Montessori, Maria, *The Secret of Childhood*, New York: Fides Publishers, 1966.

Montessori, Maria, *The Secret of Childhood*, New York: Ballantine Books, 1966.

Montessori, Maria, *Spontaneous Activity in Education*, New York: Frederick A. Stokes Co., 1917.

Montessori, Maria, *Spontaneous Activity in Education*, New York: Schocken Books, 1965.

Montessori, Maria, *Spontaneous Activity in Education*, (on line book: http://www.readcentral.com/chapters/Maria-Montessori/Spontaneous-Activity-in-Education/008).

Montessori, Maria, *To Educate the Human Potential*, India: Kalakshetra Publications, 1948.

Peikoff, Leonard, "Why Johnny Can't Think," *The Objectivist Forum*, Volume 5, Number 6, December 1984.

Pica, Rae, "More Movement, Smarter Kids" http://movingandlearning. com/Resources/Articles21.htm.

Rand, Ayn, "The Comprachicos" in *The New Left: The Anti-Industrial Revolution*, (New York: New American Library, 1971).

Rand, Ayn, *The New Left*, New York: Penguin Group 1975.

Rand, Ayn, *Introduction to Objectivist Epistemology*, New York: Penguin Group, 1979.

Ayn Rand, *Philosophy Who Needs It*, Indianapolis/New York: Bobbs-Merrill Company, 1982.

Rand, Ayn, *The Virtue of Selfishness*, New York: A Signet book from The New American Library, 1964.

Rand, Ayn, Galt's Speech in *Atlas Shrugged*, New York: Random House, 1957.

Ross, Valerie, "When the Blind Can Suddenly See, Do They Know What They're Looking At?"_http://blogs.discovermagazine. com/80beats/2011/04/11/when-the-blind-suddenly-see-do-they-know-what-theyre-looking-at/ *Discover Magazine*, April 11, 2011.

Samenow, Stanton, *Before It's Too Late*, New York: Three Rivers Press, 2001.

Saiyed, Gulnaz, "Writing by Hand Better for Learning, Study Shows," http://news.medill.northwestern.edu/chicago/news. aspx?id=177291#.UokxnwTI0p4.facebook, *Medill Reports*, Chicago, January 27, 2011.

Standing, E.M., *Maria Montessori: Her Life and Work*, New York: New American Library, 1957.

Standing, E. M., *The Montessori Method, A Revolution in Education*, Fresno, California: Academy Library Guild, 1962.

Thompson, Bradley, "Cognitive Child Abuse in Our Math Classrooms" http://www.aynrand.org/site/News2?page=NewsArticle&id=5410 The Ayn Rand Center for Individual Rights, January 25, 2001.

Winn, Harbour "A Child's Development of the Conceptualization of Time."

Walsh, David, *No: Why Kids—of All Ages—Need to Hear It and How Parents Can Say It*, New York: Simon and Schuster, 2007.

Walsh, David, *WHY Do They Act That Way?: A Survival Guide to the Adolescent Brain for You and Your Teen*, New York: Free Press, 2005.

Westminister Day School, "A Periodical Publication for Parents," (portions of the section on Separation were reprinted from this periodical).

Wolf, Aline, "Montessori or Public Kindergarten: A Parent's Decision for the Five Year-Old," Penn-Mont Academy, Altoona, Pennsylvannia, 1974.

Wolf, Anthony, *Get Out of My Life, But First Could You Drive Me & Cheryl to the Mall: A Parent's Guide to the New Teenager*, New York: Farrar, Straus and Giroux, 2002.

Wood, Paul, *How to Get Your Children to Do What You Want Them To Do*, (audio cassette), Passadena, California: Cassette Works, 1977.

Zimmerman, Sarah Cole, (paper on self-esteem presented at workshop, Berkeley, California), Feb. 20, 1983.

About the Author

Charlotte Cushman is a Montessori educator. She teaches at Minnesota Renaissance School which she owns with her husband, Dan Van Bogart.

She graduated from Lewis and Clark College, Portland, Oregon in 1972 with a B.S. Degree in Elementary Education. While attending college she went on an overseas program to Japan where she did an independent study project "Child Discipline in Japan." Immediately after graduation she took her AMI Montessori training at the Montessori Training Center, Palo Alto, California from Lena Wikramaratne, a colleague and friend of Maria Montessori.

After that she worked as an assistant teacher at Golden Montessori, Portland, Oregon, moved back to the Midwest and worked as the head teacher at Sunrise Montessori in Anoka, Minnesota. In 1985 she and her best friend, Carol Landkamer, started their own school, Independence Montessori. When Carol retired, Charlotte joined her husband's school, Minnesota Renaissance School, which he had started a few years prior.

She has authored numerous articles about child development and has been published in periodicals such as "Montessori Life," "The Montessori Courier," "Public School Montessorian," "Minnesota Parent," "The American Thinker" and the newsletter for Putting People First. She has also delivered presentations to various community groups and numerous parent groups on child development, discipline and the Montessori philosophy and method.

She is a parent and grandparent and enjoys spending time with her family at their cabin in Northern Minnesota. She also enjoys sewing, quilting, reading, knitting, music, genealogy, talk radio, doll collecting, psychology, and discussing ideas.

PLEASE RETURN TO:

Montessori Children's House of Durham
Montessori Education Since 1977
2800 Pickett Road
Durham, NC 27705

CPSIA information can be obtained
at www.ICGtesting.com
Printed in the USA
LVOW06s1237010816
498294LV00009B/3/P